# MOVING ON FROM CRIME AND SUBSTANCE USE

## SUBSTANCE USE

### Transforming identities

Edited by Anne Robinson and
Paula Hamilton

P

First published in Great Britain in 2016 by

Policy Press
University of Bristol
1-9 Old Park Hill
Bristol
BS2 8BB
UK
t: +44 (0)117 954 5940
pp-info@bristol.ac.uk
www.policypress.co.uk

North America office:
Policy Press
c/o The University of Chicago Press
1427 East 60th Street
Chicago, IL 60637, USA
t: +1 773 702 7700
f: +1 773-702-9756
sales@press.uchicago.edu
www.press.uchicago.edu

© Policy Press 2016

British Library Cataloguing in Publication Data
A catalogue record for this book is available from the British Library

Library of Congress Cataloging-in-Publication Data
A catalog record for this book has been requested

ISBN 978-1-4473-2468-3 paperback
ISBN 978-1-4473-2467-6 hardback
ISBN 978-1-4473-2471-3 ePub
ISBN 978-1-4473-2472-0 Mobi
ISBN 978-1-4473-2470-6 ePdf

The right of Anne Robinson and Paula Hamilton to be identified as editors of this work has been asserted by them in accordance with the Copyright, Designs and Patents Act 1988.

The statements and opinions contained within this publication are solely those of the editors and contributors and not of the University of Bristol or Policy Press. The University of Bristol and Policy Press disclaim responsibility for any injury to persons or property resulting from any material published in this publication.

Policy Press works to counter discrimination on grounds of gender, race, disability, age and sexuality.

Cover design by Andrew Corbett
Front cover image: Getty
Printed and bound in Great Britain by CMP, Poole
Policy Press uses environmentally responsible print partners

# Contents

# Notes on editors and contributors

## Editors

**Anne Robinson** is a principal lecturer in the Department of Law and Criminology at Sheffield Hallam University and leads the programme for qualifying probation officers. She previously worked in the probation service and as a manager in youth justice. She is author of *Foundations for Offender Management: Theory, Law and Policy for Contemporary Practice* and *Foundations for Youth Justice: Positive Approaches to Practice*, as well as co-editor and contributor to *Values in Criminology and Community Justice* (all published by Policy Press). Anne holds a Master of Social Work qualification, in which her dissertation topic explored the experiences of women involved in street sex work. She is currently a doctoral candidate in the School of Applied Social Sciences at Durham University.

**Paula Hamilton** is a senior lecturer in the Department of Law and Criminology at Sheffield Hallam University. She previously worked in the probation service and then taught the BA Community Justice at Manchester University. At Sheffield Hallam University, alongside undergraduate and postgraduate criminology courses, she leads the desistance-focused strand of teaching on the programme for qualifying probation officers. Her doctoral research was a narrative study exploring the processes of change for a small group of men in one metropolitan probation trust and the role of rehabilitative efforts – primarily probation supervision – in facilitating and supporting change. With Kathy Albertson, she has written about the ethical and value issues raised in narrative inquiry in *Values in Criminology and Community Justice* published by Policy Press.

## Contributors

**David Best** is professor of research and scholarship in the Department of Law and Criminology at Sheffield Hallam University and adjunct associate professor of addictions at Turning Point, Melbourne. He gained an undergraduate degree in psychology and philosophy, a masters in criminology and a PhD in the psychology of addictions. He has authored three books on addiction recovery and has written more than 130 peer-reviewed publications and a number of book chapters and technical reports. He has worked in academic and policy research and his primary research interests are around recovery and desistance, social networks and recovery capital.

**Jacky Burrows** is a lecturer in criminology at Sheffield Hallam University. She has extensive practice experience in a variety of psychological and offender management roles in the prison and probation services. Much of this time has been spent working with sexual offenders. Jacky has degrees in both psychology and community justice as well as an MSc in Applied Forensic Psychology from the University of Leicester. She is currently studying for an MRes at the University of Manchester alongside her teaching.

**Adam Calverley** is a lecturer in criminology at the University of Hull, UK where he teaches on a range of modules in Hull and Hong Kong. He is author of a research monograph, *Cultures of Desistance: Rehabilitation, Reintegration and Ethnic Minorities* and co-author of *Understanding Desistance from Crime* with Stephen Farrall. More recently he has worked with Professor Farrall and colleagues on *Criminal Careers in Transition: The Social Context of Desistance from Crime*, published by Oxford University Press.

**Sarah Goodwin** is a doctoral candidate at the University of Sheffield and lecturer in the Department of Law and Criminology at Sheffield Hallam University. Her current work focuses on the lived experiences of women as they attempt to desist from crime. She also has interests in criminal justice arts interventions, qualitative methodologies and ethics, community sentences and the interactions between culture, desistance and integration. Prior to studying at Sheffield, Sarah completed a BA in Law and an MPhil in Criminological Research at the University of Cambridge.

**James Irving** is a senior lecturer in the Department of Law and Criminology at Sheffield Hallam University. James was employed by the University of Manchester, as a research assistant on a Nuffield funded medical-negligence project and also collected data for King's College London's ESRC, Secure Estates, young offender project. His doctoral thesis is entitled, *How does AA's 12 Steps and membership of the Fellowship of Alcoholics Anonymous work for addressing drinking problems?* Recent work includes, researcher and co-author of the *UK Life in Recovery Survey 2015*, and co-author of *A Social Capital Approach to Assisting Veterans Through Recovery and Desistance Transitions in Civilian Life* (2015). Prior to his PhD, James completed a Master's degree by research at the University of Manchester.

**Jennifer Sloan** is a senior lecturer in criminology at Sheffield Hallam University. Her work focuses on men in prison, masculinities and sexual violence. She is co-editor of the *Palgrave Handbook of Prison Ethnography*, and her doctoral thesis was a prison ethnography entitled *Men Inside: Masculinity and the Adult Male Prison Experience*. She has undertaken comparative work looking at the prosecution of sexual violence in South Africa and England and Wales with Maggie Wykes, and has written on the topics of public perceptions of justice, stigma and cleanliness in prison. Prior to her PhD, Jennifer completed a LLB in Law from Manchester University, and the MA in International Criminology at the University of Sheffield.

# Introduction

Criminology has pursued a long-standing interest in crime causation and what leads individuals into committing crime. It is striking, though, considering the extent to which state machineries are marshalled into efforts to control and reduce crime, that criminologists have only relatively recently turned their attention to the question of what prompts offenders to cease criminal activity and how they do so. Consequently, and perhaps making up for lost time, the past two decades have seen a proliferation of literature exploring the psychosocial processes of change. Recent research has also opened questions about the impact of social contexts and criminal justice interventions on desistance from crime, examining the way that individuals transform aspects of identity and social relationships as they move away from offending (for example, King, 2014, Farrall and Calverley, 2006; Farrall et al, 2014).

This book extends explorations in one critical theme in the debates around desistance – the transformation of identity and, in particular, the internal narratives that constitute a sense of self. We present fresh research on the processes of change for individuals seeking healthier and more successful futures, and propose that debates should be widened to consider past lives of substance misuse and victimisation.

Of course, there are classic large-scale studies cited frequently throughout the desistance literature, including Shover (1996), Sampson and Laub (1993; also Laub and Sampson, 2003) and, more recently, the Sheffield Pathways Out of Crime research conducted by Anthony Bottoms and Joanna Shapland. Their longitudinal design, sample sizes and methodological rigour ensure that their messages carry weight and authority (see Farrall et al (2014) for an overview). That does not mean, however, that they are the last word on desistance. The smaller studies discussed here are able to examine specific interests which larger studies have left aside. With the exception of Giordano et al (2002), women, for example, are relatively neglected within desistance studies as are the experiences of individuals from black and minority ethnic groups. Furthermore, our qualitative studies have set out to reach, as it were, some of the parts that larger studies cannot reach in terms of subjective experiences of change and the role of emotions (although, again, here, Giordano et al (2007) provide an isolated example).

For us, the critical questions have clustered around:

- the common themes in the stories that individuals tell about themselves and their processes of change;
- the differences that emerge as we consider gender, ethnicities and age;
- the particular forms of enquiry most suited to explore and investigate the internal transformations that take place;
- the benefits of moving beyond a narrow criminal justice view of desistance and returning to broad ideas and concepts of identity, change and 'de-labelling'.

The book, then, focuses on diversity and on presenting the findings of new authors in the field alongside others who are more established. It aims to add to a vigorous desistance debate and to take it in unfamiliar directions, particularly aligning with a parallel, but distinct, movement and body of thinking around recovery from addiction.

It is worth outlining our motivations in embarking on this book. In the first instance, the interest was sparked in the course of Paula Hamilton's doctoral research exploring the psychosocial processes of change and the (re-)biography of identity in a small sample of men who had previously been heavily involved in offending. Picking up a phrase used many times by her participants, our perception is that individuals are motivated to change by the desire to seek successful lives and a vision of what that future life might be. One striking finding from her study is the significance of masculine identity and, in particular, the role of fathers in these men's lives: desistance research has been curiously silent on these subjects. This led us to think about other aspects of diversity and the limited extent to which the developing thinking around desistance and the role of identity transformation within it has taken account of difference.

The second prompt, if you like, for the book is the involvement of both of the editors in professional qualifying courses for probation officers and, through that training, our awareness of how the messages from the desistance (and to a lesser extent, recovery) literature are being adopted in practice. Leading academics in the field have worked extensively with the probation service to promote understandings about the sorts of relationships, environments and interventions that are conducive to desistance. However, we are conscious that, in the UK at least, for an appreciable length of time, efforts to link desistance-thinking to social and organisational contexts moved the focus in the direction of criminal justice practice and away from a more general concern with the complexities of psychosocial processes of change. Meanwhile the recovery movement has followed its own trajectory and mode of activism, in this case reacting to the dominance of the medical/treatment rather than criminal justice orientations and promoting empowerment through mutual aid (see Humphreys, 2002, and Allan, 2014, for a more recent overview).

The third area of interest, in considering individual subjectivities, motivations and change, is inevitably the way that we formulate questions and investigate areas of enquiry. While life course perspectives on crime and substance misuse frequently rely on quantitative data, desistance studies have turned to qualitative methodologies to help uncover the experiences of individuals as they alter – or, in our terms, transform – their identities. Many contemporary researchers have looked to narrative approaches encouraging the telling of life histories and stories of self as a helpful way (although by no means the only way) of exploring how individuals make sense of change and what it means to them. This encouraged us to reflect on the relationship between researcher and research participant, the locus of power within the research process, and the benefits of co-producing rich data.

Intriguingly, the change in question may be much broader than desistance from crime. In particular we became interested in identifying where there is common ground in experiences of change and areas of difference and divergence. Some years ago, for example Teela Sanders (2007) drew parallels between the process of desistance and exiting sex work in *Becoming an ex-sex-worker: Making transitions out of a deviant career*. We are clearly not the only ones to look in this direction as is evident in a number of publications since we conceived the idea for this book. Stone (2015) has used Maruna's concept of 'redemption scripts' (Maruna, 2001) to explore identity recovery and resistance to stigma among substance-using pregnant women and mothers. Meyer (2015) discusses expectations of women's 'desistance' from intimate partner violence (IPV) in order to gain both formal and informal forms of help, and their attempts to deal with the identities that have been 'spoiled' by association with IPV and their assumed weakness or complicity. Conceptual models from the desistance literature have also been employed to look at the impacts of narrative development within 12-step programmes on identity (Marsh, 2011) and the desistance of offenders with long-term histories of drug use (Bachman et al, 2015). Elsewhere, attention has moved from the generic offender population to 'specialists' (see, for example, Walker et al, 2015, in relation to perpetrators of IPV; Weaver and Barry, 2014, and Laws and Ward, 2010, on sex offenders). This suggests that there are real possibilities in terms of looking at change processes with diverse groups, in different contexts and employing a variety of innovative methodologies.

Fortuitously, the prompts outlined above coincided with a critical moment in the development of the criminology team at Sheffield Hallam University. The past two years have seen an influx of new people into the team who were not only research active, but focused on aspects of desistance and recovery. So a further aim of this book is to provide a vehicle for the vigour, enthusiasm and expertise of these others, as well as our own developing interests.

In the initial chapter of the book, Paula Hamilton establishes an introductory discussion of conceptualisations of identity and identity transformation in processes of personal change. She starts by exploring what is meant by identity, and analyses the two theoretical frameworks most commonly employed by the writers in this collection – narrative theory and social identity theory. Despite differences in emphasis, she argues that an understanding in both frameworks of identity and identity transformation as psychosocial constructions and processes that take place in a structured society, means that there are more similarities than substantive differences. The second section draws on concepts such as Goffman's (1963) 'spoiled identity' and Braithwaite's (1989) 'master status' to consider ways in which involvement in offending, substance misuse and other 'problematic' behaviours and lifestyles can be implicated in an individual's sense of self and, of course, the views that others take of such individuals. It will consider the implications of this in terms of stigma, discrimination and cumulative disadvantage and how these processes may constitute obstacles to change.

Chapter Two turns to the question of the role of emotions in identity transformation and desistance. Here Paula Hamilton begins by critically exploring the relative neglect of the emotional realm in both mainstream criminological and desistance literatures, before going on to consider how and in what ways emotions are seen to be implicated in processes of change in the relatively few existing desistance studies which consider this dimension. She then goes on to draw on her own doctoral research to highlight the ways in which emotions were heavily implicated in the stories her cohort of men told – both in stories of their onset/persistence in offending and of their eventual desistance.

In Chapter Three, Jennifer Sloan reflects on the findings from her ethnographic study in a prison for adult males. Her focus is on the men's changing visions and expectations of their futures as men, which she frames as 'aspirational masculinities'. The experience of time in prison may encourage negative and aggressive forms of masculinity on the one hand, but does allow opportunity for reflection and a reappraisal of life priorities on the other. In particular, she highlights shifts over time in the 'audiences' that men consider important for the performance of their masculinity, reflecting changes in values, attachments and expectations of life and identities beyond the prison wall.

Sarah Goodwin in Chapter Four extends the analysis of gender, in this instance exploring the lived experience of women in a period of change. While their experiences are similar to men's in many respects, her relationships over a period of time with a sample of women attending a day centre, reveals some intriguing differences. She highlights the significance of living in long-term abusive relationships for confidence and self-perception. And she questions assumptions about desistance necessarily involving a 'replacement identity'; aspects of self may be reworked and, on occasions, the process is more akin to finding a 'lost' self after ending a violent relationship or ceasing drug use. For the women in her study, identities were often precarious, reflecting the early and fragile nature of their desistance. Being or becoming a caregiver – an obviously more socially available role for women than for men – was often a key element in the women's accounts of change.

Chapter Five considers questions of identity during adolescence and in the transition to adulthood, noting that the latter often involves a parallel transition out of youthful delinquency. The focus is on narrative identities and developing sense of biography as revealed across a range of empirical studies (rather than the author's primary research). Anne Robinson also begins to explore how young people exercise agency in their construction of life stories and narratives of self, particularly where they have few resources to enable them to present themselves 'well', and may also be designated by others as in some way 'troubled or troublesome'. Difficult or fractured transitions may have knock-on effects for developing positive adult identities and practices, and may trap some young people in a position where their 'offenderhood' is both internalised and externally reinforced in their social relations. The challenge is then how to offer meaningful opportunities for growth and early forms of generativity.

In Chapter Six Adam Calverley argues that the processes of adopting viable non-offending identities are important in the desistance of minority ethnic offenders as they are for offenders who are white. However, differences in structural location and cultural expectations and practices mean that the forms of pro-social identity that are accessible and available vary. He examines the ways that black and dual heritage and South Asian male desisters invest in available discourses of masculinity which are shaped by ethnicity (Gadd and Farrall, 2004) and how this process of identity re-construction provides a means of transitioning from an offender to a non-offender identity. He then pinpoints the ways that identity is racialised and reviews the effects this has on desistance and the different strategies employed to deal with challenges imposed by racism (which, in his research, also varied by ethnicity, with South Asian and black desisters adopting different approaches)

Jacky Burrows in Chapter Seven turns our attention to sex offenders who, perhaps more than any other 'type' of offender, have been systematically vilified, demonised, and ostracised from mainstream society. She argues that, for once, the public, the media, the government, and − worryingly − large numbers of professionals seem to be in agreement that such 'othering' is entirely right and proper in what are seen to be the larger interests of public protection. She explores the implications of this deeply entrenched culture for 'would-be desisters' and suggests ways forward that offer individuals opportunities to uncouple from the 'master status' of sex offender and to build positive social networks.

David Best picks up some parallel themes in Chapter Eight, but also takes new directions in applying a social identity model of recovery (SIMOR) (Best et al, 2015) from substance use recovery to desistance. Based on social identity theory, this approach suggests that diverse social networks, specifically those involving individuals who are non-users and/or offenders, are supportive of recovery. Such networks assist the individual in the transition 'from addict identity to recovery identity' and building 'recovery capital' created by an amalgam of personal, social and community capital that is held together by the emerging social identities. Support for this model is provided by a mixed methods study that collected data from a sample of drug and alcohol workers in recovery from previous problematic dependent use. The chapter presents quantitative analysis and powerful case studies to argue for the role of social group membership in creating and consolidating attachments to new norms, values and behaviours, and the social identities that follow.

The final presentation of findings from primary research in Chapter Nine concentrates on the practices of Alcoholics Anonymous (AA) and how they facilitate change. James Irving analysed intensive interviews with long-term members of AA using a framework that focused in on motivation to engage, structured social engagement (through the activities of AA) and personal agency. The resulting model (presented as a helix to represent progression over time) illustrates the way that individuals use support from AA and the understandings of their problem drinking − reflecting AA language and concepts in what he terms 'linguistic echoes' − to maintain sobriety. Although there may be limits to identity transformation while still engaged with the organisation as 'sober alcoholics', the programme emphasises moral reflection and commitment to new norms and beliefs which are key elements of desistance processes.

Rounding off the collection in Chapter Ten, Anne Robinson highlights the key messages from the research and thinking in this book, pointing to fruitful areas for further investigation. She ends by considering the main challenges and obstacles encountered in extending knowledge and understanding, and reviewing established and promising methodologies for enquiry.

## References

Allan, G, 2014, *Working with substance-users: A guide to effective interventions*, Basingstoke: Palgrave Macmillan

Bachman, R, Kerrison, E, Paternoster, R, O'Connell, D, Smith, L, 2015, Desistance for a long-term drug-involved sample of offenders: The importance of identity transformation, *Criminal Justice and Behaviour*, doi: 10.1177/0093854815604012

Best, D, Beckwith, M, Haslam, C, Haslam, D, Jetten, J, Mawson, E, Lubman, DI, 2015, Overcoming alcohol and drug addiction as a process of social identity transition: The social identity model of recovery (SIMOR), *Addiction Research and Theory* 24, 2, doi: 10.3109/16066359.2015.1075980

Braithwaite, J, 1989, *Crime, shame and reintegration*, Cambridge: Cambridge University Press

Farrall, S, Calverley, A, 2006, *Understanding desistance from crime: Theoretical directions in resettlement and rehabilitation*, Maidenhead: Oxford University Press

Farrall, S, Hunter, B, Sharpe, G, Calverley, A, 2014, *Criminal careers in transition: The social context of desistance from crime*, Oxford: Oxford University Press

Gadd, D, Farrall, S, 2004, Criminal careers, desistance and subjectivity, *Theoretical Criminology* 8, 2, 123–55

Giordano, PC, Cernkovich, SA, Rudolphe, JL, 2002, Gender, crime and desistance: Towards a theory of cognitive transformation, *American Journal of Sociology* 107, 4, 990–1064

Giordano, P, Schroeder, RD, Cernkovitch, SA, 2007, Emotions and crime over the life-course: A neo-meadian perspective on criminal continuity and change, *American Journal of Sociology* 112, 6, 1603–61

Goffman, E, 1963, *Stigma: Notes on the management of spoiled identity*, Englewood Cliffs, NJ: Prentice Hall

Humphreys, K, 2002, *Circles of recovery: Self-help organisations for addictions*, Cambridge: Cambridge University Press

King, S, 2014, *Desistance transitions and the impact of probation*, Abingdon: Routledge

Laub, JH, Sampson, RJ, 2003, *Shared beginnings, divergent lives: Delinquent boys at age 70*, Cambridge, MA: Harvard University Press

Laws, R, Ward, T, 2010, *Desistance from sex offending: Alternatives to throwing away the key*, New York: Guilford Press

Marsh, B, 2011, Narrating desistance: Identity change and the 12-step script, *Irish Probation Journal* 8, 49–68

Maruna, S, 2001, *Making good: How ex-convicts reform and rebuild their lives*, Washington DC: American Psychological Association

Meyer, S, 2015, Still blaming the victim of intimate partner violence? Women's narratives of victim desistance and redemption when seeking support, *Theoretical Criminology*, doi: 10.1177/1362480615585399

Sampson, R, Laub, JH, 1993, *Crime in the making: Pathways and turning points through life*, Cambridge, MA: Harvard University Press

Sanders, T, 2007, Becoming an ex-sex-worker: Making transitions out of a deviant career, *Feminist Criminology* 2, 1, 74–95

Shover, N, 1996, *Great pretenders*, Oxford: Oxford University Press

Stone, R, 2015, Desistance and identity repair: Redemption narratives as resistance to stigma, *British Journal of Criminology*, doi: 10.1093/bjc/azv081

Walker, K, Bowen, E, Brown, S, Sleath, E, 2015, Subjective accounts of the turning points that facility desistance from intimate partner violence, *International Journal of Offender Therapy and Comparative Criminology*, doi: 10.1177/0306624X15597493

Weaver, B, Barry, M, 2014, Risky business? Desistance from sexual offending, in K McCartan (ed) *Responding to sexual offending: Perceptions, risk management and public protection*, pp 153–69, Basingstoke: Palgrave Macmillan

ONE

# Extending the 'desistance and recovery debates': thoughts on identity

*Paula Hamilton*

This book is about identity and the ways in which shifts and transformations in identity are implicated in processes of personal change in those desisting from crime and/or recovering from substance use problems. More specifically, this book aims to broaden debates about identity transformation and change by exploring the experiences of diverse populations, and by considering dimensions of identity that are often neglected or marginalised – such as gender, ethnicity, the emotions, and membership of social groups and networks, in both desistance and recovery.

So, what do we mean by 'identity'? At a very basic level the *Cambridge English Dictionary* defines identity as 'who a person is, or the qualities of a person or group that makes them different from others'. This basic definition points to a number of important themes in various conceptualisations of identity: the individual, the self or the personal, the collective, social or cultural, and of similarity and difference, themes which continue to be the source of much debate (more of which later). As a starting point, Jenkins defines identity as 'the human capacity – rooted in language – to know "who's who" (and hence "what's what")' and posits that identity refers to a 'multi-dimensional classification or mapping of the human world and our places in it, as individuals and as members of collectivities' (2014, 6).

As Jenkins (2014) argues, while identity has been one of the unifying themes of the social sciences for more than a quarter of a century, concerns about identity and identity-related issues actually have a long history (he cites both the work of Locke in 1690 and Shakespeare as examples). They cannot, therefore, be seen as historically recent phenomena that are inherently tied up with post or late modern conditions. However, as Jenkins goes on to concede, *how* we talk about such concerns is of course historically and culturally specific, so the current era will have its own terms and themes, and the current volume of discourse about identity has reached new levels, if only, as he says, 'because global noise and chatter about everything has increased' with the population and the availability of communications technologies (Jenkins, 2014, 32). That said, contemporary concerns about identity and identity-related issues can be seen as reflecting the particular conditions of uncertainty produced by change in late modern conditions in, among other things, the interrelated realms of work and family relations, class and social mobility, migration, medical and technological innovation, the combination of affluence and economic insecurity, the redrawing of national borders, the intrusiveness of global news media and the 'return' of religion to global politics (Jenkins, 2014, 32).

The magnitude of contemporary concern and interest in identity is reflected in the development of approaches to understanding processes of desistance from crime and recovery from problematic substance use. In relation to desistance specifically, although analysis of large-scale quantitative data sets has played an important role in highlighting the significance of aging/maturation and increases in social capital or bonds related to transitions or 'turning points' across the life course, qualitative phenomenological research has also highlighted the importance of subjective changes and identity transformations. While some theorists have contested the idea that identity transformation is a necessary and inherent part of change (for example, Bottoms et al, 2004), this dimension of change has become an increasing preoccupation in much of both the theoretical and empirical work in the field.

One of the particular themes that can be discerned in contemporary social science thinking about identity is a focus on the individual and notions of reflexive self-identity. As Jenkins (2014, 39) points out, many different theoretical approaches to understanding identity, such as symbolic interactionism and discourse theory, typically share a focus on individuals, and 'personal' and 'social' identification are treated as different conditions or constructs.

This focus on the individual is reflected in many of the influential studies of identity and identity transformation in both desistance and recovery, particularly those which have drawn on narrative or life-story models of identity and/or notions of personal reflexivity (for example, Maruna (2001) whose work is explored in detail elsewhere in this volume). However, in some more recent work the analysis has broadened out to consider the role and significance of social relations and networks (for example, Weaver, 2016), and a counter to this (predominant) focus on the individual is offered by variants of social identity theory as offered by Best (Chapter Eight, this volume).

Narrative and social identity theories are the two main approaches to theorising, exploring and understanding identity and identity transformation employed in the studies illuminated in this collection. The work of McAdams (1985; 1993), a leading figure in narrative psychology, has made an important contribution to an understanding of narrative as constitutive of identity, and this formed the approach to identity employed by Maruna (1997) and in his seminal (2001) Liverpool Desistance Study. McAdams and Adler (2010) define identity as:

> a self-constructed configuration or patterning of the self that integrates disparate psychological elements – talents, needs, beliefs and values, goals, important memories, important roles – in such a way as to provide a person with a sense that his or her life is more or less unified over time and across life contexts and meaningfully situated within the ideological, economic, social, and cultural ecology of the adult world. (2010, 39)

In 1985 McAdams proposed the metaphor of story as identity – that identity can be viewed as an internalised and evolving story of the self or 'personal myth' that people living in modern societies begin to construct in late adolescence and young adulthood. The story is situated within an ideological setting or 'backdrop' of fundamental beliefs and values upon which the plot of the story unfolds (McAdams and Adler, 2010, 5). The story does not cover every detail of one's life, but it includes significant and prominent scenes or 'nuclear episodes' – vivid and often emotionally charged episodes from the past including high points, low points and turning points in life. The story also contains central characters or imagoes, which McAdams and Adler describe as an 'idealised personification of the self that captures a select group of important traits, goals, relationships, or identifications in a person's life and serves to function as one of the main characters of the story' (2010, 39). McAdams (1993) argues that, while life stories only begin to emerge into consciousness in late adolescence and young adulthood, people are implicitly gathering material for these stories from the first day of life onwards. Indeed this early material may set the tone for the forthcoming story – primarily in terms of whether the tone is generally optimistic or pessimistic (see Robinson, Chapter Ten, this volume). However, as he points out, it is important to recognise that identity is not simply determined by past experience, that the past is open to constant reinterpretation – 'to the selective, creative and adaptive powers of the story telling self' (McAdams and Adler, 2010, 40).

This understanding of identity as narrative is also central to Giddens' conceptualisation of identity in late modernity where in 1991 he declared that: 'A person's identity is not to be found in behaviour, nor – important though this is – in the reactions of others, but in the capacity *keep a particular narrative going*' (1991, 54, emphasis in original). For Giddens, within a post-traditional order, self-identity becomes a reflexive project, an endeavour on which individuals continuously work and reflect through the creation, maintenance and revision of a set of biographical narratives – the story of who they are, and how they came to be where they are now – a story which makes sense to them and can be explained to other people (Giddens, 1991, 5). As discussed earlier, a focus on such agentic and reflexive self-identity (re) construction is to be found in many theorisations of desistance such as the work of Vaughan (2007) and Weaver (2016) (see Hamilton, Chapter Two, this volume).

However, although many of these analyses *do* consider the role of significant others, social groups and networks in reflexive self-identity, social identity theory can be seen as offering an important counter to this predominant focus on the individual and on *personal* change. Social identity theory, as drawn on by Best (Chapter Eight, this volume), posits that 'personal identity' is different from 'social identity' which is the internalisation of collective identifications, and that social identity is sometimes the more salient influence on individual behaviour. From this perspective, group membership is meaningful to individuals, conferring social identity and permitting self-evaluation. It is a shared representation of who one is and the appropriate behaviour attached to who one is (Jenkins, 2014, 114). Best (Chapter Eight, this volume) outlines how social identity theory proposes that, in a range of social contexts, people's sense of self is derived from their membership of social groups, and that the resulting social identities structure a person's perception and behaviour – their values, norms and goals, relationships and interactions, what they think, what they do and what they want to achieve.

There are, therefore, undoubtedly some key differences between these two approaches to understanding identity and identity change. To some extent these differences can be seen as reflecting the age-old debate about the relative primacy of agency and structure – with narrative theories prioritising agentic transformations in *personal* identity which often precede (or at least accompany) changes in the exteriority of people's lives, and social identity theories stressing the importance of '*the social*' and how the individual's self-concept (and therefore changes in self-concept) is derived from perceived membership of social groups (Hogg and Vaughan, 2002). Interestingly, these differences are reflected in practice in the sense that group and community membership are key elements in the notion of a recovery *movement* (inferring collectivity) while, aside from a relatively few isolated examples (for example, Clinks, Unlock), there is much less sense of a *movement* or *community* of desisting offenders. This may well reflect the primacy of notions of empowerment and ownership in recovery, whereas in traditional 'correctional' criminal justice policy and practice offenders are typically constituted as *objects* of correctional treatment (Bazemore, 1992, cited in Maruna and LeBel, 2010, 70; and see Burrows, Chapter Seven, this volume),

While not denying the conceptual distinctions between personal and social identities, there are however some significant areas of overlap. Some analyses have sought to stress the ways in which the two are inextricably linked whereby personal identity serves to give meaning to the social categories of groups to which people belong. For example, Reid and Deaux (1996) argue that, in claiming a social identity, people use their personal attributes, traits and behaviours (or identity) to say what the category or group is and what it means to be a member. In this sense then, as Jenkins (2014) argues, 'identity' is a meta-concept that, unusually, makes as much sense individually as collectively, and is therefore strategically significant for social theoretical debates about 'structuration' and the relationship between the individual and collective (Martin and Dennis, 2000; Parker, 2000; Stones, 2005, cited in Jenkins, 2014, 17). Jenkins goes on to propose a dialectical approach to understanding identity made up of three distinct 'orders'; the individual order – the human world as made up of embodied individuals, and what- goes-on-in-their-heads; the interaction order – the human world as constituted in the relationships between individuals, and what-goes-on-between-people; and the institutional order – the human world of pattern and organisation, of established-ways-of-doing-things (Jenkins, 2014, 42) which he argues allows for an understanding of both individual and collective identities (Jenkins, 2014, 48).

At base, both approaches to understanding identity and identity transformations highlighted in these volumes understand identity as a set of psycho-social processes, although their emphases may differ. For example, Maruna (2001) in discussing personal or ontological narratives or self-stories, stresses that they cannot be understood outside of their social, historical and structural context. Self-narratives are developed through social interaction; appraisals from those around us, modelling, and structural obstacles and opportunities all influence personal identity and identity change. Moreover, he argues, each person adopts a self-story based on the limited range of interpretations or narrative archetypes 'proposed, suggested and imposed on him by his culture, his society and his social group' (Foucault, 1998, 11, cited in Maruna, 2001, 8). The differentially structured nature of availability of and exposure to 'positive' and prosocial archetypes and cultural repertoires obviously has important implications for those seeking to desist and/ or recover, as explored in various chapters in this collection.

What is inarguable is that both of these approaches to understanding and identity and identity transformation share a conceptualisation of identity as an on-going project, a process Jenkins (2014, 6) terms 'identification'; that identity is not a 'thing', not something that one can 'have' or not, but rather something that one *does*. In contrast to classic scholarship in the field which centred on stage-models of identity and focused particularly on identity formation in adolescence (for example, Erikson, 1950; 1958; 1968; Goffman, 1959), both narrative and social identity conceptualisations of identity eschew essentialist notions of a categorical or trait-based core self, which remains largely fixed throughout the life, and instead view identity or identification as a reiterative activity and a situated accomplishment (Stevens, 2012). In both approaches identity is understood as:

> inherently fluid and fragile, actively and selectively constructed and repeatedly reconstructed, dramaturgically performed and achieved, in response to one's both maturing and mutable cognitions, desires, expectations, choices and conduct, and one's relationships, of similarity and difference, with others and the social structure. (Stevens, 2012, 528)

However, as Maruna (2001) so cogently argues this contemporary understanding of identity as negotiated, fluid, situationally accomplished and mutable is not extended to 'deviants' who tend to be viewed as people with immutable and essentially flawed natures (Gendreau and Ross, 1979, cited in Maruna, 2001, 4). As Maruna highlights, Irwin (1985 cited in Maruna, 2001, 4) called this the myth of the 'bogeyman' – the belief that some individuals are fundamentally and permanently different from 'normal' people. Indeed, as Maruna goes on to point out, when an offender *does* seem to have changed, the 'paradigm of criminal essentialism' means that the usual response is the view that he or she was never *really* a criminal from the start (Lofland, 1969,

289, cited in Maruna, 2001), thereby making it almost impossible to contradict the idea that 'real criminals' cannot change (Maruna, 2001, 5). This paradigm of criminal essentialism is undoubtedly supported and exacerbated within a wider contemporary political and popular context where penal marking, 'Othering' and constructions of 'dangerousness' abound (Garland, 2001). Within such a stigmatising, exclusionary and segregative context, 'deviants' often have to labour under the weight of a 'spoiled identity' (Goffman, 1963) or 'master identity' of offender or addict (Braithwaite, 1989). Desisting from crime and/or recovering from substance use problems must be recognised as often hugely difficult endeavours, particularly for those deeply entrenched in criminal and/or substance using networks and living in disadvantaged circumstances (Maruna and LeBel, 2010). As such, change requires a tremendous amount of self-belief and is made highly difficult, if not nigh on impossible, if those around the individual believe that change is not possible (Maruna and LeBel, 2010). Braithwaite (1989) argues that, when society's response to 'deviants' is to stigmatise, segregate and exclude, they are left with little opportunity for achieving self-respect and affiliation in the mainstream, although they are welcomed by groups of other stigmatised 'outcasts'. Repeated exclusion and stigmatisation leads only to reinforcement and internalisation of the 'master status' or 'master identity' of 'deviant', 'offender' or 'addict' and to lack of access to various forms of 'positive' capital which research has consistently shown is so significant in desistance and recovery processes.

In contrast to notions of 'criminal essentialism' and despite these significant obstacles, the empirical reality is, of course, that most 'deviants' *do* change. As discussed earlier, a substantial and ever-growing body of theoretical and empirical work has highlighted the importance and significance of identity (or identities) and of identity transformation in people's change processes. The seminal work in this area, both in the fields of desistance and recovery, are well-known and discussed in the following chapters so they will not be rehearsed here, but it is perhaps worth highlighting some of the key concepts and debates that have been raised in this literature. Of course, one of the key debates which this chapter has attempted to address – and which is considered by Best (Chapter Eight, this volume) – is around the nature of identity itself and which dimensions of identity and identity transformation are prioritised in accounts of change. As discussed earlier, this can be seen, to some extent, as reflecting the age-old debate about structure versus agency in the social sciences which has been a recurring and enduring preoccupation. For example, in the field of desistance debates have centred around which comes first and which matters most – agentic changes in self-identity or self-concept or changes in the exteriority of people's lives. In contrast to social control theories of desistance (most notably those of Laub and Sampson, 1993; Sampson and Laub, 1992; Sampson and Laub, 1993) some analyses, perhaps most notably Vaughan (2007) and Paternoster and Bushway (2009), clearly prioritise agency, subjective changes and identity transformations. These analyses often incorporate notions of personal reflexive dialogues and processes in identity transformations, which are seen to precede, and indeed determine, subsequent external changes. However, reflecting the increasing recognition of the interplay between agency and structure – of the personal and the socio-structural – an increasing number of interactionist or integrative theories of desistance have emerged whereby desistance is seen as the outcome of an individual seeking to alter their socio-structural context (Weaver, 2016).

Another key debate in the field centres around how far change necessitates a 'knifing off' of a previous problematic or 'spoiled identity' as suggested by Laub and Sampson (2003). Although less viscerally perhaps, this idea is also reflected in Giordano et al's (2002) idea of a 'replacement self', and by Paternoster and Bushway's (2009) notion of the 'feared self'. However, a contrasting view, offered by Maruna (2001), is that change instead involves reaching back into early experiences to find and re-establish an 'old' or 'real me', a process of 'reverting to an unspoiled identity' (Goffman, 1961, cited in Maruna, 2001, 89) through creation of a coherent self-narrative which allows the individual to 'rewrite a shameful past into a necessary prelude to a productive and worthy life' (Goffman, 1961, cited in Maruna, 2001, 87).

This chapter has sought to explore conceptualisations of identity and identity transformations in both the desistance and recovery literatures. In doing so, it has attempted to argue that, despite some not insignificant conceptual differences in the approaches most commonly employed in the field and by the authors in this volume, there are also areas of significant commonality and overlap. One further area of common concern in both the desistance and recovery literatures is the need for personal change and identity transformation to be recognised, validated, supported and endorsed, not only by significant others in people's lives, but by communities and the wider society. It is being increasingly recognised that personal change is not enough, and that change requires not only a transformation in an individual's identity but also the recognition and corroboration of that new identity within a (moral) community (McNeill, 2014). Desistance and recovery are not one way streets – communities and societies need to play their part in change, and it is only through such efforts that the stigmatising and excluding effects of 'spoiled identities' can be eliminated and transformational change aided and supported. The chapters that follow engage with the debates highlighted here in their efforts to 'unpack' the 'black box' of processes of identification (Jenkins, 2014), through their consideration of dimensions of transformational identity change that are so far under-developed and the, as yet, rather neglected experiences of a range of diverse populations.

## References

Bottoms, A, Shapland, J, Costello, A, Holmes, D, Mair, G, 2004, Towards desistance: Theoretical underpinnings for an empirical study, *Howard Journal of Criminal Justice* 43, 4, 368–89

Braithwaite, J, 1989, *Crime, shame and reintegration*, New York: Cambridge University Press

Erikson, EH ,1950, *Childhood and society*, New York: Norton

Erikson, EH, 1958, *Young man Luther: A study in psychoanalysis and history*, New York: Norton

Erikson, EH, 1968, *Identity: Youth and crisis*, New York: Norton

Garland, D, 2001, *The culture of control*, Oxford: Oxford University Press

Giddens, A, 1991, *Modernity and self-identity: Self and society in the late modern age*, Cambridge: Polity Press

Giordano, PC, Cernkovich, SA, Rudolph, JL, 2002, Gender, crime and desistance: Toward a theory of cognitive transformation, *American Journal of Sociology* 107, 990-1064

Goffman, E, 1959, *The presentation of self in everyday life*, Garden City, NJ: Doubleday-Anchor Books

Goffman, E, 1963, *Stigma: Notes on the management of spoiled identity*, Englewood Cliffs, NJ: Prentice-Hall

Hogg, MA, Vaughan, GM, 2002, *Social psychology* (3rd edn), London: Prentice Hall

Jenkins, R, 2014, *Social identity* (4th edn), London: Routledge

Laub, JH, Sampson, RJ, 1993, Turning points in the life course: Why change matters to the study of crime, *Criminology* 31, 301-325

Laub, JH, Sampson, RJ, 2003, *Shared beginnings, divergent lives: Delinquent boys to age 70*, Cambridge, MA: Harvard University Press

McAdams, DP, 1985, *Power, intimacy and the life story: Personological inquiries into identity*, New York: Guilford Press

McAdams, DP, 1993, *The stories we live by: Personal myths and the making of the self*, New York: Guilford Press

McAdams, DP, Adler, JM, 2010, Autobiographical memory and construction of a narrative identity: Theory, research and clinical implications, in JE Maddux, J Tangney (eds) *Social psychological foundations of clinical psychology*, New York: Guilford Press

McNeill, F, 2014, Desistance, rehabilitation and reintegration, in J Shapland (chair), How best to stop offenders reoffending and reintegrate them into civil society, Symposium conducted at the seminar series of the University of Sheffield Centre for Criminological Research, London, England

Martin, PJ and Dennis, A, eds, 2000, *Human agents and social structures*, Manchester: Manchester University Press

Maruna, S, 1997, Going straight: Desistance from crime and self-narratives of reform, *Narrative Study of Lives* 5, 59–93

Maruna, S, 2001, *Making good: How ex-convicts reform and rebuild their lives*, Washington, DC: American Psychological Association

Maruna, S, LeBel, T, 2010, The desistance paradigm in correctional practice: From programmes to lives, in F McNeill, P Raynor, C Trotter (eds) *Offender supervision: New directions in theory, research and practice*, Cullompton: Willan

Parker, J, 2000, *Structuration*, Buckingham: Open University Press

Paternoster, R, Bushway, S, 2009, Desistance and the feared self: Toward an identity theory of criminal desistance, *Journal of Criminal Law and Criminology* 99, 4, 1103–56

Reid, A, Deaux, K, 1996, Relationship between social and personal identities: Segregation or integration?, *Journal of Personality and Social Psychology* 7, 6, 1084–91

Sampson, RJ, Laub, JH, 1992, Crime and deviance in the life course, *Annual Review of Sociology* 18, 63-84

Sampson, RJ, Laub, JH, 2005, A life-course view of the development of crime, *The Annals of the American Academy of Political and Social Science* 602, 1, 12–45

Stevens, A, 2012, 'I am the person now I was always meant to be': Identity reconstruction and narrative reframing in therapeutic community prisons, *Criminology and Criminal Justice* 12, 5, 527–47

Vaughan, B, 2007, The internal narrative of desistance, *British Journal of Criminology* 47, 3, 390–404

Weaver, B, 2016, *Offending and desistance: The importance of social relations*, Abingdon: Routledge

# TWO

# Emotions and identity transformation

*Paula Hamilton*

## Introduction

The emotional dimensions and trajectories of crime and of desistance have, at least until relatively recently, been more or less neglected in mainstream theorising. This chapter draws on a small-scale narrative inquiry with a group of desisting men to explore the ways in which their emotions were implicated both in their offending behaviour and in their re-biography of their sense of themselves as men; a transformation in their narratised identities which appeared to underpin their desistance. The chapter begins by providing a brief critical exploration of the 'place' of emotions in criminology and in theorisations of desistance. It then highlights the relatively few existing studies of desistance which pay attention to the role and significance of emotions in change and explores the implications of such work. Finally, the chapter draws on empirical work to show how emotions, particularly fear and shame, were key to the transformative experiences of participants.

## Emotions, crime and criminology

The role of emotions, particularly vengeance and revenge, were clearly visible in pre-Enlightenment thinking and practices around punishment and social control, and a return to 'emotive' and 'ostentatious' punishments has been seen as characteristic of a shift in penal (and popular) sensibilities which has marked late modernity (Pratt, 2000). However, for much of its history criminology has neglected emotions, viewing them with suspicion and as unworthy of serious attention or investigation (Farrall et al, 2014). This neglect is noted to have its roots in criminology's Enlightenment origins whereby offenders were characterised as free-willed, *rational* actors, responsive to deterrent penalties. Since that time a defining feature of western thinking has of course been the way in which reason and emotion have been regarded as opposing and differently valued forces, with the emotional seen as 'less than' the rational – more lowly, primitive, natural and also feminine. Since the 1970s, not least due to feminist scholarship which challenged these assumptions and highlighted their damaging implications, there has been a resurgence of interest in the emotions across the humanities and many of the social sciences. However, criminology's origins along with its enduring commitment to what Garland (2002) terms the 'Lombrosian' and 'governmental' projects means that it has been particularly slow to embrace thinking about emotions. There have, of course, been a few notable exceptions including: Cohen's (1955) work around the humiliating 'status frustration' experienced by working-class boys and links with delinquency; Goffman's (1963) work around how people manage the pain and shame of 'spoiled identity'; Matza's (1969) notion of the 'invitational edge' offered by the 'drift' into delinquency; and Jack Katz's (1988) seminal work around the emotional 'seductions of crime'.

As Farrall et al (2014) point out, underpinned by the emotional embeddedness of some of the major movements in criminal justice in recent years: the victim's movement, restorative justice, the emergence of an emotional and punitive public discourse around crime and punishment (Karstedt, 2011, cited in Farrall et al, 2014) and particularly the interest in the effects of shame on offenders, one of the discernible developments in criminology in recent years is the (re)emergence of interest in emotions. This has been found in the work of, among others, Karstedt, Loader and Strang (2011), de Haan and Loader (2002) and Braithwaite (1989). However, as de Haan and Loader highlight, emotions remain 'a somewhat peripheral topic in theoretical criminology' and:

> Many established and thriving modes of criminological reflection and research continue to proceed in ways that ignore entirely, or at best gesture towards, the impact of human emotions on their subject matter – if you doubt this, take a quick glance at almost any criminology textbook, whether of a conventional, radical, or integrating bent. (2002, 243)

These authors call for criminological theorising to 'take more serious account of the affective dimensions of criminal behaviour; something that requires more active engagement with – and in – the sociology of emotions' (2002, 245).

## Emotions and desistance

Reflecting the relative neglect of the emotions in criminological theorising about the onset and persistence of criminal behaviour, relatively little explicit attention has been paid to the emotional dimensions of desistance. This is perhaps not surprising in the substantial body of (post-positivist) desistance research which draws on large-scale quantitative data to emphasise the importance and primacy of aging/ maturation and changes or 'turning points' in the exteriority of desisters' lives. It is more surprising however in the phenomenological and narrative desistance research which emphasises the role of subjective changes and identity transformation. For example, Maruna's (2001) seminal work around how desisters are able to re-biography their lives and identities into what he terms the 'redemption script', fails to explicitly consider how desisters' emotional states and responses may be implicated in and shape this process. Similarly, Giordano et al's (2002) influential study employed a symbolic-interactionist perspective to challenge Sampson and Laub's (1993) age-graded theory of informal social control and highlighted a central role for the actor and actor-based changes in desistance. In analysis of both quantitative and life history data the authors concluded that a series of intimately related cognitive transformations, culminating in the envisioning of an appealing and conventional 'replacement self' or identity, were crucial in changes in criminality. However, the authors explicitly acknowledge that their study, at this stage, did not engage with the 'arena of the emotions' and argue that given that both 'emotional and corporeal processes' undoubtedly play important roles in change, and also in 'derailments or setbacks', that future research should focus attention on emotions and how they may affect behavioural change and the nature and timing of cognitive shifts (Giordano et al, 2002, 1055).

In their later 2007 follow-up study, Giordano and her colleagues revised their theory, arguing that such a strictly cognitive approach to explaining desistance is incomplete, and broadened their analysis to include consideration of the role of emotions and the offender's 'emotional self' as well as social influences and cognitions in the desistance process. Again from a symbolic-interactionist perspective, and drawing on Meadian conceptualisations of role taking,[1] the interconnectedness of emotions and cognitions, and of developmental changes,[2] Giordano et al argue that three life-course changes in the emotional realm have direct effects on desistance. First, they posit that as young people mature into adulthood and experience more role-taking opportunities across a wider set of social arenas, this may result in a diminution of the negative emotions that may have originally connected to criminal behaviour (they focus particularly on the role of anger) (Giordano et al, 2007, 1610). Second, they argue that this increase in role-taking opportunities associated with the move into adulthood may also facilitate a diminution of positive emotions connected to crime (as first highlighted by Katz, 1988). Finally, they argue that as the various coping strategies delinquents have hitherto employed to deal with their emotions are increasingly disapproved of and viewed by others as childish and inappropriate, the third life course change in the emotional realm with implications for desistance is an increased ability to regulate or manage the emotions in socially acceptable ways (pp 1610–11). The authors argue that analysis of their quantitative data lent support to this theorisation where their participants showed changes in emotions and emotional responses over time, and that depression and an 'angry identity' both reduced the likelihood of desistance. In an important further rejoinder to social control theories, Giordano et al argue that what they term 'emotional mellowing' may indeed be associated with life course transitions (such as marriage), but that this may also occur as part of development – it does not fundamentally depend on the actions of a spouse or other obvious catalyst; patterns of stability and change in emotions can proceed alongside or completely independent of major role or life transitions.

The authors assert that they have not abandoned their prior emphasis on cognition, but that analysis of their data and their sample's life history narratives have revealed the ways in which the types of cognitive transformations they previously highlighted and emotions are mutually supportive, and how in turn these are both shaped by social processes. For example, they argue that in the early stages of change emotions can play an important role in how and why the individual develops a general openness to change and in a varying receptivity to 'hooks for change'. In relation to later stages of the change process they argue that positive emotions and a strong emotional connection to a prosocial lifestyle can help solidify the individual's cognitive transformations that resulted in their new prosocial identity and rejection of deviant behaviours.

As previously discussed, allied with the (re) emergence of restorative justice interest in the effects of shame on offenders has been particularly notable in recent years. Liebrich's (1996) analysis of her study of 48 former offenders highlights shame as the most commonly mentioned reason given by her participants for going straight and the most commonly mentioned cost of offending. Liebrich outlines three kinds of shame discernible in her participants' accounts: public humiliation, which was the experience of having their offending behaviour exposed in front of total strangers; personal disgrace related to having their offending behaviour exposed to people they either simply knew or loved and respected; while private remorse was the experience of having offended against one's own personal morality. Liebrich asserts that this latter form of shame, private remorse, seemed to be the most painful and most enduring in its effects. Liebrich argues that while most of her participants *decided* to go straight, and that their decision seemed to have a rational cost–benefit analysis basis, there was also an important affective and moral dimension to it. This determined how people perceived costs and benefits, with feelings of shame and, conversely, feelings of self-respect being most significant. Liebrich goes on to explore the policy and practice implications of her findings, arguing that there is a role for shaming in restorative practices in the form of reintegrative shaming which, she posits, is likely to be most effective when it results in both personal disgrace and private remorse. However, she highlights how shaming which continues beyond offenders' decisions to go straight will only serve to stigmatise and, in doing so, may well impede desistance.

A further exception to the relative neglect of the role and significance of emotions in desistance is found in the work of Farrall et al (2014). In analysis of the latest sweep of interviews with a sample of Farrall's (2002) original cohort of participants, the authors explicitly consider the 'emotional trajectory of desistance'. Through development of a schema whereby recent and long-term desisters were ranked along a continuum in terms of the emotions which they said that they had felt, Farrall et al argue that five rough 'phases' of the emotional trajectory of desistance were discernible: 'early hopes', 'starting to break away', 'becoming accepted', 'feeling accepted' and 'acceptance achieved'.

The authors argue that the emotional experiences of those in the early stages of desistance are very much linked to and shaped by their recent proximity to their offending. These individuals' fairly recent experiences of crime, substance misuse and, in some cases, of relapse, tended to produce negative feelings of guilt, shame and regret. While the authors note that these emotions may play a positive role in terms of increasing motivation to make the most of the future, they also argue that such introspection can be painful, not least due to feelings of self-blame and responsibility, and the fact that these emotions are on-going. They argue that for these reasons, individuals in this 'phase' may need to protect themselves from fully acknowledging this regret and guilt lest this undermines their efforts to change.

Farrall et al report that as individuals move further along the emotional trajectory the associations they have with offending and seeing themselves as 'offenders' become progressively weaker and, as a result, negative emotions recede. They report that feelings of uncertainty quickly all but disappear, feelings of guilt and shame gradually diminish, and regret (with the exception of the 'normalcy' phase) fades away as individuals become more confident and assured of their success in desisting (2014, 213). The authors also note that as individuals move along the emotional trajectory while some of the same emotions remain, their nature and focus change as the temporal distance from offending increases. They report that hopes grow firmer and more related to specific conventional aspirations, feelings of happiness refer to life in general rather than to having ceased offending, and negative feelings such as guilt and shame relate to specific anecdotal examples from their past – painful memories from which individuals now feel far removed.

Farrall et al argue that at the same time, as people move through the emotional trajectory of desistance, new positive emotions start to emerge. They argue that by the 'starting to break away' phase, the majority of desisters report feelings of pride and achievement related to their desistance, and by the 'becoming accepted' phase, reports of feeling trusted and belonging steadily increase, with these feelings becoming more pronounced as desisters' change efforts are recognised by others.

They report, however, that by the latter stages of the emotional trajectory these feelings had largely faded, and that those at the end of the emotional trajectory felt little sense of achievement at having desisted. They argue that this is perhaps not surprising if, with the passage of time, an individual's past offending shapes their identities less and less until, by the final stages of the trajectory, it forms no part of their personal or social identities (2014, 214). They argue that their findings suggest that a sense of achievement at desisting gives way to other feelings of pride related to more conventional achievements such as family and careers. They also note that the strength of feelings around these achievements, as well as feelings of (re)gaining trust and belonging, gradually fade away as these achievements become more 'mundane' and taken-for-granted aspects of the desister's current identity and so they cease being felt as 'sensations on their emotional radar' (2014, 214).

These authors conclude that their exploration of the emotional trajectory of desistance suggests that the latter stages are characterised by 'normalcy' – becoming much 'like everyone else'. So the end point of the desisters' journey was not simply about demonstrating non-offending for a significant number of years, but as much about a mindset and lifestyle demonstrated though engagement with wider signals of social respectability such as paying tax, voting and looking after children. However, Farrall et al note that there are rare times when a desister's past reminds them of its presence, such as situations when they need criminal records checks. They therefore conclude that over time desisters' memory of their offending identity becomes ever fainter, all but disappearing, until these sorts of incidents remind them of its existence. Thus, although it will fade away again, their offending past will remain part of their identity (2014, 214).

In summary, Farrall et al conclude that analysis of their data suggests that individuals' desistance journeys progress through different phases characterised by the presence of particular emotions and the absence of others. Building on previous analysis (Farrall and Calverley, 2006), they conclude that their findings reaffirm that desistance is not confined to 'external' social factors but also comprises a significant emotional dimension. They argue that it is through these emotions that individuals interpret the meaning of their past, make sense of their present and re-orient their future. Farrall et al therefore argue that 'how desisters feel about their desistance matters' (2014, 215), and how desisters manage their emotions will have implications for success in avoiding offending.

In exploring the subjective, agentic and identity-making dimensions of desistance (located within social structures and contexts), several recent studies have employed the notion of personal reflexivity in their analyses, and have offered some consideration of the role of emotions in this process. For example, Vaughan's (2007) theoretical work draws on the work of Archer (2000; 2003) to foreground the notion of an 'internal narrative of desistance', arguing that when faced with the possibility of changing their life individuals engage in a 'moral conversation' with themselves which he describes as:

> 'a process of judgement where the agent estimates how the choices most relevant to them can be reconciled with his or her ultimate concerns and then proceeds upon the most appropriate course of action' – a process whereby what truly matters to the individual is reassessed and recast and their identity transformed. (Vaughan, 2007, 393)

Vaughan highlights how this 'moral conversation' is not merely a cognitive or 'intellectual' endeavour, but also involves the realm of the emotions whereby emotions often signal likely reactions to a situation before an individual begins to explicitly reflect on a situation. As he puts it, 'emotions provide signals for reason to decode' (2007, 293).

Vaughan outlines three stages in this internal narrative of change or 'moral conversation'. The first, discernment, is where the individual reviews possible choices and views them alongside the concerns around which they have hitherto structured a life dominated by crime. The second is 'deliberation', where the individual reviews the pros and cons of potential courses of action and compares them with the option of continuing with their current situation or lifestyle. This involves the individual comparing these different potential options in terms of how far they are congruent with their commitments and what matters most to them. Vaughan argues that what ultimately emerges here is a comparison of selves – 'who one is and who one wishes to be' (p 394). Again Vaughan highlights the role of emotions at this stage, arguing that 'emotional commentary' often helps the individual to clarify whether a particular course of action is really appropriate, and how this often also involves thinking about the reactions and feelings of others whereby 'the fashioning of a new identity for oneself is often dependent on considering one's current identity as viewed by others' (p 394). The third and final stage is 'dedication' where the individual re-orders their concerns and interests in order to allow a new commitment to the new identity to emerge. He argues that in order to establish desistance agents must regard their new identity as incompatible with continued criminality (p 394).

However while acknowledging a role for emotions in this reflexive 'moral conversation', Vaughan does not elaborate on the types of emotions that may be in play, nor exactly how they might be implicated. Archer's work, upon which Vaughan bases his analysis, similarly posits emotions as 'among the main constituents of our inner lives' and that they are 'the fuel of our inner conversations' (Archer, 2000, 194, cited in Burkitt, 2012). However, Burkitt (2012) argues that what Archer misses in her account of emotional reflexivity is other people and our emotional relationships with them. As Burkitt elaborates, emotions are seen in her theorisation (merely) as a commentary on our concerns (how we rank, pattern and pursue our beliefs and desires). Yet little is said about how these have become concerns in the first place, Burkitt (2012) argues that this is a process in which our interactions and relationships with others and our emotional connection to them (through which we interpret and imagine the way they evaluate and judge us) – a process that evokes strong emotions – are key.

The relational dimensions of personal reflexivity in desistance is a central concern of Weaver's (2016) recent work which examines the role of a co-offending peer group in shaping and influencing offending and desistance. Weaver's analysis, like Vaughan's (2007), also draws on the work of Archer (2000; 2003) and her theorisation of personal reflexivity (manifest in the 'internal conversation') as the mediating force between structure and agency. However, echoing Burkitt's (2012) position, Weaver argues that because Archer's focus is essentially individualistic she is unable to elaborate on the relational context in which our cares or concerns, or our beliefs and desires, emerge. Therefore, Weaver goes on to draw on the work of Donati (2011, cited in Weaver, 2016) to argue that it is our relationships that constitute 'who we are' and are thus the context within which our ultimate concerns arise (Weaver, 2016, 48). Through examination of the life stories and social relations of six Scottish men, Weaver's analysis posits a central role for friendship groups, intimate relationships and families of formation, employment and religious communities in variously constraining, enabling and sustaining both criminality and desistance. Therefore, although not an explicit central unit of analysis or discussion in her theorisation, emotional connectedness with others (in such friendship groups, intimate relationships and families and so on), through which these individuals interpreted and imagined how others saw them and how they saw themselves, triggered reflexive evaluation of their priorities, behaviours and lifestyles, leading to change for many, although not all, of these men.

Therefore, while still arguably a fairly marginal concern within criminology and within the desistance literature, these studies offer a significant contribution to putting emotions onto the 'desistance agenda' and to aiding our understanding of the ways in which emotions may play a role in people's change processes over time. The findings of my own study, based on small-scale, qualitative, exploratory research, echo this work in highlighting the crucial significance of emotions in prompting, shaping and sustaining the transformations in identity which appeared to underpin participants' desistance.

## Narratives of emotions and desistance

The study that forms the basis of discussion in this chapter originally set out to build on the findings of existing qualitative research around the phenomenology or lived experience of desistance. It also aimed to consider the role of 'rehabilitative efforts' – primarily probation supervision – in desistance thus understood. However, the decision to employ a narrative inquiry approach where desisters' psycho-social self-narratives were viewed as the phenomena of interest and narrative methods were employed to explore this, ultimately led the study in a very different direction. Consequently, the significance of emotions in participants' offending and eventual desistance emerged as a key finding.

Arguably, this is an inherent advantage of narrative inquiry over more traditional (qualitative) methodologies. It avoids imposing the researcher's agenda and the academic 'story so far' of desistance, and allows more freedom and opportunity for themes and issues, as yet un-explored or under-developed in the existing literature, to emerge directly from participants' narrative accounts. This was definitely the case in this study. As discussed above, the relationship between emotions and desistance rarely feature in the existing research literature – certainly at the time this study began – and was therefore an area that I was unlikely to ask about. Arguably, narrative or biographical methods are also inherently suited to studies such as this which seek to explore participants' psycho-social meaning-making frameworks and subjective experiences. It is perhaps questionable how far more traditional methods, such as question-and-answer interviews, allow researchers to 'tap into' such realms and meaningfully explore them (Hollway and Jefferson, 2000).

## Methodological approach

In an effort to explore desisters' self-narratives, a series of narrative interviews were conducted with a small cohort of desisting men (based on the men's own assessment, my own, and that of their supervising probation officer). The final cohort of eight participants was made up entirely of men on the basis that the overwhelming majority of offenders are men, and also given that the time and resource constraints of doctoral research would make it difficult to meaningfully compare men's and women's experiences. All of the men had substantial offending histories, often dating back to childhood, and all had substantial experience of the criminal justice system, including both custodial and community sentences. Their offending histories were made up of what can be regarded as 'conventional' crimes in the sense that although some of the offences were very serious in nature, they did not include recorded offences relating to domestic abuse or sexual offences. The time elapsed since last conviction (while in the community) ranged from nine months to over three years.

Three interviews were conducted with each participant over a fairly short time frame. The first of these interviews focused on establishing a time line of significant life events with each participant in an effort to contextualise their later narratives and on building rapport between myself and the narrators. The second interview was the main narrative interview in the sense that this is where I sought to elicit the men's narratives of desistance simply by asking them to 'tell me about when you first started to get into trouble, how that progressed and about more recent times when you've been trying to turn things around and make changes'. In the third and final interviews I asked participants to theorise their experiences, asked questions about areas underdeveloped in their narratives, and shared my initial interpretations with them. Each participant's narrative was analysed holistically for content leading to the identification of special foci or themes in their stories. This then allowed for comparisons and identification of similarities and differences in the stories of participants across the cohort.

While the cohort of participants were fairly typical of the wider offender population in terms of socio-demographic factors and offending histories, the small-scale exploratory nature of this study raises issues around representativeness and generalisabilty. However, the study sought to gain rich in-depth understanding of the participants' subjective experiences of desistance, and this approach, and use of a small sample is suitable for theory building and generalising to theoretical propositions. As Maruna and Matravers argue, while such a case study approach is not without its methodological limitations, the deep exploration of life narratives can 'generate at least as much insight ... as getting to know a little bit about 200 or 2000 human beings in a large-scale survey' (2007, 437).

## Narratives of identity, emotions and offending

Emotions featured heavily in the stories these men told of the onset and persistence in their offending and, in many cases, their associated substance misuse. Most of their stories told of how they built their early identities around the external performance of the 'hard man' character or imago expressed through crime, violence and substance misuse. However, rather than a straightforward, positive process of identification, where they internalised the codes and values of such identities, these men experienced a great deal of inner ambivalence and conflict. They used this imago and behaviours strategically, as a way to manage painful emotions stirred in them by early life experiences, including, in many cases, their troubled relationships with their fathers. They also used them as a way to search for agency – a desire for power, for feeling strong, for having an impact on the world: to assert, protect and expand the self and separate from others. For these men, the external performance of the 'hard man', expressed through these behaviours, was used as a way of mastering and separating from these early experiences and their emotional responses to them. These themes dominated their stories of the escalation in their offending and substance misuse.

For example, Steven's[3] story told of how his relationship with his father and his type of masculine performance stirred feelings of fear, shame and powerlessness in him. It also described how the early construction of his identity around the 'hard man' role, expressed through crime and substance misuse, and the emergence of strongly agentic motivations, were strategic responses related to his desire to 'block out' his emotions and separate himself from others, both physically and emotionally:

> *This* [his father's abuse] *was going on for years, you know what I mean? It just got to a point where I thought, you know what, fuck this, I've had enough, you know what I mean? I was just like doing my own thing...I started getting into drugs and all that, you know what I mean? Committing crime and all that, going to prison you know and all that shit. But basically yeah, when you're getting abused and things for years...and obviously I found something in drugs, you know what I mean?...I was just trying to escape what I was feeling or what was going on, you know what I mean? And of course to maintain that it all needs money, so I used to have to commit crime for it.*

In a similar vein, the role of fear in the early construction of his masculine identity is clear in Dave's story. He describes being a 'frightened kid' but how, actively encouraged by his father, his early masculine identity was built around the use of violence and aggression as a way of negating his overriding feelings of fear – not only of other men or boys and their violence, but fear of failing to measure up as a 'real man' as conventionally understood and as endorsed by his father:

> *I was picked on at school and my father always said 'always go for the big 'un, give him a good hiding and then they become scared of you. And that's what I used to do...I always wanted to be part of that, not 'cause I was the bully, 'cause I was always a frightened kid with being small...and nine times out of ten I would get battered, but I'd accept that beating to show them that you're accepted within that group....And that's the way I was brought up and that's the way I went, into a violent...But I was always a scared child, you know, I was always scared of violence and that.*

His story went on to describe how his alcohol misuse, and adoption of what he terms 'machismo', allowed him to 'mask' his emotions, particularly his overriding feelings of fear:

> I was always scared of violence and that, but when I started drinking about the age of twelve, thirteen…it gave me this macho…you know, like I wasn't scared anymore, it took away that fear, you know?

Often related to fear, the emotion of shame was also central to these men's stories. Their feelings of shame were often linked to their fathers' abuse and to what they perceived as their failure to protect themselves, their mothers and siblings from the violence. For some of these men, shame was also related to their families' poverty and the often accompanying stigma, bullying and social isolation they experienced. Marshall's story perhaps expressed shame most strongly. It told of a great deal of shame in his childhood which was dominated by his mother's drinking and drug misuse. But he also felt fear and shame around the abusive treatment he, his siblings and mother suffered at the hands of various men who spent time at his home, and about his inability to prevent this. He went on to describe his drug misuse, which began at a very early age, as a way of escaping his home situation and his feelings of embarrassment and shame about it:

> You know, I was doing it with me father [taking drugs]. And then after that me mother's behaviour and then me doing, taking these recreational drugs to the point of addiction, to block out you know, their lifestyles erm, embarrassing, embarrassment you know?…I mean when I took I could go 'Ah', I could stick two fingers up to it…it was you know, a psychological reddening, but not going red do you understand? Like of your lifestyle, your house, your mother you know?

The complex ways in which masculinities, masculine self-identities, emotions and offending interacted in these men's narratives are beyond the scope of this discussion, but the gendered nature of these emotions is highly significant in terms of the experiences and relationships that gave rise to them, how they were subjectively experienced by these men, and in terms of the emotional expression afforded, or more accurately not afforded, to young men and boys in our society.

Objectification and denial of emotion is widely regarded as a key feature of conventional or hegemonic masculinity. However, many researchers and theorists (for example, Kimmel,1994) have highlighted how the overriding emotion of masculinity is fear – fear of sexuality, fear of emotion, fear of other men, and ultimately fear of being exposed as 'less than' a 'real' man as conventionally understood. These men's stories reflected this, suggesting that key to the construction of their early identity, which underpinned their offending and substance misuse, was the need to negate their feelings of fear. This meant not only fear of their father's (and others') violence towards them, but also, and significantly, fear that they would be 'found out'– that they would not be able to 'measure up' to the masculine 'ideal', often exemplified by their fathers and endorsed more widely in our society.

Closely allied and related to these men's fears was the emotion of shame. Scheff and Retzinger (1991) argue that due to limitations in the conceptualisation of shame in western societies it is difficult to convey the importance of shame dynamics for understanding both 'normal' and pathological behaviour, and in a similar vein Nathanson (1997, cited in Costello et al, 2010) argues that shame is a critical regulator of human social behaviour. There is a substantial body of psychological, sociological and criminological literature which suggests a link between shame and anti-social and offending behaviour (Ahmed and Braithwaite, 2011). As noted above, the (re)emergence of interest in restorative and re-integrative justice and practices has led to a renewed interest in this link and in the role shame can play in appropriate and meaningful responses to these behaviours.

Scheff et al (1989) contend that most analyses of masculine behaviour simply link it to power and domination and so neglect what they term its emotional/relational aspects. To counter this, they set out to explore the role of emotions, particularly shame, in men's use of violence. They describe shame as a primary emotion generated by a negative evaluation of self, and one that is generally unacknowledged and seen as socially unacceptable or taboo in our society. They propose self-esteem as a 'summary concept' which represents how well a person manages shame. People with high self-esteem, they argue, have sufficient experience of pride to outweigh their experience of shame; they can manage shame, whereas people who have had very little experience of feelings of pride cannot. When someone with little pride experiences some sort of humiliation (real or imagined), Scheff et al argue that rather than acknowledging this, it is masked with anger, and the person is then caught in a 'shame–rage feeling trap' where violence is the consequence of trapped, unacknowledged shame.

In later work, Scheff and Retzinger (1991; 1997) developed these ideas, and in addition to this 'shame–rage loop' identified a 'shame–shame loop' where unacknowledged shame and shame about being ashamed can result in withdrawal and depression. As highlighted by Scheff and Retzinger (1991; 1997), both these ways of repressing unacknowledged shame involve separation and alienation from others. These ideas are reflected in Nathanson's (1992, 132, cited in Costello et al, 2010) 'Compass of Shame' which explores the various ways that human beings react when they feel shame – ideas which have been influential in the development of restorative practices such as conferences and circles. The four poles on this compass of shame and behaviours associated with it are: Withdrawal – isolating oneself, running and hiding; Attack self – self put-down, masochism; Avoidance–denial, abusing drugs, distraction through thrill seeking; Attack others – turning the tables, lashing out verbally or physically, blaming others.

Shame, like fear, is also gendered in the sense that it is linked to societally expected gender norms. While for women shame may be related to a range of competing and often conflicting expectations, for men in contemporary western societies, shame is primarily linked to the 'hegemonic ideal' – the need to never be perceived as weak, and to live up to what it means to be a 'real man' – powerful, protector/provider, unemotional, successful and so on. As with fear, feelings of shame are also gendered in the sense that to experience or struggle with emotion is in itself seen to run counter to what it is to be a 'real man' as conventionally understood in our society, and in terms of the emotional expression permitted to boys and men in our culture. In later work Scheff (2006) argues that a socially constructed and endorsed 'cult of masculinity' in western societies involves isolation from others, the suppression of fear and acting out of anger. In contrast, the 'cult of femininity' involves reciprocal engulfment with others, the suppression of anger and acting out of fear. He argues that when boys are taught to suppress their emotions, first in their families, and later by peers, this results in a 'silence/violence pattern' where vulnerable feelings are first hidden from others and, after repetition, even from the self. He argues that, as a result of this emotional 'distancing', when men face what they perceive to be threatening situations, they are compelled to either silence or to rage and aggression.

These conceptualisations of the dynamics of shame were clearly reflected in many of these men's narratives, where their shame was primarily generated by their negative evaluation of themselves against the masculine 'ideal' as exemplified by their fathers and endorsed culturally. For many of these men, this negative evaluation stemmed from what they saw as their inability to prevent or stop their father's abusive behaviour towards themselves, and from what they perceived as their failure to protect their mothers and siblings from the violence of their father (and other males). For some of these men, these negative self-appraisals also related to what they perceived as their failure to live up to others' expectations of them, to their families' poverty, social circumstances and subsequent stigmatisation, and to their parents' lifestyles and behaviours. Their stories clearly suggest that these men had very little experience of pride and, consequently, had low self-esteem. So when they experienced what they perceived as some sort of humiliation – at the hands of their fathers or others – they were unable to acknowledge their feelings of shame. They masked this with anger, resulting in violence and harmful behaviour to others and/or they avoided or 'retreated' from their feelings of shame (the shame–shame trap) through the misuse of drugs and/or alcohol. As referred to above, Scheff and Retzinger (1991; 1997) suggest that both these ways of repressing unacknowledged shame involve separation and alienation from others and this was reflected in the highly agentic motivational themes in these men's stories of the onset and persistence of their offending.

## Narratives of identity, emotions and desistance

Of course each participant's experience of the process of change was unique to them and their own lived experience. Yet across their stories it was evident that their desistance processes involved a complex and on-going re-biography of their narratised identities – a process in which their emotions were key.

Reflecting existing empirical and theoretical work in the field (for example, Giordano et al, 2002; Rumgay, 2004), a common feature of these men's stories of desistance was that the process began with an increase in their general openness or readiness to change. Themes included a growing dissatisfaction and weariness with aspects of their offending lifestyles – primarily in terms of being a focus of police and other authorities' attention and, overall, a shift towards viewing their offending, and often their substance misuse, more negatively. Again reflecting Rumgay's (2004) theoretical work and also research in the field of addictions, a further common theme in their stories was the considerable length of time that it took for these cognitive shifts and readiness to change to emerge and develop.

Their narratives revealed, however, that the crux of change for these men was undergoing some sort of, what Evans and Wallace (2008, 502) term, 'corrective emotional experience' or 'nuclear episode' (McAdams,

1985; 1993) which entailed these men acknowledging, admitting, and then eventually valuing their emotions.

Their stories tell of how these corrective emotional experiences followed significant events in these men's lives. Some of these were positively attuned, such as becoming a parent for the first time, entering into a meaningful relationship and getting clean from drugs for the first time (if only temporarily at this stage). Others were more negatively attuned, including bereavement, breakdown and experience of long-term imprisonment. Significantly, their stories suggest that, while many of these men had experienced similar life events before, an increase in their general willingness and openness to change and increased levels of motivation, meant that these events, at this particular time in their lives, were interpreted differently in terms of the *meanings* ascribed to them, whereby they were now perceived as significant potential turning points or opportunities for change.

These life events, whether positively or negatively attuned, aroused strong emotional responses and feelings of vulnerability in these men. As a result they were compelled to engage in 'emotional labour' – acknowledging, confronting and admitting their emotions, both those they had experienced in the past, and those aroused by these contemporaneous life events. Doing this 'emotional labour' prompted a realisation in these men that the 'hard man' imago and the agentic codes, attitudes, values, beliefs and behaviours around which they had constructed their identities were inherently flawed, particularly in their insistence that men do not (and should not) feel emotion, and that emotions can be successfully negated or denied through the use and pursuit of power, domination, violence and unmitigated agency (Evans and Wallace, 2008). These experiences therefore challenged these men's ability to maintain the incongruence between their performance of the 'hard man' imago or character and their internal, emotional worlds, and this experience was therefore akin to the collapse of the 'false self' (Winnicott, 1960, cited in Evans and Wallace, 2008).

Their narratives suggest that in light of and prompted by these corrective emotional experiences, these men entered into a period of intense reflexive dialogue where they began to examine, question and reflexively reappraise what they knew of themselves – their stories so far – and, as a result of these experiences, who they now wanted to be. These men's stories therefore reflect Vaughan's (2007, 393) assertion of the importance of a 'moral conversation' in desistance whereby individuals reflexively construct their own identities through an internal 'conversation' which enables them to determine what is of most importance to them. When people are faced with the possibility of changing their lives, as was the case for these men, this entails the individual reflecting on who they were in the past in relation to who they want to be in the future.

While the relational aspects of these men's reflexive experiences are largely beyond the scope of this discussion, their stories do highlight the importance of their emotional connectedness to others and how (significant) others' appraisals of them, (or at least imagined appraisals of them) their behaviour and lifestyles played an important role in this process. Furthermore, reflecting Burkitt's (2012) theorisation of reflexivity, their stories highlighted how feelings and emotions were not merely attendants or commentary to reflexivity, they appeared to be the very basis and motive for reflexive thought: colouring these men's perceptions of their selves, others and the social world, and influencing the way they deliberated on choices they faced (2012, 458). As Burkitt puts it, these men's reflexivity did not 'emerge out of nowhere, nor is its source the various founts of knowledge; behind every thought is the emotional–volitional sphere and this is also true of reflexive thought' (2012, 469)

This reappraisal, following the collapse of their 'false self' or 'mask of emotional bravado' (Pollack, 1995, 42, cited in Evans and Wallace, 2008), can be seen as exposing these men to a risk of 'identity nakedness' (Lofland, 1969, 282) However, reflecting Maruna's (2001) findings, the men in this study were able to reinterpret the *meaning* of events in their past and restructure the story of their lives so far into a 'positive' and progressive one, where past negative and traumatic events and the feelings of fear and shame they engendered were now acknowledged and reinterpreted as supplying learning, wisdom and hope – that they made these men, in a positive sense, who they are today.

For example, Marshall described how he sought to make sense of his past traumatic experiences and his emotional responses to them and was able to re-interpret or re-biography them into positive experiences:

> *That's what I mean by finding myself like, you know? When you realise, when you go through these situations where you have these feelings that hurt or upset you or make you feel magnified… And you try and understand, understand and reconcile, and make sense of it bit by bit…because maybe I wouldn't be as thoughtful as I am, I wouldn't be as deep thinking as I am and I wouldn't be who I am now and basically I'm, I am happy with who I am!* [his emphasis]

For these men, this process of reflexive reappraisal of who they were and who they now wanted to be involved the acknowledgement, acceptance and valorisation of their emotional worlds, which were now admitted a place in their re-biographied sense of self. Common themes in their narratives were the importance of making peace for what they had done – sometimes with their God, sometimes with others, but always with themselves, of finding inner peace and peace of mind, happiness and inner contentment. Many participants also spoke about an increasing awareness of and concern about the impact of their lifestyle and behaviour on others, and of recognising a need and desire to become less self-interested and motivated and to change their lives positively for the benefit of others. As a result of their acknowledgement of their emotions, and acceptance and reinterpretation of their past experiences, their narratives suggest that these men were now able to begin to recognise and value more communal life goals, and strivings for communion – which, in contrast to agency, refers to strivings for love, friendship, intimacy, care-giving and belongingness – became much more dominant motivational themes in their stories.

Their narratives suggest that these men now began to deliberate on how far different potential courses of action and identities would resonate with their new emotional and communal value commitments. They no longer felt that they needed, or wanted, to adopt the 'mask' of the 'hard man' character – which was now seen as incongruent with who they wanted to be. Instead they began to envision and then make conscious and intentional moves towards new, more emotionally 'balanced' and prosocial behaviours and roles, for example as father, partner, scholar and so on, which allowed for the development of new, non-criminal identities. Their narratives therefore suggested that the 'corrective emotional experiences' or 'nuclear episodes' that these men underwent appeared to act as 'hooks' for a reflexive reappraisal of their lives and subsequent re-biography of their masculine identities which in turn acted as a 'hook for change' towards desistance.

While their narratives suggested that the moves towards non-criminal behaviours, roles and identities were conscious and intentional, this does not mean that this process should be understood as unproblematic. Indeed, reflecting existing research in the field, the stories these men told of their efforts to change were ones characterised at times by ambivalence and vacillation, and punctuated by obstacles. However, their narratives suggest that when faced with such obstacles these men were able to reflexively adjust their goals and strategies. Yet also key to 'keeping desistance going' in the face of these obstacles and frustrations was the way in which their new narrative structures or identities –

particularly the integration of more emotional and communal value commitments, goals and beliefs – functioned to regulate their self-concept, mood and motivations (Pillemer, 1992, cited in Singer, 2001): offending and substance misuse were seen as incompatible with these new commitments, and therefore no longer viable or credible options. Reflecting the latter stages of Farrall et al's (2014) emotional trajectory, striking themes in participants' stories of their lives today included the importance of 'normalcy' and assimilation – becoming 'just like other people'. They also spoke of the importance of contentment, inner peace, happiness and joy, and how these goals or goods could be pursued and achieved through generative activities, but also through more 'mundane' day to day activities. Dave, for example, describes his life today in the following way:

> I just try and live a normal life, well, as normal as possible, you know, and enjoy life…I was out on my bike the other night and I thought this is great, that simple thing…lovely evening, the sun just going down, nice and warm and you're just free…I'll go for a walk, go sit in the garden…so yeah, life's good at the moment, nothing's changed, but it's good. You know, feeling good about how I feel about myself, things are good, there are positive things, you know?

## Conclusion

The findings of this study highlight the significance of emotions in both these men's early identities, which underpinned their offending, and their re-biographied identities, which underpinned their eventual desistance. The findings suggest that undergoing some form of 'corrective emotional experience' played a key role in prompting these men's reflexive reappraisals of their lives and eventual shifts in their identities. A common criticism of studies, such as this, which emphasise the role of cognitive and subjective shifts and transformations, is that they often do not explain what triggers these processes (Weaver, 2015). Arguably this study makes a contribution to this area by suggesting that emotions played a key role in triggering, but also shaping, colouring and underpinning these men's reflexive reappraisals and subsequent re-biography of their identity.

Weaver (2016) also highlights how such principally agentic theories are also often unable to explain why and how individuals are able to sustain their investment in prosocial behaviours, roles and identities, particularly during challenging times when their investment in these may be diminished. Again, this study arguably makes some contribution to understanding how such investment can be sustained. These men's narratives of their moves to such new, non-criminal identities did indeed highlight how their efforts were sometimes frustrated by societal and structural 'roadblocks'. However, they also highlighted how their new narrative structures or identities – particularly the integration of their emotions and communal value commitments – functioned to regulate their self-concept, mood and motivations (Pillemer, 1992, cited in Singer, 2001), leading them, when appropriate, to adjust their goals/strategies for change, but also meaning that they no longer saw criminal behaviour and criminal lifestyles as congruent with their new sense of self.

In conclusion, while emotions have, at least until very recently, been largely neglected in theorisations of both crime causation and desistance, the findings both of this study and of recent large-scale studies such as that by Farrall et al (2014) suggest that they are a significant component of desistance. It would seem that emotions play a key role in shaping how people make sense of and interpret their pasts, present and possible futures, and that to not take the links between emotions, crime and desistance seriously would be a disservice to those harmed by crime as well as to offenders and desisters themselves.

## Notes

[1]  Shott, 1979, 1323 cited in Giordano et al, 2007, 1607, describes role taking as 'the process of putting oneself in another's position and taking that person's perspective'.

[2]  In contrast with psychological stage models, development from this perspective is seen as arising in social experiences and activities where the individual develops as a result of their relations to these processes as a whole and to other individuals within them.

[3]  All participants' names have been changed to ensure their anonymity.

## References

Ahmed, E, Braithwaite, J, 2011, Shame, pride and workplace bullying, in S Karstedt, I Loader, H Strang (eds) *Emotions, crime and justice*, Oxford: Hart Publishing

Archer, MS, 2000, *Being human: The problem of agency*, Cambridge: Cambridge University Press

Archer, MS, 2003, *Structure, agency and the internal conversation*, Cambridge: Cambridge University Press

Braithwaite, J, 1989, *Crime, shame, and reintegration*, Cambridge: Cambridge University Press

Burkitt, I, 2012, Emotional reflexivity: Feeling, emotion and imagination in reflexive dialogues, *Sociology* 46, 3, 458–72

Cohen, S, 1955, *Delinquent boys: The subculture of the gang*, Glencoe, IL: Free Press

Costello, B, Wachtel, J, Wachtel, T, 2010, *Restorative circles in schools: Building community and enhancing learning*, Bethlehem, PA: International Institute for Restorative Practices

Evans, T, Wallace, P, 2008, A prison within a prison? The masculinity narratives of male prisoners, *Men and Masculinities* 10, 4, 484–507

Farrall, S, 2002, *Rethinking what works with offenders: probation, social context and desistance from crime*, Cullompton: Willan

Farrall, S, Calverley, A, 2006, *Understanding desistance from crime: Theoretical directions in resettlement and rehabilitation*, Maidenhead: Open University Press

Farrall, S, Hunter, B, Sharpe, G, Calverley, A, 2014, *Criminal careers in transition*, Oxford: Oxford University Press

de Haan, W, Loader, I, 2002, On the emotions of crime, punishment and social control, *Theoretical Criminology* 6, 3, 243–53

Garland, D, 2002, *Of crime and criminals: The development of criminology in Britain*, in M Maguire, R Morgan R Reiner (eds) *Oxford Handbook of Criminology* (3rd edn), Oxford: Oxford University Press

Giordano, PC, Cernkovich SA, Rudolph, JL, 2000, Gender, crime, and desistance: Toward a theory of cognitive transformation, *American Journal of Sociology* 107, 4, 990–1064

Giordano, PC, Schroeder, RD, Cernkovich, SA, 2007, Emotions and Crime over the Life Course: A neo-Meadian perspective on criminal continuity and change, *American Journal of Sociology* 112, 6, 1603–61

Goffman, E, 1963, *Stigma: Notes on the management of spoiled identity*, Harmondsworth: Penguin

Hollway, W, Jefferson, T, 2000, *Doing qualitative research differently: Free association, narrative and the interview method*, London: Sage

Karstedt, S, Loader, I, Strang, H, 2011, *Emotions, crime and justice*, Oxford: Hart Publishing

Katz, J, 1988, *Seductions of crime: Moral and sensual attractions of doing evil*, New York: Basic Books

Kimmel, M, 1994, Masculinity as homophobia: Fear, shame and silence in the construction of gender identity, in H Brod, M Kaufman (eds) *Research on men and masculinities series: Theorising masculinities*, Thousand Oaks, CA: Sage

Liebrich, J, 1996, The role of shame in going straight: A study of former offenders, in B Galaway, J Hudson (eds) *Restorative Justice: International Perspectives,* Monsey, NJ: Criminal Justice Press

Lofland, J, 1969, *Deviance and identity*, Englewood Cliffs, NJ: Prentice Hall

McAdams, DP, 1985, *Power, intimacy and the life story: Personological inquiries into identity*, New York: Guilford Press

McAdams, DP, 1993, *The stories we live by: Personal myths and the making of the self*, New York: Guilford Press

Maruna, S, 2001, *Making good: How ex-convicts reform and rebuild their lives*, Washington, DC: American Psychological Association

Maruna, S, Matravers, A, 2007, N = 1: Criminology and the person, *Theoretical Criminology* 11, 4, 427–42

Matza, D, 1969, *Becoming deviant*, Englewood Cliffs, NJ: Prentice Hall

Pratt, J, 2000, Emotive and ostentatious punishment: Its decline and resurgence in modern society, *Punishment and Society* 2, 417–39

Rumgay, R, 2004, Scripts for safer survival: Pathways out of female crime, *Howard Journal of Criminal Justice* 43, 4, 405–19

Sampson, RJ, Laub, JH, 1993, *Crime in the making: Pathways and turning points through life*, Cambridge, MA: Harvard University Press

Scheff, TJ, 2006, *Goffman Unbound!* Boulder, Colorado: Paradigm

Scheff, T, Retzinger, S, 1991, *Emotions and violence*, Lanham, MD: Lexington Books

Scheff, T, Retzinger, S, 1997, Shame, anger and the social bond: A theory of sexual offenders and treatment, *Electronic Journal of Sociology* 3, 1, www.sociology.org/content/vol003.001/sheff.html

Scheff, T, Retzinger, S, Ryan, M, 1989, Crime, violence and self-esteem, in A Mecca, N Smesler, J Vasconcellos (eds) *The social importance of self-esteem*, Berkley, CA: University of California Press

Singer, JA, 2001, Living in the amber cloud: A life history analysis of a heroin addict, in DP McAdams, R Josselson, A Lieblich (eds) *Turns in the road: Narrative studies of lives in transition*, Washington: DC American Psychological Society

Vaughan, B, 2007, The internal narrative of desistance, *British Journal of Criminology* 47, 3, 390–404

Weaver, B, 2015, *Offending and desistance: The importance of social relations*, London: Routledge

# THREE

# Men, prison and aspirational masculinities

*Jennifer Sloan*

## Introduction

'Masculinities' as a topic for analysis is now increasingly recognised in academic criminological literature. Yet, in the majority of cases the 'masculinity' in question is seen in a particularly negative light. Violence (Butler, 2007; Ellis, 2013; McCorkle, 1992; Monaghan, 2002; Winlow et al, 2001) and sexual harm (Hayes, 2014; Howe, 2008; Moolman, 2011) as demonstrations of masculinity are not new associations, and neither is the use of masculinity-in-association as an analytical tool in criminology: men and race (Phillips, 2012), men and age (Crawley and Sparks, 2005; Harvey, 2012; Nayak, 2006) and men and class (Ellis, 2013; Nayak, 2006) are often seen discussed together. However, what is regularly missing in criminology is an analysis of masculinity as a standalone issue. Bearing in mind that 95 per cent of the prison population is male, there is an undeniable underpinning connection of masculinity that runs throughout criminal justice, but criminologists rarely engage with this, looking instead at other features of these men such as class, race and age. Interestingly, these 'other' features are often used to differentiate criminal men from 'ordinary' men and this process of differentiation in itself is inherently masculine in use (see Sloan, 2011): men often compare themselves to other men (and women) in order to place themselves on the hierarchy of hegemonic masculinity (Connell, 2005).

As such, looking at the similarities between men (in this case, within prison) can be useful in better understanding wider masculinities. This was one of the purposes of the doctoral research that is the basis of this chapter, which looked at masculinities and the adult male prison experience (Sloan, 2016; 2011). The research was an ethnographic study of an adult, male, category C prison in England: over a period of four months in 2009, I spent time on the wings, observed prisoners' day-to-day lives, interviewed 31 male prisoners (aged between 21 and

55, with an average age of 31), and collected personal research diaries. Such an approach allowed the gendered dimension of incarceration to be somewhat triangulated for greater authenticity – from the words the men used to their lived behaviours, and the reactive reflections of an observer from the opposing gender. The sample was self-selecting but, when analysed, shared many of the common findings of other research studies into the lived prison experience and the implications for masculinity, which are rarely discussed.

Although my sample was small relative to the prison population, the research was informative with regard to men's experiences of being men within the prison setting. More research is needed to confirm the external validity of these findings, but the research as a whole gives a good initial indication of men's gendered experience of the general prison experience in a field where the focus tends to be on the negative and extreme manifestations of incarcerated masculine identity. A key issue here relates to the lack of consistency of application of the terminology surrounding masculinities (Sloan, 2016; 2011). In this research, the focus was on male behaviours that related to the individual and group identity of being a man in prison.

The interviews asked men generally about their day-to-day lives in prison and did not focus in any detail on particularly negative or positive experiences. Looking beyond the purely negative aspects of male identity in prison is very useful in gaining a fuller picture of the adult male prison experience. This chapter considers one such positive aspect of masculinity that was identified in the doctoral research project. Aspirational masculinities are a particularly interesting topic in the context of desistance, in that men's aspirational masculinities can (and often do) change during the course of their lives and criminal careers, generally depending upon the 'audience that matters' to them at that particular time in their lives (be that peers, family or the self) (see also Sloan, 2016, for a more detailed discussion of this notion). In many cases, prison can give men the thinking space and subsequent opportunity to re-evaluate these 'audiences who matter', although only in certain contexts. My argument builds on the existing conceptualisations of identity transformation and the importance of social capital in existing desistance literature through the addition of the notion of gender – specifically masculinity, an area which is generally neglected in all areas of criminological research, not least desistance literature.

The aspirational masculine identity was clearly relevant in the mental lives of men at all stages of their criminal careers, before, during and after prison. It is thus an important factor to consider when analysing criminal men, not least because many of the aspirations that men have are directly linked to their masculine identities and the sorts of men they believe they want to become. This links with existing literature by Ricciardelli et al, who note that many men in prison respond to issues of uncertainty and risk which can affect their own identities, 'in ways that present their masculinity as empowered rather than submissive' (2015, 492). In this sense, then, aspirational masculinities were central to men's journeys of identity transformation within the prison environment, whereby they changed their behaviours in order to seek successful lives in the future. I did not keep in touch with the men I interviewed. My naivety as a new researcher, coupled with security consciousness imposed by the institution, meant that I have no knowledge of whether men achieved their ambitions or aspirations. Some will still be in prison now, others may well have returned after release (although I hope not). For some, though, facing up to the challenges of life outside prison may well have paid off.

## Aspirational masculinities

The intersection of aspiration and masculinity is not a new idea. In fact, it is central to some of the key theories about masculine behaviour. Connell coined the term 'hegemonic masculinity', based on Antonio Gramsci's theory of hegemony as class relations, whereby:

> At any given time, one form of masculinity rather than others is culturally exalted. Hegemonic masculinity can be defined as the configuration of gender practice which embodies the currently accepted answer to the problem of the legitimacy of patriarchy, which guarantees (or is taken to guarantee) the dominant position of men and the subordination of women. (Connell, 2005, 77)

Connell goes on to note that hegemonic masculinity is 'historically mobile' (2005), and others have identified the concept as being aspirational in nature (Howson, 2006; Wetherell and Edley, 1999). Hegemonic masculinity is what men aspire to achieve. Indeed, Connell makes this clear, identifying hegemonic masculinity as 'a position always contestable' (2005, 76). Wetherell and Edley question 'the appropriateness of a definition of dominant masculinity which no man may ever actually embody' (1999, 337). I would argue that this is the very point of masculinity and its achievement, as personal aspirations are always changing from day to day – and from man to man

– depending on the life each man is living at the time, the people with whom he interacts, the television he watches and the newspapers he reads. However, the challenge to hegemonic masculinity as a theoretical device, along with its culturally imperialistic nature (Gerami, 2003), goes beyond the scope of this chapter, and is a subject for another time.

In today's society, although highly fluid, the most valorised men tend to be those with successful careers and good jobs, beautiful wives, toned bodies and money to buy expensive goods, fast cars and travel the globe. Achieving the masculine heights of people like Brad Pitt, José Mourinho or Simon Cowell is, in practical terms, unachievable for most men. For those lacking educational skills, jobs, disposable income and access to institutions of social power such as sports clubs, politics or celebrity fame (that is, the majority of men in prison), it becomes nigh on impossible, but is readily grasped as an aspiration. Men can (and do) try, and often the achievement of an element of these hegemonic ideals is good enough – the toned body, the cash, the fast car. All of these can be achieved in one of two ways – legitimately, through legal means, and illegitimately, through criminality and harmful behaviours.

Another theoretical position that highlights the aspirational nature of masculinity more broadly is that of Kimmel who posits that masculinity is granted by others, generally men. He notes that:

> Masculinity is a constantly changing collection of meanings that we construct through our relationships with ourselves, each other, and with our world. Manhood is neither static nor timeless; it is historical. Manhood does not bubble up to consciousness from our biological makeup; it is created in culture. Manhood means different things at different times to different people. (1994, 120)

As such, men strive for masculinity within specific cultural contexts, which, again, change from man to man. Kimmel goes on to suggest that other men play an important role in the establishment of masculine credentials. He thus argues that masculinity is performed (see also Butler, 1999; West and Zimmerman, 1987; Connell, 1996) for the benefit of other men from whom men aspire to receive collective male approval. He claims that such 'homosociality' actually results in a form of homophobia. Men go on to fear other men as a result of their power to grant masculine status and, by extension, to undermine an individual's masculine identity. Thus 'being seen as unmanly is a fear that propels American men to deny manhood to others, as a way of proving the unprovable – that one is fully manly' (Kimmel, 1994, 135).

The aspirational nature of the masculine position, then, becomes clear: men aspire to become – and to be seen as – certain *kinds* of men. This takes on a new dimension, however, when power structures among men are brought into play. Connell and Kimmel both recognise the existence of subordinated masculinities – those who are seen as lesser men in the hegemonic 'competition'. The very process of aspiring to be masculine results in power hierarchies and subsequent marginalisation which is 'always relative to the *authorisation* of the hegemonic masculinity of the dominant group' (Connell, 2005, 80–1). The dominant group is that selection of men who hold power and authority, and who – when contextualised with Kimmel's theory – are key gatekeepers in wider society's acceptance of certain masculine performances as demonstrative of 'worthy' masculine identity.

When the criminal justice system is brought into play, it is clear to see how certain demonstrations of masculinity – violence, sexual harm, theft as a mechanism to achieve 'consumer masculinity' (Crewe, 2009, 277) – are punished as negative behaviours of domination and harm. Yet, men in all cultures aspire to achieve power in some form or another. Indeed, Kimmel states that 'the hegemonic definition of manhood is a man *in* power, a man *with* power, and a man *of* power' (1994, 125). The form of that power may be manifested in different ways, but in no culture are all men seen as equally manly. Men in the terrorist group *ISIS/ISIL/DAESH*, for example, view men that do not conform to their cultural beliefs to be 'infidels' and of lesser value; some people/groups in India still use the caste system in some areas; and in Britain, the 'chav' or benefits 'scrounger' is seen as a lesser man (see Jones, 2012).

Although criminal justice institutions attempt to encourage legitimate masculinities through prosocial modelling (Cherry, 2004) and the punishment of harmful behaviours, this has two potential outcomes. On the one hand, those who associate with, and follow, the prosocial modelling of the staff (where such behaviours exist at all), are seen as betraying the solidarity of the prisoner collective if they get too close to authorities. Platek observed that, of the group assigned the non-'man' status of 'mug', 'the most odious of "mugs" are prison functionaries. A "man" may have no contact whatever with a jailer' (1990, 462). On the other hand, the impact of punishment potentially has similar effects to martyrdom (Gerami, 2003). Men are granted status for overcoming the challenges imposed upon them by the authorities. In essence, the criminal justice system creates a two-tiered system of masculinity: legitimately performed and illegitimately performed, which ultimately shapes the aspirations felt by men at different points in their life courses.

Within the category C adult male prison where I was researching, participants discussed a range of different aspirational masculinities. Some men focused upon education and attending college upon release. Others spoke of wanting to gain employment, mostly using their qualifications for personal training acquired during their incarceration. Perhaps the most poignant group was of those men who wanted to be good fathers on release even if that meant taking a step back and sorting out their own lives and ability to be good role models before taking on the responsibility of caring for their children again. In general, however, the key aspiration was to avoid returning to prison. Yet such aspirations had clearly changed from how they wanted to be seen before they went to prison.

## Before prison

Men who are imprisoned have been deemed in law to have committed a criminal offence. The overwhelming correlation between manhood and offending behaviour has resulted in various theories attempting to explain the relationship between the two. One of the more convincing is that of James Messerschmidt (1993), who argues that:

> When men enter a setting, they undertake social practices that demonstrate they are 'manly'. The only way others can judge their 'essential nature' as men is through their behaviour and appearance. Thus, men use the resources at their disposal to communicate gender to others. For many men, crime may serve as a suitable *resource* for 'doing gender' – for separating them from all that is feminine. Because types of criminality are possible only when particular social conditions present themselves, when other masculine resources are unavailable, particular types of crime can provide an alternative resource for accomplishing gender and, therefore, affirming a particular type of masculinity. (1993, 84)

This is somewhat similar to Merton's suggestion that 'Every social group invariably couples its scale of desired ends with moral or institutional regulation of permissible and required procedures for attaining these ends' (1938, 673). If we apply these words to a gendered context, it is clear to see how certain men end up on the wrong side of the law:

'The technically most feasible procedure, whether legitimate or not, is preferred to the institutionally prescribed conduct' (Merton, 1938, 674). Crime allows men to practice hegemonic masculinity for the audience that matters most to them – usually their peers (thereby demonstrating a somewhat homogenous, and therefore limited, source of social capital).

In both cases, the theorics take into account the fact that other men are granting and guiding masculine behaviours according to certain gendered social norms (as per Kimmel's theory) which are of restricted accessibility: not all men can achieve them legitimately, yet all men are encouraged to aspire to them in order to conform to societal expectations.

The men in my research were incarcerated for a wide variety of offences including sexual offences, violence, murder, robbery and burglary. While the subject of their offences was not actually a topic for discussion in the interviews, many of them spoke of their pre-prison lives, which were often chaotic and characterised by time in the social care system, drugs, alcohol and the negative influences of others:

> *And like there's a connection between that, like social services, such as like going into care from your, from your, like, your own home, and then, um, peer pressure kind of brings drugs into the circle, and then you just find yourself in a little vicious circle.* (Zachary)

And

> *It's just a way of life ent it, coz when I, coz from a young age I was brought up in care and things like that, in secure units, detention centres and everything like that, so I just learnt to live by myself, by my own rules, and I've learnt to live on the street as well, you know what I mean, you pick things up on the street, so I'm very street wise, me, you know what I mean, so that's just how it is.* (Isaac)

This is not unusual. The Ministry of Justice in 2012 reported that 7 per cent of prisoners interviewed had been in some sort of public care (MoJ, 2012c, 7). Such chaotic lives and the lack of stable, legitimate masculine figures from whom to learn masculinity can be highly influential on the types of men that boys aspire to be, and develop into:

> *Just follow in my father's footsteps, yeah, he's a mug, no, he's alright but he's in prison, he obviously aint that good is he, at*

*the end of the day I followed in his footsteps and just carried on,*
*carried on.* (Evan)

Phillips makes the point that, in contrast to women learning from other women, boys' ability to learn from the men in their lives is limited by the secretive state of masculinity. Masculinity is often performed outside the home and away from domestic life. Phillips argues that this results in boys learning more from their peers in a 'collective process of masculinism' (1994, 29), which is not always a positive process. The men that these prisoners aspired to be could be inherently limited by virtue of the lack of positive men from whom to learn more socially legitimate forms of masculine identity signifiers. Add to that the fact that committing crimes can grant these boys masculine credentials from the peers with whom they *do* socialise, and prison becomes an important signifier of masculinity for young men with few other options. Prison itself can then shape these men in different ways.

## In prison

Masculinity is seen to be synonymous with prisons. In representations of prisons, the masculine is emphasised (generally in a negative light through violence, rape, gangs and drugs). As such, men often enter prison with preconceived ideas of the types of men they are expected to be, which can shape their initial aspirational masculinities around the avoidance of victimisation:

> *My biggest worry about coming to prison was the things what you*
> *hear on the outside, you know, people getting beat up, what you*
> *see on the TV ... And um, you find out ... trouble, if you're*
> *looking for trouble, you'll find it. If you're not then you're pretty*
> *much ok.* (Joshua)

In relation to violence in the US prison system, McCorkle found that many younger inmates respond to threats of violence through proactive attitudes. Indeed, '
Many believe that unless an inmate can convincingly project an image that conveys the potential for violence, he is likely to be dominated and exploited throughout the duration of his sentence' (1992, 161).
Yet, in adult prison the feelings are slightly different. Many of the men I spoke to noted how Young Offender Institutions (YOIs) were much more violent than adult prisons. In the latter, men just wanted to 'do their time' and get out, potentially indicating the well-known

notion of 'growing out' of criminality (Rutherford, 2002). They also spoke of wanting to change themselves while in prison, moving away from masculinity-through-violence, to a more controlled masculine identity:

> *And I'm in a much better space than I've ever been before in my life, I can recognise my problems a lot easier, I'm able to, um... control myself and conduct myself in a...orderly manner if you like, without...if somebody says something to me that I don't like, fair enough, that's your opinion. Whereas before I'd have probably back chatted and ended up in an argument.* (Samuel)

This differentiation can be explained through the various 'audiences that matter' across the different men in prison. For some (generally young men), the audience that matters most is their peers, and this is similar to the situation outside of prison and in line with expectations of hegemonic masculine practices. However, other men in prison are able to use the time more effectively as an opportunity to re-evaluate the audience that matters most to them (which, of course, depends to a great degree on the social capital they already have on the outside), and how they should perform their masculinities accordingly.

For example, one prisoner went on to explain his reasoning for a change in identity, which in part was guided by the type of sentence he was serving (an Imprisonment for Public Protection or IPP sentence). These sentences – now abolished by the Legal Aid, Sentencing and Punishment of Offenders Act 2012 – were indeterminate in the sense of release being conditional upon the views of the Parole Board, and required post-sentence monitoring for at least ten years. Targeted at serious violent and sexual offences, IPP sentences require prisoners to prove a reduction in risk – and therefore, a behavioural change – before they can be considered for release (see Sloan, 2014, for more discussion on IPP sentences and masculinities):

> *I've got to bite my lip, I've got to learn to walk away, because if I don't I'll end up, I'll be coming back to prison. And then something happened with my sister, something, a guy spat in her face, anyway, in front of my little nephew, bla bla bla, so, I mean, I was angry, I'm saying to her when I get out I'm gonna, you know, I'm gonna kill him. But then I sat down and I thought about it and I thought, well, I know it's my sister, but if I go doing anything, I'm not changed at all, and I'll be coming back to prison. So I sat there and I...of course I'd like to stick up for*

*my sister, but you know, I'm not doing anything. Coz if I did do something, that means I'm coming back to prison, that means I've learnt nothing for the whole time I've learnt in prison. And I'll be coming back here, and I wouldn't have changed one bit. And I'd be letting other people down as well.* (Oliver)

From this, we can see a change in masculine self both in the light of the future man Oliver wants to be – that is, *not* a prisoner – and the importance of the performance of his identity for the benefit of others who may – or may not – be watching and judging his masculine performance, in what is in essence, a masculine panopticon. In prison, it is not only other prisoners who act as an audience for masculine performances but also prison staff, who are important in the policing of masculinities. They have the power to grant masculine status, or – what is more important – to take it away through infantilisation processes that occur by virtue of their powers of control over the individual. In my research, this often affected the relationships between prisoners and staff – in particular, psychologists are seen negatively by incarcerated men due to the immense power they have over a prisoner's sentence progression (Maruna, 2011). This created difficulties for me when researching, as most of the men mistook me for a psychologist!

The change of identity on entering and leaving prison has been theorised, yet not from a directly masculine perspective (Schmid and Jones, 1991). Schmid and Jones propose the existence of a 'pre-prison' identity – which is suspended during incarceration – a prison identity, and a 'release identity', closely followed by the development of a 'post-prison identity', based upon the ex-prisoner's definitions of his prison experience (1991, 427). Such identities will undoubtedly be shaped by the expectations that the male prisoner has of himself and who he wants to be, and also who he thinks he should be in the eyes of others. Thus, his aspirational masculinity takes on a different light in different settings. One thing that my participants did note was that being in prison provides time in which to take stock and evaluate their lives and aspirations:

*The best thing is…the time to reflect on stuff…Positives…positive reflection, memories, stuff like that, when you're outside you're generally not, you don't have time really to think about stuff like that.* (Kai)

Many prisoners made use of the resources that were available to them – however limited – to attempt to develop a masculine self that they could continue to achieve and ultimately take forward upon release. Such resources included the education system:

> *Yeah, you know...it'll be even better once, once I get on my education the days, the days, you know, once you get your days go, everything's a...I put, I put everything into sections, you know... even my sentence, you know, do my exams, get that done, get to D cat, that...that's my goals, when you make short goals for yourself, tends to go a lot quicker I think.* (Joshua)

and the gym facilities:

Researcher: *Have you always been into the gym and weights and stuff?*

Zachary: *I think I have, I think that was a little side effect of prison...Like a good thing that came out of it, the only good thing I think is that now I've got lots of qualifications in that area and um, yeah because if I didn't come to I don't think I would have lifted up a weight and that's when it first started when I was 15 and uh, then I obviously realised that it was something I liked doing, you know.*

Prisoners used the resources available to alter and develop more legitimate aspirational masculinities in the prison (although some participants spoke of their misuse by a certain few). Yet, ultimately, when in prison, there is only so far that these men can go. The skills learned in prison are mostly useful for their identities upon release rather than their incarcerated masculinities, which are kept in a state of limbo while always being subject to potential challenge by other men. In addition, such opportunities to develop skills are limited, are prison dependent, and are subject to the routines and overarching security restrictions of the prison. As I have noted elsewhere:

> Whilst work is of central importance to all our lives, it has particular significance to men in prion who, ironically, are often distanced from its opportunities the most...What is important, however, is giving men the *opportunity* to take on work which can act as a socially legitimate and positive masculine signifier in a world where many men's only means

to prove their masculinity is through violence, domination and harm. (Sloan, 2015, 92)

Such opportunities ultimately shape the types of men that prisoners are able to try to become upon release.

## After prison

Men's aspirations for the sorts of men they wanted to be after prison tended to be guided by the skills that they had learned in prison, although some referred to identity signifiers that were only just becoming available to them, such as fatherhood. As Hamilton notes (Chapter Two, this volume), the role of fathers in offending men's lives is highly significant, and this has been seen elsewhere in the context of prisons (Earle, 2012). The importance of being a significant member of the family unit and fulfilling one's role as a father and/or partner was key to many men I spoke to:

> In the first month I knew my girlfriend was pregnant I went out, bought cot, bottles, steriliser, a Moses basket, pram, pushchair thing, everything, then with like the first month, and now I feel good, coz I paid for it all. Even though I'm in here, my girlfriend doesn't have to want for anything, because when I was working, I've got enough money saved in the bank to keep her like…not wanting anything basically, if she wants something, then she can just go to the bank, she don't need to ask me, if the baby needs something, milk, whatever, clothes, she can just go and buy them, and that's what makes me feel good. (Harrison)

And

> All I can do is just, is just show my kids for the first time in their life that someone in their family is doing something right man, um I'm looking forward to doing that. (Ethan)

The aspirations of other men related to their future careers which were linked to the skills that they had managed to develop during their time in prison. The majority of such 'careers' revolved around the gym, one of the main recreation activities out of the cell available to prisoners:

*My end objective, if you like, is probably to, like, open a gym...
If I could do that then...that would be me, that would be all my
dreams come true.* (Zachary)

Such aspirations all clearly show how the audiences that mattered to
these men had changed, representing a shift from peer influence to
other forms of masculine social capital resources such as employment
and family. In contrast, some did not have audience that mattered
to them that was not predominantly peer-based and it is notable
that these prisoners did not generally aspire to leave their criminal
lifestyles. Nevertheless, the aspirations of many prisoners revolved
around changing their identities so as not to return to prison. They
recognised the influence of others in the shaping of their performance
of self, and often spoke of having to re-evaluate friendship groups; in
essence, changing their audience for masculine performance:

*Yeah, yeah it does, it does yeah, it kinda scares me in some respects
that I'm going out at the age of [X] to start life fresh, you know
meeting, making new friends, uh maybe finding a new relationship,
having to work at that at some, you know, in a clear frame of
mind, there's a lot of stuff that scares me but I do think that I can
do it, I know that I've got the ability to do it.* (Kai)

This even extended to religious audiences. Prison is a key site for
religious transformation, and this can influence the types of men
whom prisoners want to try to be upon their release. Indeed, it has
been noted that, 'for those individuals who convert to Islam in English
prisons, Islam provides them with a moral framework from which to
rebuild their lives' (Spalek and El-Hassan, 2007, 99):

*This time, I want to go out, go Mosque, go Mosque every week,
yeah.* (Jack)

So, the aspirational masculinities shared with me by male prisoners
tended to revolve around them changing their behaviours so that
they would be able to access socially valued structural power ladders
of masculinity through the relevant masculinity-granting audiences
(whether these be employment, family or religion). There may be
differences in the forms of masculinity that men aspire to depending
upon those factors that differentiate them (factors such as class, age,
wealth and ethnicity). Yet, the power structures that run throughout are
essentially the same. These men ultimately attempt to access the realms

where *men of power* reside and can subsequently, as an audience, grant legitimate masculine status – men that they as individuals, and society in general, respect and afford masculine power and credentials. In essence, the 'positive' aspirations that these male prisoners display actually conform to the system of hegemonic inequality posited by Connell, whereby certain men are able to dictate the limits and dimensions of masculinity that are granted status and esteem, thus marginalising and subordinating those who do not aspire to such heights of manhood. Yet aspiration and achievement are two very different states to occupy.

## Discussion

Changing aspirations may well provide opportunities for desistance, but there are many potential roadblocks along the way, often dependent upon the social capital that is available to these men in the community even before they enter prison. So does aspirational masculinity mean that men are ultimately doomed to fail? As we have already seen, before prison, men often commit crime as a way to achieve masculine status when other, legitimate, mechanisms for masculine identity achievements are (perceptibly) unavailable to them (Messerschmidt, 1993). When in prison for such criminal actions, men are yet again limited in the masculine resources (and audiences) available to them and only too often opt for the 'easy' route to achieving masculinity through reputation, power, dominance and violence, performing for an audience of their male peers. Upon release, many men aim to achieve a masculine identity through their positioning within families, for example, or the world of work. The goals of achieving masculinity are still there. Such goals may be enabled by those who support the prisoner's life upon release – family, friends, employers: those who accept the individual in spite of his offending past. Barriers exist where such relationships are not there to support identity change and those structural changes that they need to make to their lives in order to move onto a different path (Laub and Sampson, 2003). Interestingly, the key difference throughout the process of imprisonment (before, during and after) in terms of shaping aspirations, is the 'audience that matters' to individuals. Before prison, peers often influence men to commit illegitimate behaviours, be that through criminal friends who encourage the behaviours that lead to offending such as drinking and drug taking, or gangs and crime networks. These men require a certain kind of – generally illegitimate – masculine performance in order to grant the individual masculine status (or at least status as the individual perceives it).

During imprisonment in YOIs, aspirational masculinities tend to be shaped by fears and routes to avoid victimisation in a hyper-masculine world. The audience of the YOI community is highly influential (and yet often extremely vulnerable and uncertain as these young men are still learning their masculinities). In the adult estate, men's audience-who-matters is subject to change with reflection and time: those on longer sentences often get the chance to re-evaluate what and who 'matters' to them and their futures. Those without the time or inclination to change the performative 'audience that matters' to them will generally return to the same behaviours of crime and harm upon release. They will not change, as they 'do not need to' – their masculine performances of illegal masculinities suit the audience that matters to them at the time. This may well explain why these men tend to be reconvicted so often. In 2010, those receiving a sentence of immediate custody of less than 12 months compared with matched offenders receiving one to four years, had a one year proven reoffending rate of 62.5 per cent (MoJ, 2013, 19). There is no time for change to their masculine aspirations or valued audiences, or to develop alternative skills for performing legitimate masculinity to take them away from criminality.

According to the men I spoke to, those who do change their aspirations and their 'audience that matters' will try to focus upon performing for their families, employers, and/or gaining favour with other more socially legitimate purveyors of masculine credentials, therefore having the potential to move away from crime and offending behaviours. This fits with the desistance literature that states that social bonds are important as a catalyst for change (Laub and Sampson, 2003), and the findings of Cid and Marti (2012) regarding the impact that maturation into adulthood can have upon offenders' interpretations of institutions such as the family.

Yet, these men are still in positions where they may feel that legitimate resources for masculine performance are not available to them. It is unlikely that their positions within the world of work are improved by being in prison. Indeed, in 2011/12 only 26.59 per cent of prisoners nationally (both men and women) entered employment upon their release from prison (MoJ, 2012a, 35). The fact that this was above the national target is a sad indictment of what is expected of ex-offenders. The Ministry of Justice also found that: 'Both having been employed in the year before custody and having a qualification were associated with a lower likelihood of reconviction in the year after release than being unemployed and not having a qualification (40 per cent compared with 65%, and 45 per cent compared with 60%, respectively)' (MoJ, 2012b, ii).

Family ties are also highly strained by imprisonment. Not only are there serious implications for how men can act as fathers when they are separated from their children (Earle, 2012; Roy, 2005), many relationships are strained – some to the point of no return – by the prison process: '43 per cent of sentenced prisoners and 48 per cent of remand prisoners say they have lost contact with their families since entering prison' (NACRO, 2000, cited in SEU, 2002, 112) and '22 per cent of the prisoners who were married on entering prison are now divorced or separated' (Dodd and Hunter, 1992, cited in SEU, 2002, 112). In addition, the financial (and practical) implications of imprisonment of a family member on the remaining family are huge, as well as resulting in issues such as physical and mental illness (Smith et al, 2007).

Although men's masculine aspirations may have changed during their prison careers, their pasts play an important role in affecting who they are able to become: 'The factor *most strongly* independently associated with increased likelihood of employment after release from custody amongst the SPCR longer-sentenced prisoners was *employment before custody*' (MoJ, 2014, 3). Yet 13 per cent of the prison population have never had a job (MoJ, 2012b). This was an issue recognised by the men themselves:

> In a way I don't, I don't ever want to come back but now I've got a criminal record it's harder to get jobs and that out there, so… dunno really. If you can't get a job and…it's hard, d'you know what I mean…everyone needs money to survive, so…dunno what's round the corner do ya. (Jayden)

If these men struggled to perform their masculinity legitimately (that is, through employment) *before* prison, the imposition of a prison sentence is not going to help much, particularly if prisons fail to recognise such needs. Greater policy focus on men's goals for masculine identities and the routes available to such men to 'act out' their masculinities, is required inside and outside of prison in order to address such issues. Within the prison this may be difficult, given the tensions between prisoners and staff regarding power differentials and not wanting to appear 'too close', as well as budgetary issues and balancing the ever prioritised matter of 'security'.

Prison policy has a key focus upon rehabilitation and reducing reoffending. HM Prison Service states that it 'serves the public by keeping in custody those committed by the courts. Our duty is to look after them with humanity and help them lead law-abiding and useful lives in custody and after release' (www.justice.gov.uk/about/hmps/). Yet very few of the practical policies put in place actually encourage positive aspirational masculinities. Although programmes within prison have attempted to deal with masculinity, these are rare. 'Safe Ground' is an example of one of the few. This charitable organisation runs a number of masculinity-focused courses within some prisons and YOIs in England. One such programme, entitled 'Man up' is 'designed to support men and young men to explore the ways in which the concept of masculinity contributes to shaping individual identity' (Safe Ground, 2015).[1] Yet, this programme is only run in a tiny proportion of prisons and YOIs in the country (though it is expanding). Although other offending behaviour programmes have operated on a similar basis – Potts (1996) details a prison group run by the Probation Service in West Yorkshire which focused on masculinity in the 1990s – out of the 48 current programmes listed as available by the Ministry of Justice, none focus explicitly upon masculinities (MoJ, 2011, 47–72). This is strange: 'After all, if we believe that alcohol or drugs related crime can be reduced by work intended to reduce such abuse, then surely gender related crime – and that's most of it – can be reduced by developing interventions which deconstruct traditional masculinity' (Potts, 1996, 31).

Indeed, public debate needs to engage with the very goals of achieving masculinity impressed upon men from a young age through the media, popular culture, film and peer pressures, in the same way that the pertinent issues affecting young women are debated: issues such as body image, sexism and harassment. When it comes to engaging with men's issues and masculine performativity, the debate goes strangely quiet.

This is not surprising: masculinity has been controlled by other men for thousands of years: a minority of men are in positions of power that enable them to dictate what 'good' masculinity is. Bibbings has considered cases in history which demonstrate the end of the 1800s as 'a period when worries about men resulted in efforts to rein in male behaviour and attempts to legally bind men by delineating the parameters of unacceptable and unlawful violence' (2014, 190). Arguably, that process continues today, but has spread well beyond the courtrooms to the media, public policy, and general stereotypes and stigmas which form mechanisms through which masculinity is policed by more powerful and influential men – editors, politicians, commentators, sportsmen, celebrities, comedians and so on. Extremes of gender are ultimately penalised by those in power with influence, where they can be criminalised, demonised or stigmatised to such a degree that achieving masculinity becomes almost impossible legitimately and legally.

## Conclusion

All men aspire to be a certain kind of man in their own eyes and in the eyes of those whose opinions they value. In the majority of cases, these are other men, although not always:

> *I don't, I don't want to embarrass my Mum, my Mum's she's...I've not had a bad upbringing, I've had a brilliant upbringing you know, never wanted for anything, we were quite well off and stuff so it's no reflection on her and I don't...want her to think that, you know, any of her family are judging her or, you know, she just wants to be proud of me at the end of the day and I want to make her proud of what, you know, it's an awkward situation.* (Sebastian)

The audience who actually matter, however, tends to change throughout the prison life stages of an offender. Prior to prison, men's aspirational masculinities tend to be shaped by their peers, from whom they learn what it is to 'be a man' – not always with the most positive results. When in prison, these aspirations change. In YOIs, aspirations are shaped by fear and avoiding victimisation through violence, yet in adult prisons, men's aspirations turn to who they want to be upon release and how they can get there (not least because the violence and hyperactivity seen in YOIs is neither valued, nor particularly tolerated, by adult prisoners). Such aspirations are often made possible through the provision of time to think (although for short sentence prisoners, such breathing space is generally unavailable).

Upon release, men attempt to put these aspirations – often based on families, employment and/or gaining favour with other more socially legitimate purveyors of masculine credentials – into action. Yet the means through which they are able to achieve masculinity are still limited, if not more so through stigma. The key factor that may have changed is the masculine 'audience' for performance, and the change in perspective of the offender (and what he views to be important to his masculine identity).

This chapter has attempted to show how aspirational masculinities are key to the behaviours and actions of criminal men who come into contact with the prison system. Clearly there will be exceptions to the theoretical ideas being proposed here. If we believe that masculinities are fluid and plural (Connell, 2005), we must acknowledge that not every man will fit the same theoretical mould. Yet it is clear that men's masculine aspirations shape them in clear ways during their prison lives and beyond. Achieving such aspirations is dependent upon the resources made available to these men. Therein lies the problem, as men who have experienced prison often have fewer, rather than more, legitimate masculine and social capital resources at their disposal. It is the provision of such resources, as well as the encouragement of positive aspirational masculine identities and positive potential audiences that matter to these men, which needs greater focus in policy and practice in order to support those positive aspirations to become desistance-inducing realities.

## Note

[1]   Please note that all opinions and critiques made are made by the author and not in any way endorsed or supported by *Safe Ground*.

## References

Aresti, A, 2010, *'Doing time after time': A hermeneutic phenomenological understanding of reformed ex-prisoners experiences of self-change and identity negotiation*, Unpublished PhD Thesis, Birkbeck, University of London

Bibbings, LS, 2014, *Binding men: Stories about violence and law in late Victorian England*, London and New York: Routledge

Butler, J, 1999, *Gender trouble: Feminism and the subversion of identity*, London and New York: Routledge

Butler, M, 2007, *Prisoner confrontations: The role of shame, masculinity and respect*, Unpublished PhD Thesis, University of Cambridge

Cherry, S, 2004, Pro-social modelling in prisons, *Prison Service Journal* 156, 46–7

Cid, J, Martí, J, 2012, Turning points and returning points: Understanding the role of family ties in the process of desistance, *European Journal of Criminology* 9, 6, 603–20

Connell, RW, 1996, New directions in gender theory, masculinity research, and gender politics, *Ethnos* 61, 3–4, 157–76

Connell, RW, 2005, *Masculinities* (2nd edn), Cambridge: Polity Press

Crawley, E, Sparks, R, 2005, Older men in prison: survival, coping and identity' in A Liebling, S Maruna (eds) *The effects of imprisonment*, Abingdon and New York: Routledge

Crewe, B, 2009, *The prisoner society: Power, adaptation, and social life in an English prison*, Oxford and New York: Oxford University Press

Dodd, T, Hunter, P, 1992, *The national prison survey 1991*, London: HMSO

Earle, R, 2012, 'Who's the Daddy?' – ideas about fathers from a young men's prison, *The Howard Journal of Criminal Justice* 51, 4, 387–99

Ellis, A, 2013, *'Handy lads': An ethnographic research study of men and violence in northern England*, Unpublished PhD Thesis, University of Sheffield

Ellis, A, Wykes, M, 2013, Bringing the boys back home: Re-engendering criminology, in M Cowburn, M Duggan, A Robinson, P Senior (eds) *Values in Criminology and Community Justice*, pp 77–92, Bristol: Policy Press

Gerami, S, 2003, Mullahs, Martyrs, and men conceptualizing masculinity in the Islamic Republic of Iran, *Men and Masculinities* 5, 3, 257–274

Harvey, J, 2012, *Young men in prison*, Abingdon and New York: Routledge.

Hayes, S, 2014, *Sex, love and abuse: Discourses on domestic violence and sexual assault*, Basingstoke: Palgrave Macmillan

Howe, A, 2008, *Sex, violence and crime: Foucault and the 'man' question*, Abingdon and New York: Routledge-Cavendish

Howson, R, 2006, *Challenging hegemonic masculinity*, London and New York: Routledge

Jones, O, 2012, *Chavs: The demonization of the working class*, London: Verso Books

Kimmel, MS, 1994, Masculinity as homophobia: Fear, shame, and silence in the construction of gender identity, in H Brod, M Kaufman (eds) *Theorizing masculinities*, Thousand Oaks, CA and London: Sage

Laub, J, Sampson, R, 2003, *Shared beginnings, different lives: Delinquent boys to age 70*, Cambridge, MA: Harvard University Press

McCorkle, RC, 1992, Personal precautions to violence in prison, *Criminal Justice and Behaviour* 19, 2, 160–73

Maruna, S, 2011, Why do they hate us? Making peace between prisoners and psychology, *International Journal of Offender Therapy and Comparative Criminology* 55, 5, 671–5

Merton, RK, 1938, Social structure and anomie, *American Sociological Review* 3, 5, 672–82

Messerschmidt, JW, 1993, *Masculinities and crime*, Lanham, MD: Rowman and Littlefield Publishers

Messerschmidt, JW, 2001, Masculinities, crime, and prison, in D Sabo, TA Kupers, W London (eds) *Prison Masculinities*, Philadelphia, PA: Temple University Press

MoJ (Ministry of Justice), 2011, *Correctional Services Accreditation Panel Report 2010-11*, London: MoJ

MoJ, 2012a, *National Offender Management Service annual report 2011/12: management information addendum, Ministry of Justice Information Release*, www.gov.uk/government/uploads/system/uploads/attachment_data/file/218333/noms-annual-report-2011-12-addendum.pdf

MoJ, 2012b, The pre-custody employment, training and education status of newly sentenced prisoners: Results from the Surveying Prisoner Crime Reduction (SPCR), longitudinal cohort study of prisoners, *Ministry of Justice Research Series 3/12*, London: MoJ

MoJ, 2012c, Prisoners' childhood and family backgrounds, Results from the Surveying Prisoner Crime Reduction (SPCR), longitudinal cohort study of prisoners, *Ministry of Justice Research Series 4/12*, London: MoJ

MoJ, 2013, 2013 Compendium of re-offending statistics and analysis, *Ministry of Justice Statistics Bulletin*, London: MoJ

MoJ, 2014, The impact of experience in prison on the employment status of longer-sentenced prisoners after release, Results from the Surveying Prisoner Crime Reduction (SPCR), longitudinal cohort study of prisoners, *Ministry of Justice Analytical Series*, London: MoJ

MoJ, 2015, *Offender Behaviour Programmes (OBPs)*, London: MoJ, www.justice.gov.uk/offenders/before-after-release/obp

Monaghan, LF, 2002, Hard men, shop boys and others: Embodying competence in a masculinist occupation, *The Sociological Review* 50, 3, 334–55

Moolman, B, 2011, *Permeable boundaries: Incarcerated sex offender masculinities in South Africa*, Unpublished PhD Thesis, University of California, Davis

NACRO, 2000, *The forgotten majority: The resettlement of short term prisoners*, London: NACRO

Nayak, A, 2006, Displaced masculinities: Chavs, youth and class in the post-industrial city, *Sociology* 40, 5, 813–31

Phillips, A, 1994, Learning masculinity, in A Coote (ed) *Families, children and crime*, London: Institute for Public Policy Research

Phillips, C, 2012, *The multicultural prison: Ethnicity, masculinity and social relations among prisoners*, Oxford: Oxford University Press

Platek, M, 1990, Prison subculture in Poland, *International Journal of the Sociology of Law* 18, 459–72

Potts, D, 1996, *Why do men commit most crime? Focusing on masculinity in a prison group*, Wakefield, UK: West Yorkshire Probation Service

Ricciardelli, R, Maier, K, Hannah-Moffat, K, 2015, Strategic masculinities: Vulnerabilities, risk and the production of prison masculinities, *Theoretical Criminology* 19, 4, 491–513

Roy, K, 2005, Nobody can be a father in here: Identity construction and institutional constraints on incarcerated fatherhood, in M Marsiglio, K Roy, G Litton Fox (eds) *Situated fathering: A focus on physical and social spaces*, Lanham, MD: Rowman and Littlefield Publishers

Rutherford, A, 2002, *Growing out of crime: The new era*, Winchester: Waterside Press

Safe Ground, 2015, *Man up*, www.safeground.org.uk/programmes-services/man-up/

Schmid, TJ, Jones, RS, 1991, Suspended identity: Identity transformation in a maximum security prison, *Symbolic Interaction* 14, 4, 415–32

SEU (Social Exclusion Unit), 2002, *Reducing re-offending by ex-prisoners*, London: Social Exclusion Unit

Sloan, J, 2011, *Men inside: Masculinity and the adult male prison experience*, Unpublished PhD Thesis, University of Sheffield

Sloan, J, 2014, Masculinity and imprisonment for public protection, *Prison Service Journal,* 213, 30–4

Sloan, J, 2015, Masculinity, imprisonment and working identities, in C Reeves (ed) *Experiencing imprisonment: Research on the experiences of living and working in carceral institutions*, London and New York: Routledge

Sloan, J, 2016, *Masculinity and the adult male prison experience*, Basingstoke: Palgrave Macmillan

Smith, R, Grimshaw, R, Romeo, R, Knapp, M, 2007, *Poverty and disadvantage among prisoners' families*, York: Joseph Rowntree Foundation

Spalek B, El-Hassan, S, 2007, Muslim converts in prison, *The Howard Journal* 46, 2, 99–114

Sykes, G, 1958, *The society of captives: A study of a maximum security prison*, Princeton, NJ: Princeton University Press (2007 edn)

West, C, Zimmerman, DH, 1987, Doing gender, *Gender and Society* 1, 2, 125–51

Wetherell, M, Edley, N, 1999, Negotiating hegemonic masculinity: Imaginary positions and psycho-discursive practices, *Feminism and Psychology* 9, 3, 335–56

Winlow, S, Hobbs, D, Lister, S, Hadfield, P, 2001, Get ready to duck: Bouncers and the realities of ethnographic research on violent groups, *British Journal of Criminology* 41, 3, 536–48

Wykes, M, Ellis, A, Sloan, J, 2013, 'Motifs' of masculinity: The stories told about 'men' in British newspaper coverage of the Raoul Moat case, *Crime, Media and Culture* 9, 1, 3–21

# FOUR

# Lived desistance: understanding how women experience giving up offending

*Sarah Goodwin*

## Introduction

Given the proportion of women in the criminal justice system, and particularly those in prison, it is perhaps understandable that the overwhelming focus in desistance research has been on men. Many important studies either neglect to include women, or ignore the differences in experience between genders (for example, Sampson and Laub, 1993; Maruna, 2001; Bottoms et al, 2004). In many ways desistance is experienced similarly despite gender, and this can be a wholly acceptable reason for a lack of research interest. However, research indicates that there are some common features of women's desistance that are markedly different to (or significantly more pronounced than) men's researched experiences (for example, Giordano et al, 2002; Leverentz, 2006). In addition, while many researchers talk of desistance as a process rather than an event, it is still rare to encounter a qualitative research design which attempts to take this position seriously in the *investigation* of desistance. With some exceptions, the desire to identify 'successful' desisters understandably proves more pressing than the possibility of examining the process of desistance as it unfolds. Yet this need not be the case.

Through the use of a micro-longitudinal, relational interviewing approach (Soyer, 2014; Leverentz, 2014), I followed a number of women through some months in their lives where they had experience of desisting from crime to some extent. This approach offers unprecedented access to the daily experience of women as they face the challenge of desisting, and lessens problems of retrospective interviewing after many months or years of offending-free behaviour. Yet this intensive qualitative approach raises questions of whether my findings are specific to women, or whether men would report similar experiences if they were interviewed in comparable circumstances.

In this chapter, I first look at understandings of lived desistance, introducing existing research on female desisters, particularly the role of identity in their experiences. Next, I introduce my own study and the methods used. Turning to explaining my findings, I examine why identity change may be important to female desisters and explore the impact of participants' lack of confidence in themselves on their understanding of their own identities. In contrast to some other desistance literature (Maruna, 2001) which discusses people exerting an identity which they had not previously embodied, I show that many of my participants reclaimed a previous identity rather than creating a brand new identity in their desistance. This re-discovery of a lost 'self' was particularly evident in women who had lived many years in controlling and abusive relationships. The most common identity to be (re-)claimed among the participants was that of a mother or carer, which raised questions about the social availability of various alternative identities to the participants. However, a 'caring' identity also provided opportunities for strengthening desistance through providing a cognitive blueprint (Giordano et al, 2002) and generative potential (Maruna, 2001) – although these opportunities were not always realised. When it came to experiencing desistance as a process, the most obvious impacts of a (re-)establishment of a prosocial identity were the accompanying increases in confidence. Whether directly or indirectly, questions of identity did have an appreciable effect on women's experiences of desistance, and throughout this chapter I consider the extent to which discussions of identity were shaped by the research methods themselves.

## Lived desistance?

Before outlining the details of the study which form the basis of this chapter, it is beneficial to spend some time explaining what I mean by the use of the term 'lived desistance'. Studies in the area have long agreed that desistance is best understood as a process and not an identifiable point in time (Weitekamp and Kerner, 1994; Bushway et al, 2001; Laub and Sampson, 2001; Barry, 2006; Kazemian, 2007; Weaver and McNeill, 2007). This process is not linear and straightforward but almost inevitably includes periods of backsliding, relapse and uncertainty (Glaser, 1969; Maruna, 2001). By following participants through the desistance process, insights are gathered into their experiences (both positive and negative) *as they live them*. To examine this process in-situ, there is therefore no inherent need to require potential research participants to be crime-free for any period of time before the start of the study (Mulvey, 2004). Moreover, given the relapse-filled nature of the desistance process, further criminal behaviour during the course of the research need not invalidate a participant's continued involvement. While some research requires self-reported intentions to desist to be supported both by the absence of further criminal convictions and a corroborating opinion from a professional (Maruna, 2001), others solely rely on a self-definition of being a desister (McNeill and Weaver, 2010).

In the current study, I take a mixed approach, which is primarily based on participants' stated intentions and desires to desist, but requires some corroboration in the form of an assertion from a professional that they have seen some (unspecified) signs of participants' sincerity in desistance. Other studies have used a wide range of measures to determine whether participants' previous criminality was serious enough to allow for the possibility of desistance. While many different choices could be justified, it seems that, at the very least, participants should have committed more than one crime (even if not officially recorded) before they can be said to be able to desist. This is therefore the approach I take – although admittedly the limited previous criminal involvement I required was partly influenced by concerns over recruiting sufficient numbers of participants. In summary, to investigate 'lived desistance' means following participants who can be viewed as desisting from some level of repeated criminal behaviour, over time, to see what their experiences are (both successful and otherwise) of giving up offending.

Perhaps at this point it is necessary to justify discussing 'desistance' and not 'recovery' when so many female offenders are convicted of crimes inherently linked to alcohol and drug addictions (Caddle and Crisp, 1997; Malloch, 2004; Morash, 2010; Leverentz, 2014). Indeed, 12 of the 15 participants in my study referred in interview to struggles with substance abuse. In addition to being common practice in criminological studies to look at the desistance of addicted offenders (Maruna, 2001; Bottoms and Shapland, 2011; Leverentz, 2014), drug use is technically offending behaviour whenever the substances in question are illegal (Malloch, 2004). Similarly strong associations exist among those previously convicted of crimes between alcohol abuse and offending to access funds for the purchase of that alcohol (Malloch, 2004; Morash, 2010). Not all offenders have addiction problems, but constraining my discussion of desistance to those unaffected by substance abuse would only address a small number of offenders in the criminal justice system. Furthermore, questions of identity, in particular, appear to be similar across experiences of both desistance and recovery. Colman and Vander Laenen (2012) found that desisters viewed previous identities as 'criminals' as subordinate to previous identities as 'addicts' when they retrospectively interviewed those desisting and recovering from serious offending and addiction. However, this might be an artefact of their recruitment strategy, which relied on treatment and social care services. Yet identities as recovering addicts were not always prominent in the current study, even where participants were recovering from severe addictions or in treatment. Both those with substance abuse struggles and those without frequently referred to a range of previous identities (naturally including that of 'addict'), and these identities shared similar effects on participants as they tried to desist. For example, both addicted and offending women face stigma from society which labels them as both uncaring and unfeminine (Worrall, 1990; Smart, 1992; Zaplin, 1998; Carlen, 2002; Malloch, 2004), necessitating a change in how they see themselves to achieve successful desistance. The difficulties of adverse circumstances, damaged relationships and bruised self-confidence affect both groups of women as they renegotiate their own identities. Undoubtedly, recovery and desistance are not fully interchangeable terms, but the connections and similarities between the two are striking. What is important is that recovery and desistance are not experienced as separate processes by those women in the present study where both are subsumed into the overall process of (re-)creating a prosocial identity and lifestyle. With this in mind, I discuss desistance from crime here even where it is inextricably bound up with recovery from addiction.

## Female desisters

Female offenders face many challenges in desisting from crime. Many are exposed to poverty (Loucks, 2004; NOMS and NPS, 2006; McIvor, 2007; Morash, 2010) and have few workplace skills (Loucks, 2004; NOMS and NPS, 2006). In addition, many are mothers (although some no longer have care of their children) (Loucks, 2004; Corston, 2007). They often face fractured family and personal relationships (Morash, 2010), and experience of abuse (either as children and/or as partners) is common (Loucks, 2004; NOMS and NPS, 2006; McIvor, 2007; Morash, 2010). Indeed in the current study, 10 out of 15 participants disclosed experiences of abuse. In addition to widespread misuse of alcohol and drugs (Loucks, 2004; NOMS and NPS, 2006; McIvor, 2007), physical and mental health problems are common (Loucks, 2004;

McIvor, 2007; Debidin, 2009; Morash, 2010), and around a third of women in contact with probation services in England and Wales have admitted self-harm or attempted suicide (Debidin, 2009). Yet despite all this, and in common with male offenders, there are several accounts of female offenders leaving crime behind them (for example, Eaton, 1993; Leibrich, 1993; Giordano et al, 2002).

Nevertheless, research into the experiences of female desisters remains relatively scarce. Many of the largest and most influential studies in the area either focus exclusively on men (Laub and Sampson, 2003; Bottoms et al, 2004) or fail to analyse their mixed (but male-heavy) samples by gender (Maruna, 2001; Farrall et al, 2014). Yet some important contributions do exist. Of particular note is Giordano and colleagues' (2002) study and their theory of cognitive transformation. Based on a mixed methods study with over a hundred initially incarcerated boys and girls over many years, such a robust approach to studying female desistance is yet to be matched. However, due to the impressive size of the sample, the study can only provide a few snapshots into desisters' experiences, and is hampered by gaps of many years – risking greater use of reconstruction, improvisation and speculation in participants' accounts (Graham and Bowling, 1995). On the other hand, and providing a detailed exploration of female desisters' lived experiences through the process of desistance, Leverentz's (2014) qualitative study of female ex-prisoners in Chicago is based on interviews with 49 women every three to four months over the course of a year. Naturally, several other useful studies into women's desistance exist (for example, Sommers et al, 1994; McIvor et al, 2009; Sharpe, 2011), and they provide further insight into women's experiences of giving up crime.

Within both gender-aware studies and desistance research in general, the necessity of a change in identity is often viewed as central to long-term success (Baskin and Sommers, 1998; Giordano et al, 2002; Bottoms et al, 2004; Sanders, 2007; Byrne and Trew, 2008; Paternoster and Bushway, 2009). Some writers assert that such a change is necessary for both male and female desisters in order to shed the problematic and shame/stigma-inducing identity of 'offender' and to provide a satisfactory 'replacement self' (Giordano et al, 2002). Giordano and colleagues (2002) expand this concept, explaining that replacement selves which provide more detailed 'cognitive blueprints' – in other words, guides to behaviour in those roles – are particularly helpful to a desister as they attempt to claim a new identity. Others focus on the gendered aspects of the desisters' identity, claiming that being at once 'female' and an 'offender' is inherently problematic to women because of the assumed maleness of offenders (Byrne and Trew, 2008). Rumgay (2004) suggests that this strained understanding of identity is precisely what prompts female offenders' experiences of intense shame and powerlessness. Therefore, a change in identity is necessary to reconcile these conflicting views of the self and in order to provide a foundation for successful female desistance. Yet some other studies claim that identity change is not necessarily crucial for desistance at all (Bottoms et al, 2004; Farrall et al, 2014). With such conflicting viewpoints, it can be difficult to conclude whether an identity change is truly necessary to desistance and, if so, for what reason – and especially whether this is inherently tied to gender. In the current study, it is particularly interesting to consider these questions in the context of investigating lived desistance. It may be that issues of identity are not particularly relevant to desisters in their everyday lives and are instead later superimposed onto experiences or recognised only with the benefit of hindsight. I now turn to providing more details of my approach to the study

## Methods

Over the course of a year, I was a regular volunteer at Together Women Sheffield – a community 'one-stop-shop' (Corston, 2007) which caters to women either involved, or at risk of becoming involved, in the criminal justice system. Many of their service users come to the centre via court, receiving either a tailored Specified Activity Requirement on their community order, mandating sessions at Together Women, or through attending Probation appointments with officers who are, in effect, seconded to the centre. From this attendance at Together Women, I was able to meet many women with recent offending histories who were trying to desist. I interviewed 15 of them between one and seven times – a total of 44 interviews – and also conducted a focus group with most of the staff members.

The repeated nature of interviewing within such a short time-frame led me to characterise the study as 'micro-longitudinal'[1] – a type of qualitative longitudinal research (Thomson, 2007). Before, after, and in-between formal interviews, I often had interactions with participants – which were not recorded as formal data but which instead informed and fed into our discussions at interview (as well as contributing to continued rapport). As such, I considered this study to be relational qualitative research, with the development of good relationships with participants consisting not only of time together in interview as a core aim. All participants had recent histories of more than one instance of criminal activity, and many had extensive previous involvement in crime. These crimes were not always officially recorded, and ranged from minor public disorder, shoplifting and drug possession offences to violence, drug dealing, drug production and fraud. First interviews often occurred within a few months of the most recent instance of criminal behaviour. As such, I was able to see the early emergence of desistance in participants' lives as they were experiencing it.

I first analysed the interview and focus group data by transcribing recordings and creating pen portraits of each participant's experiences. I then iteratively coded all the transcripts using NVivo, initially using around 30 themes that had emerged during fieldwork, transcription and creating the pen portraits. Data from interviews are presented with the participant's pseudonym and the interview number, thus data from Beth's fourth interview is tagged as (Beth, 4). As the focus was on female offenders , there is no direct gender comparison available within the study and there has not yet been a fully comparable micro-longitudinal study conducted elsewhere with male desisters in the community (although see King (2013a) for the closest attempt to date). In the discussion that follows, I examine the various aspects of identity that were discussed by women in my research and suggest the extent to which these novel insights can be viewed as either gendered and/or generated by a closer methodological focus on the process of desistance.

## Previous problematic identities

In some cases, the reasons for needing a new desisting identity were evident in interviews. Previous offending could be so tightly bound up with how a participant saw one of their core identities that a 'replacement self' (Giordano et al, 2002) seemed crucial for the desister's progress. Megan, who had a history of drug-related minor offending and was living in residential rehabilitation at the time of the interviews, demonstrated this in her description of her partner compared with herself: 'But he was a drinker and I'm a, I was heroin' (Megan 1). Here, Megan showed that her recent addiction to heroin was central to her understanding of her identity when she compared herself to her partner. Interestingly, she does not describe herself as an addict but refers merely to the drug itself. Even though this seemed to be a speech shortcut rather than an explanation that she viewed herself as fundamentally subsumed by the drug, it is indicative of the importance heroin played in her life. Supporting existing findings that problematic offending identities are prolific among offenders, regardless of gender (Giordano et al, 2002; Baskin and Sommers, 1998), the implication of Megan's words was that she could not desist without shedding her drug-using identity, echoing findings on the primary importance of recovery to desisters elsewhere (Colman and Vander Laenen, 2012).

Yet it was not just among drug-users that an identity which was fundamentally problematic for desistance was evident. In interview, Nicole discussed a number of incidents where she had violently offended against both people and property as a result of neighbourhood disagreements. When asked whether she was more serious or excitable as a person, Nicole replied that she could be either very excitable or very serious – but both to extremes:

> There's nothing, I've always described myself like there's no middle, like, me anger. I'm either the softest, stupidest, daftest person ever, like where people walk all over me, or I'm losing the plot and I'm smashing someone's car up on front, there's no in-between and I get het [worked] up, oh, to the point where I can't control myself, that's a big part of my problem. (Nicole 1)

As a person that was either letting herself be taken advantage of, or whose anger was out of control, Nicole realised that her character of extremes would not be helpful in her desistance. Both the soft and the explosive sides of her fed into her identity, but she thought that both needed to be modified if she was to succeed in maintaining a prosocial life. The problems that Nicole saw in these aspects of her identity would presumably be relevant to any desister, whether male or female, and require a similar 'replacement identity' for those, like Megan, whose identities as substance abusers were prominent. Yet, other parts of Nicole's identity that she valued – specifically her role as a leader among her peers – did not, in her mind, necessitate a change in identity, despite their significant contribution to her past offending. In the past, her desire to lead others had led her to make rash and dangerous decisions rather than taking time to listen to other viewpoints and suggestions – a tendency that had led to some of her offending when a local feud became unmanageable. In desistance, Nicole instead re-defined what it meant for her to be 'a leader', and incorporated taking advice from others as an important aspect of that role. In this way, Nicole dealt with a previous problematic identity without the need for a 'replacement self' (Giordano et al, 2002). Instead, she could be seen as re-writing the detail of the 'cognitive blueprint' of her existing identity. Nevertheless, in both these approaches – looking to shed or re-define a problematic identity, the link between identity work and desistance is straightforward. Perhaps due to the repeated interviewing method, such stark discussion about previous identities and desistance was uncommon beyond the first interview. It seemed that either participants did not think much about their identities in their everyday lives, their perspectives on identity did not much effect their daily experiences, or the relevance of identity was complexly connected to a number of other topics which were easier to express. Once such topic was participants' confidence, and I turn next to discuss its interaction with concerns of identity in desistance.

## Lack of confidence and precarious identities

(Self-)confidence can be understood as the knowledge of oneself as a person and the valuing of one's skills and character (Oxford English Dictionary, 2014).[2] Many studies on desistance make use of the concept of confidence, suggesting that a new identity (or indeed, any lesser changes) cannot happen without the presence of self-confidence in desisters (Shover, 1996; O'Brien, 2001; Burnett, 2010; Myers, 2013). Such claims are supported by the wider psychological literature which asserts that behavioural change is enabled by confidence (Bandura, 1977). While some suggest that confidence is an emotional aspect of desistance (Farrall and Calverley, 2006), I argue more specifically that a lack of confidence can inhibit the development and maintenance of a stable, prosocial, desisting identity. It is necessary here to point out the gender differences previously detected in levels of confidence among offenders. Some studies on male offenders have found no perceptible lack of self-esteem (Burnett, 1992), but female offenders have been found to exhibit especially low levels of confidence in themselves (Worrall, 1990; Davidson, 2011). It may be that some of this difference is attributable to differing research methods and the likely self-presentation of people from each gender. However, whether these findings mask lower confidence in male offenders or higher confidence in female offenders (or both) is unclear. Questions of data reliability elsewhere notwithstanding, many participants in this study shared feelings of extremely low self-confidence, often with credible stories explaining the causes for those beliefs. It was evident that this lack of confidence profoundly affected their lives as they desisted, particularly through its interaction with their identities.

I return to discussion of Nicole for a clear example of the effect of low confidence on identity. Her lack of confidence was particularly apparent when I asked her how she would describe herself to someone who had never met her before:

*Em, see this is where I do go wrong, I doubt meself before I've even, I don't know. I've sorta like, it depends who I meet, depends who it is, if it's someone really important I'll just, I don't know, I'll not let them in too much.* (Nicole 1)

Nicole's doubts as to how to describe herself, and her uncertainty of what to say depending on who she was talking to, suggested that she was unsure of who she really was. Her low confidence and lack of a clear identity appeared to feed into each other. As a result, Nicole maintained a distance with those who were 'really important' – presumably those who had some power over her, such as probation officers. Despite her discussing various specific aspects of her identity in interview (as mentioned earlier), my sense of her not really knowing who she was persisted. If a strong identity, or identity change, is truly necessary for successful desistance, Nicole had some way to go in asserting such an identity.

Yet for some, it was not a case of low confidence and vague identities being concurrent, but instead a previous clear identity was damaged by attacks on their confidence. This was particularly true of participants who talked at length about their experiences of domestic abuse. Ten of the fifteen women in the study disclosed historical or ongoing domestic abuse, with a couple of older-than-average offenders (in their 50s and 60s) having recently ended seriously controlling and abusive relationships of many years' standing. Beth was one of those women, and had not considered herself to be a victim of domestic violence until she was sent to prison for workplace theft and heard other prisoners discuss their experiences. Despite presenting a chronic lack of confidence in herself, she described the reasons for this powerfully:

*But I didn't ever think I were very strong, because of what he'd manipulated me and everything, but I've told everybody now what he's done and that and, so suppose I'm starting to be me again, I don't know.* (Beth 1)

In telling a personal history of being a capable and confident young woman, Beth explained that her identity had been damaged by her abusive partner. His constant criticisms and manipulations had made her question herself to the extent that she became unsure of herself and lost her previous identity. Her tentative recognition that her old identity was coming back (reflecting part of Maruna's (2001) redemption scripts) was accompanied by a recovery of some confidence. This recovery was, in turn, triggered by the recognition that speaking about her victimisation was a strong and brave thing to do, and echoed the experiences of female desisters elsewhere (Rumgay, 2004) who gained confidence as a result of establishing their identity. In the quote above, it is apparent that Beth considered her 'starting to be me again' as a process, rather than an event – she was 'starting', she had not yet achieved success. Beth described this whole process as something which followed her resolve never to offend again, but as she gradually grew in confidence and understanding of herself, her position as a free and prosocial member of society likewise stabilised and strengthened.

This process of gaining self-confidence was a long and difficult one, however, and was certainly not linear. In a later interview, Beth shared that she continued to struggle with seeing herself as a strong and capable woman:

> *Me daughter said to me the other day, 'I think you've done really well, you've not had no major blow-outs or owt like that' and I don't see myself like that, I see meself…pathetic, really.* (Beth 2)

As she continued with the difficult job of rebuilding her life without her husband, it could be hard for Beth to see an attractive identity emerging for herself. She faced struggles in finding suitable accommodation in a new area (living by herself for the first time in many years), grieving for the breakdown of her abusive relationship (with a husband that she nevertheless loved) negotiating with the Department for Work and Pensions for financial support, re-establishing relationships with her adult children and her grandchildren, avoiding the shame of old friendships, navigating a new church and the people involved there, and filling her time on a daily basis. Little wonder that it could be hard for her to see who she was becoming or how she could value herself in the midst of these difficulties. As the difficulties Beth faced in forming and maintaining a prosocial identity seem particularly testing because of her experiences of domestic abuse, it may well be that any desister who faced recovery from abuse-based trauma would encounter similar struggles.

## Increased confidence and identity change

Yet when participants had experienced some success in accessing a desisting identity, they exhibited increased self-confidence. It seemed unlikely that identity change solely promoted self-confidence, or that self-confidence only enabled identity change. Instead, it seemed that both interacted in a virtuous circle, with increased self-confidence and identity change both contributing to the other's development. Twenty-two year-old Rachel (whose self-belief had been seriously damaged through a long-term abusive relationship with a much older man while she was a teenager) talked of the difference her desistance had made to how she felt about herself and how she wanted former friends to see her:

> *I can look myself in the mirror without cringing, you know what I mean, I'm not ashamed of who I am, I'm happy to be me.* (Rachel 3)

> *What they've gotta remember, I'm not the person I was when I come here, that fragile person that had been in a domestic violence relationship for seven years, I'm stronger and better than that now.* (Rachel 3)

Both Rachel's new identity and her new confidence in herself had benefits in many other areas of her life as she desisted. The first benefit, as shown in her first quote, is the removal of shame. An attribute of feeling one's identity to be degrading (Goffman, 1963; Bartky, 1990), the shame that Rachel had previously felt, had disappeared once she could claim a new, desisting identity. Despite some limited evidence of reintegrative shaming aiding desistance (Leibrich, 1996), Rachel experienced the removal of shame as beneficial to her view of herself. In addition, the strength and belief in herself demonstrated in the second quote gave Rachel the ability to stand up to her former friends and refuse to take drugs from them. The confidence she had gained had a direct effect on her ability to persevere in her desistance even when her existing relationships made that difficult for her.

Rachel was not the only participant to experience multiple advantages from a changed identity and a related increase in confidence. Steph was in her 40s, and desisting from alcohol-related shoplifting which she had begun to commit as an adult. A large part of her daily experience revolved around being 'prosocial' enough to once again take care of her primary-school-aged daughter (who was living by mutual agreement with Steph's parents). When she had progressed enough to have frequent visits and care of her daughter, Steph exhibited more self-confidence and became more certain of who she was. As a result, she appreciated being seen as trustworthy and trusted, and reported being more at ease with her life and the process of desisting:

*But, yeh, I feel like I'm more coming back to me and that responsibility's there again with [daughter] and the trust, em, I'm more, I'm just more comfortable.* (Steph 7)

Steph was evidently pleased with the effects of returning 'back to me'. In reclaiming her previous identity, she was able to again inhabit roles that she used to have as a responsible and trusted mother and which had been denied her during her offending. It was also evident that Steph's relationships with her parents and her daughter improved as she resumed her role as a mother. Given the importance of social relationships in desistance (Eaton, 1993; Baskin and Sommers, 1998; Giordano et al, 2003; Rumgay, 2004; Burnett et al, 2005; Farrall, 2005; Barry, 2010; Goodwin, 2014; Leverentz, 2014), this impact of a new identity could be significant in Steph's continued desistance. While Steph experienced these advantages as she reclaimed who she used to be, Rachel was very clear that she had become a new person in her desistance – finding a replacement self (Giordano et al, 2002). I now turn to examine this difference in experience in more detail.

## A new identity or the return of an old self?

Those, like Rachel, who spoke of a new identity had, without exception, recent histories of serious substance abuse and had been exposed to many recovery narratives through a variety of services. Yet others with similar histories, like Steph, talked of rediscovering who they used to be. It was, however, rare for participants from any background to talk about being able finally to be who they truly were, as though they had never before presented their real self. As such, there were some points of connection with the desistance narratives in Maruna's (2001) study, but the desisters did not perfectly echo the sentiment of being liberated to be their true selves. This again perhaps reflects the prominence of domestic victimisation in the sample as opposed to Maruna's sample. I now examine the differences in experiences of those who had re-asserted a lost identity and those who had created a brand new self.

As already seen, Beth mentioned several times that she was aiming to be more like how she was before her abusive marriage:

*And I'm trying to be me again, which I think I got lost before, so I'm trying to, yeh, trying to get myself in a nice place.* (Beth 1)

*I think I were always held back, always walking on eggshells and I suppose I lost my identity a bit really, didn't say owt [anything] in case it were the wrong thing and, I loved him…I have always been the one that dealt with everything, and then I suddenly met him and I've gone down to this, bit of a no mark, really that didn't do owt, didn't say owt, so I think I'm getting back now to maybe what I were before.* (Beth 2)

Her love for her husband meant that she had subsumed her identity into her efforts not to say 'the wrong thing'. His influence drained Beth's identity (and worth) away until she was unable to do or say anything for herself. Beth was always very clear that she wanted to be the same person that she was many years ago. She did not need to find a new identity, as her old identity was prosocial and a 'nice place'. While her offending did occur at a time when she considered herself to be acting out of character (like the scripts in Maruna's (2001) study), she had previous experience of being her true self (unlike Maruna's (2001) desisters). Desistance thus became a process of reclaiming that identity for herself.

While Beth's experiences in re-asserting her previous identity were echoed by some participants, others were clear that their desistance required them to be a new person. Rachel had started to take heroin as a 14-year-old who was trying to self-medicate for mental health problems. Her drug-taking had led to a long-term abusive relationship with an older man and a variety of offending behaviours. Eight years later, she was in residential rehabilitation for addiction to a number of drugs and alcohol. As seen earlier, her aim was to keep the new identity that she had formed there in the rehab:

*Yeh, I know I've changed and I know how much this place has done for me, I know that I'm not going back to that, no shape or form.* (Rachel 3)

Perhaps because of her comparatively young age (at 22, Rachel was the youngest participant in the study) and her long-lasting addictions, Rachel did not feel that she had a suitable previous prosocial identity to which to return. She talked at other points of not knowing who she was before she started to take drugs, and this is hardly surprising given her young age. Thus, Rachel fitted the standard 'replacement self' model of desistance (Giordano et al, 2002) much more closely than anyone else in the study. For her, the person she had become while at the rehabilitation facility was a new self. Her continued desistance depended on not returning to her previous self. While Rachel's new primary identity was described here as being a sober, contributing member of society, she talked elsewhere of being a 'good mum'. Indeed, the primacy of a specific identity as a carer – usually as a mother or grandmother – was evident in the majority of participants' accounts.

## 'I know I'm a caring person': a gendered identity?

Several studies have commented on the frequency of female offenders both defining themselves primarily as caregivers (Katz, 2000) and being primarily defined by others as caregivers (Leverentz, 2014). However, before examining the data from the current study which supports these findings, it is important to note that not all participants focused on a caring identity. Megan was one of only three participants who did not have any children. She was ending her time at a residential rehabilitation centre at the time of the first interview, and reflected on the identity she could now present to potential future employers:

> At least it's just me, with the qualifications, rather than Megan the drug addict, but I'm a recovering addict now anyway, so [laughs]. (Megan 1)

There was some indication that Megan's assertion that she was a *recovering addict* was a learned script from the rehabilitation centre, as she caught herself halfway through her description of herself as a drug addict and corrected her own perspective. Nevertheless, her view of herself as a person with qualifications centred not on caring responsibilities but rather her educational achievements. While both men and women have been found elsewhere to base a desisting identity on being a worker (Farrall, 2002; Giordano et al, 2002; Byrne and Trew, 2008; King, 2013b), Megan was the closest in this study, through the central role of her qualifications, to base her new self on being a worker (although perhaps, more accurately, a potential worker). This discrepancy in findings may be due to the recent and fragile nature of desistance for the participants – although similar studies of early desistance in men have found that employment remains crucial (King, 2013b). Of the 15 women in the study, 11 were in receipt of Employment Support Allowance for health problems. For many, these health problems (or at least their acute nature) were short-term and caused by recent addictions. However, for all, this benefit was granted because they were not (yet) well enough to undertake employment. As their desistance progressed, one or two participants proceeded to gain work, but this was not the case for most of them. With employment at best a distant hope for most at this early stage in their desistance, it was unsurprising that it did not feature as a basis for a desisting identity. Yet even when participants were in receipt of Job Seekers Allowance, and so judged by the state to be fit for work, talk of seeing themselves as a worker was rare. Despite the stigma attracted from society and the media by being on benefits (Valentine and Harris, 2014), participants did not see the possibility of work as something that could shape their identities. This was also true for the few that did various jobs in the grey economy. It is possible that this was, in part, due to the lack of suitable work that allowed them to also care for their children (Fawcett Society, 2012). In addition, most participants were from working-class backgrounds, where mothers are encouraged to stay at home to care for children (Leverentz, 2014). In light of all these factors, it may be that participants' focus on being primarily a caregiver was a fair reflection of their experiences, expectations and opportunities – at least in the early stages of desistance.

In addition to relational and micro-longitudinal interviews with desisters themselves, I also conducted a focus group with members of staff at Together Women. The staff provided deep insight into the relevance of identity to desisters' lives, gleaned from years of observation and listening to service users. The danger of the focus group was that too much importance was extrapolated about influences which were peripheral to the actual experience of desistance and, indeed, I did find that the staff discussed identity much more frequently and explicitly than the participants. Alternatively, it may have been that the importance of existential factors could only be fully recognised in hindsight. Nevertheless, staff were aware of the potential problems that a desister could have in asserting a primarily caring identity:

> *Like you say, they feel like they take, maybe, and that becomes their identity, and that becomes, they kind of, can accidentally embody that and that's who they are, and then become too dependent.* (Staff Focus Group)

Here staff raised an interesting paradox: by thinking of themselves primarily as mothers (they said), desisters became too dependent on other people and therefore less capable of directing their own lives. I remain unsure of why this should be the case – if the very nature of care is providing for others' needs, how can it engender a habit of dependence? However, perhaps this is linked to assumptions that those who do not earn an income have a dependent nature because they are financially dependent on the state. Dependence could then be seen as primarily financial rather than the absence of a more general capability.

Nevertheless, it was not only staff who identified difficulties with a caregiving identity. At our first interview, Rachel (introduced earlier) immediately claimed a caring identity and then proceeded to highlight the tensions which that view of herself was causing in her desistance:

> *I struggle to find out about myself and, I know I'm a caring person and I'm a bit, I am a bit soft, you know what I mean. And I like to take care of people and make sure everyone's alright and stuff, but I'm struggling to do that at the minute because I'm not caring for myself so how can I care for other people?* (Rachel 1)

Rachel's core identity here is firmly described about caring for others. However, she identifies that she is incapable of properly caring for others because of the early stage of her desistance. Therefore, although she still has concern for others (attentiveness), she shows that she cannot fulfil a core part of caring because she currently lacks the competence to provide for their needs (Sevenhuijsen, 2003). This temporary inability to fulfil her identity provided Rachel with additional motivation to succeed in desistance.

There was the potential for a caregiving identity to be of even greater worth in desistance, but this was a challenging prospect given existing cultural beliefs. Maruna (2001) found that 'generativity' – the desire to give something back – was important in desisters' stories. Participants in the current research also echoed desires to give something back to the community as an acknowledgement of the harm which they had caused. It seemed to me that a valuable and natural way of doing this was through the conscientious fulfilment of the caring roles that participants occupied, but this was not recognised by the participants themselves. Staff explained why they thought that this was the case:

> *Oh, and that's all that they've ever known if they've come from a family who had just had children young and they've had children young, and you know, and you get a lot of these big families, that's all they know a woman to be, so they don't see it as anything, as an achievement, it's just life, 'That's who I am, I'm just mum.'* (Staff Focus Group)

In being a mother, the potential to contribute to society through raising children was nonetheless taken for granted. In caregiving, there was a ready-made identity with a detailed cognitive blueprint, easily able to support desistance (Giordano et al, 2002, Rumgay, 2004), but the generative possibilities of such an identity were unrecognised by desisters and society. While employment was perhaps an ambitious goal for these female desisters (see earlier), being a good mother could be adopted as a generative action as well as a core identity – if it would only be accepted and valued as such.

## Conclusion: '[The] best thing is me, knowing what I want, wanting my life back'

As Steph showed in the above quote, understanding her identity was a crucial part of her desistance. It provided her with a positive aim in desistance – she wanted more than to 'not offend' – and a clear view of what that might look like. Similarly for many of the participants, the person they saw themselves to be did have a significant influence on their desistance experiences. Looking at their experiences as they lived them highlighted a number of complexities as yet unexplored in the research on identity and desistance. Previous problematic identities had to be discarded or more creatively re-imagined. Low self-confidence and uncertain identities conspired against successful desistance while increased self-belief and certain identities provided further perceived benefits to desisters. Some shaped a new identity for themselves, but it was particularly common for women with experience of domestic abuse victimisation to re-discover a previous self. In both cases, being or becoming a caregiver was prominent in participants' accounts. While this aspect of desisting identity did appear to be closely tied to gender, it brought its own potential pitfalls. Nevertheless, there remains the possibility of applying the research on generativity in desistance to female desisters' caregiving identities in a way that further supports them as they attempt to give up offending. Some of the insights gathered here on the development of identity during the desistance process may have been gained through the unique methods used and could be equally relevant to male and female desisters. For example, there is evidence to suggest that such trauma is particularly common among female offenders (Bloom et al, 2003), but there is also a subset of male offenders who exhibit comparable rates of victimisation (Prison Reform Trust, 1991). Therefore, the constraining role of low self-confidence on the assertion of identity could conceivably be experienced by desisters of both genders with histories of abuse victimisation. Nevertheless, my study supports previous findings that suggest the desistance experience is generally different for women than for the typical male desister.

## Notes

1    Thanks to Stephen Farrall for the suggestion of this term.

2    Although I liken it here to self-esteem, it is not my intention to similarly equate it
     to broader concepts such as self-efficacy or agency. However, confidence appears
     to be a crucial part of these concepts (Stajkovic, 2006) and therefore academic
     work on both self-efficacy and agency is relevant to the discussion.

## References

Bandura, A, 1977, Self-efficacy: Toward a unifying theory of behavioral
    change, *Psychological Review* 84, 191–215

Barry, M, 2006, *Youth offending in transition: The search for social recognition*,
    Abingdon: Routledge

Barry, M, 2010, Youth transitions: From offending to desistance, *Journal
    of Youth Studies* 13, 121–36

Bartky, SL, 1990, *Femininity and domination: Studies in the phenomenology
    of oppression*, London: Routledge

Baskin, DR, Sommers, IB, 1998, *Causalities of community disorder:
    Women's careers in violent crime*, Boulder, CO: Westview

Bloom, B, Owen, B, Covington, S, 2003, *Gender-responsive strategies:
    Research, practice, and guiding principles for women offenders*, Washington,
    DC: National Institute of Corrections, US Department of Justice

Bottoms, A, Shapland, J, 2011, Steps towards desistance among male
    young adult recidivists, in S Farrall, M Hough, S Maruna, R Sparks
    (eds) *Escape routes: Contemporary perspectives on life after punishment*,
    Oxford: Routledge

Bottoms, A, Shapland, J, Costello, A, Holmes, D, Muir, G, 2004,
    Towards desistance: Theoretical underpinnings for an empirical study,
    *Howard Journal of Criminal Justice* 43, 368–89

Burnett, R, 1992, *The dynamics of recidivism*, Oxford: Centre for
    Criminological Research, University of Oxford

Burnett, R, 2010, The will and the ways to becoming an ex-offender,
    *International Journal of Offender Therapy and Comparative Criminology*
    54, 663–6

Burnett, R, Batchelor, S, McNeill, F, 2005, Reducing reoffending:
    Lessons from psychotherapy and counselling, *Criminal Justice Matters*
    61, 32–41

Bushway, SD, Piquero, AR, Broidy, LM, Cauffman, E, Mazerolle, PJ,
    2001, An empirical framework for studying desistance as a process,
    *Criminology* 39, 491–515

Byrne, CF, Trew, KJ, 2008, Pathways through crime: The development
    of crime and desistance in the accounts of men and women offenders,
    *Howard Journal of Criminal Justice* 47, 238–58

Caddle, D, Crisp, D, 1997, Imprisoned women and mothers, *Home Office Research Study*, London: Home Office Research and Statistics Directorate

Carlen, P, 2002, *Women and punishment: The struggle for justice*, Cullompton: Willan

Colman, C, Vander Laenen, F, 2012, 'Recovery came first': Desistance versus recovery in the criminal careers of drug-using offenders, *The Scientific World Journal*, doi: 10.1100/2012/657671

Corston, J, 2007, *The Corston Report: A report by Baroness Jean Corston of a review of women with particular vulnerabilities in the criminal justice system: The need for a distinct, radically different, visibly-led, strategic, proportionate, holistic, woman-centred, integrated approach*, London: Home Office, www.justice.gov.uk/publications/docs/corston-report-march-2007.pdf

Davidson, JT, 2011, Managing risk in the community: How gender matters, in R Sheehan, G McIvor, C Trotter (eds) *Working with women offenders in the community*, Cullompton: Willan

Debidin, M, 2009, A compendium of research and analysis on the offender assessment system (OASys) 2006–2009, *Ministry of Justice Research Series*, London: Ministry of Justice.

Eaton, M, 1993, *Women after prison,* Buckingham: Open University Press

Farrall, S, 2002, *Rethinking what works with offenders: Probation, social context and desistance from crime*, Cullompton: Willan

Farrall, S, 2005, On the existential aspects of desistance from crime, *Symbolic Interaction* 28, 367–86

Farrall, S, Calverley, A, 2006, *Understanding desistance from crime: Emerging theoretical directions in resettlement and rehabilitation*, Maidenhead: Open University Press

Farrall, S, Hunter, B, Sharpe, G, Calverley, A, 2014, *Criminal careers in transition: The social context of desistance from crime*, Oxford: Oxford University Press

Fawcett Society, 2012, *The impact of austerity on women*, London: Fawcett Society

Giordano, PC, Cernkovich, SA, Rudolph, JL, 2002, Gender, crime and desistance: Toward a theory of cognitive transformation, *American Journal of Sociology* 107, 990–1064

Giordano, PC, Cernkovich, SA, Holland, DD, 2003, Changes in friendship relations over the life course: Implication for desistance from crime, *Criminology* 41, 293–328

Glaser, D, 1969, *The effectivenes of a prison and parole system*, Indianapolis, IN: Bobbs-Merrill

Goffman, E, 1963, *Stigma: Notes on the management of spoiled identity*, Upper Saddle River, NJ: Prentice-Hall

Goodwin, S, 2014, Relatively supported? Desisting women and relational influences, in A Crawford, J de Maillard, S Farrall, A Groenemeyer, P Ponsaers, J Shapland (eds) *Desistance, social order and responses to crime: Today's security issues*, Antwerpen: Maklu

Graham, J, Bowling, B, 1995, Young people and crime, *Home Office Research Study* 145, London: HMSO

Katz, RS, 2000, Explaining girls' and womens' crime and desistance in the context of their victimization experiences: A developmental test of strain theory and the life course perspective, *Violence Against Women* 6, 633–60

Kazemian, L, 2007, Desistance from crime: Theoretical, empirical, methodological, and policy considerations, *Journal of Contemporary Criminal Justice* 23, 5–27

King, S, 2013a, Early desistance narratives: A qualitative analysis of probationers' transitions towards desistance, *Punishment and Society* 15, 147–65

King, S, 2013b, Perceptions of work as a route away from crime, *Safer Communities* 12, 122–32

Laub, JH, Sampson, RJ, 2001, Understanding desistance from crime, in MH Tonry, (ed) Chicago, IL: University of Chicago Press

Laub, JH, Sampson, RJ, 2003, *Shared beginnings, divergent lives: Delinquent boys to age 70*, Cambridge, MA: Harvard University Press

Leibrich, J, 1993, *Straight to the point: Angles on giving up crime*, Dunedin: University of Otago Press

Leibrich, J, 1996, The role of shame in going straight, in B Galaway, J Hudson (eds) *Restorative justice: International perspectives*, Monsey, NY: Criminal Justice Press

Leverentz, AM, 2006, The love of a good man? Romantic relationships as a source of support or hindrance for female ex-offenders, *Journal of Research in Crime and Delinquency* 43, 459–88

Leverentz, AM, 2014, *The ex-prisoner's dilemma: How women negotiate competing narratives of reentry and desistance*, New Brunswick, NJ: Rutgers University Press

Loucks, N, 2004, Women in prison, in G McIvor (ed) *Women who offend*, London: Jessica Kingsley Publishers

McIvor, G, 2007, The nature of female offending, in R Sheehan, G McIvor, C Trotter, (eds) *What works with women offenders*, Cullompton: Willan

McIvor, G, Trotter, C, Sheehan, R, 2009, Women, resettlement and desistance, *Probation Journal* 56, 247–7

McNeill, F, Weaver, B, 2010, *Changing lives? Offender engagement: Key Messages from the desistance research*, Glasgow: Glasgow School of Social Work and Scottish Centre for Crime and Justice Research, Universities of Glasgow and Strathclyde

Malloch, MS, 2004, Women, drug use and the criminal justice system, in G McIvor (ed) *Women who offend*, London: Jessica Kingsley Publishers

Maruna, S, 2001, *Making Good: How Ex-Convicts Reform and Rebuild their Lives,* Washington, D.C, American Psychological Association

Morash, M, 2010, *Women on probation and parole: A feminist critique of community programs and services*, Lebanon, NH: University Press of New England

Mulvey, EP, 2004, Introduction: Pathways to desistance study, *Youth Violence and Juvenile Justice* 2, 211–12

Myers, RR, 2013, The biographical and psychic consequences of 'welfare inaction' for young women in trouble with the law, *Youth Justice* 13, 218–33

NOMS (National Offender Management Service), NPS (National Probation Service), 2006, *Delivering effective services for women offenders in the community: A good practice guide*, London: National Offender Management Service and National Probation Service

O'Brien, P, 2001, 'Just like baking a cake': Women describe the necessary ingredients for successful reentry after incarceration, *Families in Society: The Journal of Contemporary Human Services* 82, 287–95

*Oxford English Dictionary*, 2014, Confidence, n, *Oxford English Dictionary*, Oxford: Oxford University Press

Paternoster, R, Bushway, S, 2009, Desistance and the 'feared self': Toward an identity theory of criminal desistance, *The Journal of Criminal Law and Criminology* 99, 1103–56

Prison Reform Trust, 1991, *The identikit prisoner*, London: Prison Reform Trust

Rumgay, J, 2004, Scripts for safer survival, *Howard Journal of Criminal Justice* 43, 405–19

Sampson, RJ, Laub, JH, 1993, *Crime in the making: Pathways and turning points through life*, London: Harvard University Press

Sanders, T, 2007, Becoming an ex-sex worker, *Feminist Criminology* 2, 74–95

Sevenhuijsen, S, 2003, The place of care: The relevance of the feminist ethic of care for social policy, *Feminist Theory* 4, 179–97

Sharpe, G, 2011, *Offending girls: Young women and youth justice*, Abingdon: Routledge

Shover, N, 1996, *Great pretenders: Pursuits and careers of persistent thieves*, Boulder, CO: Westview

Smart, C, 1992, *Regulating womanhood: Historical essays on marriage, motherhood and sexuality*, London: Routledge

Sommers, IB, Baskin, DR, Fagan, J, 1994, Getting out of the life: Crime desistance by female street offenders, *Deviant Behavior* 15, 125–49

Soyer, M, 2014, The imagination of desistance, *British Journal of Criminology* 54, 91–108

Stajkovic, AD, 2006, Development of a core confidence: Higher order construct, *Journal of Applied Psychology* 91, 1208–124

Thomson, R, 2007, The qualitative longitudinal case history: Practical, methodological and ethical reflections, *Social Policy and Society* 6, 571–82

Valentine, G, Harris, C, 2014, Strivers vs skivers: Class prejudice and the demonisation of dependency in everyday life, *Geoforum* 53, 84–92

Weaver, B, McNeill, F, 2007, Desistance, in R Canton, D Hancock (eds) *Dictionary of probation and offender management*, Cullompton: Willan

Weitekamp, EGM, Kerner, HJ, 1994, Epilogue, in EGM Weitekamp, HJ Kerner (eds) *Cross-national longitudinal research on human development and criminal behavior*, Dordrecht: Kluwer Academic Publishers

Worrall, A, 1990, *Offending women: Female lawbreakers and the criminal justice system*, London: Routledge

Zaplin, RT, 1998, *Female offenders: Critical perspectives and effective interventions*, Gaithersburg, MD: Aspen Publishers

FIVE

# Growing out of crime? Problems, pitfalls and possibilities

*Anne Robinson*

## Introduction

This chapter differs from most others in this book as it is based on reflections that inform plans for my doctoral studies rather than analysis of data already collected. It also differs in taking two separate areas for consideration. The first of these is my own main interest in the development of identity during the mid-teenage years, both in terms of narrative identity (developing a sense of auto-biography) and identity-in-action (developing a sense of self through social relations and 'performance'). The second area focuses more firmly on transitions and specifically what happens in the process of maturation and creating – or at least assuming – adult identities. There are relatively few biographical studies offering close up examination of young people and their involvements in crime, and, other than Giordano et al (2002; 2007) long-term qualitative studies starting in adolescence are surprisingly thin on the criminological ground. Nevertheless, there are valuable insights from UK-based research with young adults on Teesside (for example, MacDonald and Marsh, 2005; MacDonald et al, 2011)) and in Sheffield (Bottoms and Shapland, 2011; Shapland and Bottoms, 2011). More pertinently, Halsey and Deegan's (2015) recent longitudinal study of young offenders in South Australia follows their lives from the mid-teenage years onwards. I draw on each of these to consider the development of identities in transition and the salience of social context, specifically criminal justice involvements, in opening up or foreclosing possibilities for positive change.

## Crime over the young life course

Both these areas, of course, can be related back to the classic pattern of the age–crime curve. It has been noted elsewhere that, with some variation, the familiar bell-shaped curve, showing an increase and then a tailing off of anti-social activities, is still apparent whether the graph is plotted by age, the number of young people offending (prevalence), or the quantity of offences committed by young people (incidence) (see, for example, McVie, 2004). Bottoms and Shapland (2011) also suggest that charting the frequency of offending over time for a given population of offenders tends to produce similar bell-curves to the more familiar cross-sectional analyses. And this is despite these longitudinal measures excluding young people for whom offending is one-off or of short-term duration. A rudimentary analysis would indicate that this supports Moffitt's (1993) proposition that most offending is limited to the adolescent period, but it does raise questions about her contrasting category of life-course persistent offenders: it is increasingly acknowledged that, even for these individuals, offending ceases or typically reduces in frequency and seriousness with age.

In the decades since Moffitt (1993) first distinguished between adolescent-limited and life-course persistent patterns of offending (and offenders), her taxonomy has been both challenged and refined. One recent example of trajectory modelling from the Pathways to Desistance Study (Mulvey et al, 2010; Steinberg et al, 2015) identified five separate pathways. Between 2000 and 2003, this study enrolled a sample of 14–17 year olds from Philadelphia after conviction for a serious (in US terms, felony-level) offence and followed them for seven years. Analysis of interviews with 1,119 male participants at the three-year point suggested five distinct groups characterised by:

- low offending at both base line and follow up;
- relatively low offending at baseline but with a more marked decline at follow up;
- moderate levels of offending throughout;
- 'desisters' – high initial offending but significant reduction at follow up;
- 'persisters' – high initial offending that remains relatively high throughout.

Together Groups 1 and 2 represent almost 60 per cent of the sample, which is significant in itself, confirming that even for what the authors refer to as 'serious adolescent offenders', an early decrease or cessation of offending is common. The latter two groups are of most interest, and specifically the question of why certain young people have desisted before or during their early 20s while others starting with similar entrenched patterns sustain their involvement in offending (these 'persisters' being roughly 7.5 per cent of the total).

From a psychological perspective, one of the pertinent areas of enquiry for these researchers is psychosocial maturity and its impact on 'aging out of offending'. In previous research, Steinberg and Cauffman (1996; and see also Cauffman and Steinberg, 2000) had suggested three relevant dimensions of maturity: *temperance*, including the ability to control impulses and aggression; *perspective* or the ability to consider different points of view, consideration of longer term consequences and the vantage point of others; and *responsibility*, which includes the ability both to take responsibility for one's own behaviour and to resist coercive influences from other people (Steinberg et al, 2015). Across the groups over the seven-year study period, these young people evidenced varying levels of psychosocial maturity judged against these three dimensions. As expected, persisters and late desisters were less mature than early desisters at age 16. However, there is mounting evidence that neurological, cognitive and emotional development continues well into the 20s (see Prior et al (2011) for a review of literature) and, in this research, late maturation is so marked for some young people that Steinberg et al comment that their 'chronic offenders show a lack of psychosocial maturation that might be characterised as arrested development' (2015, 9). Interestingly, as maturation is a social as well as a psychological process, they ask whether experiences of institutionalisation or criminal justice involvement might have a detrimental impact on maturation. For me, in fact, the more intriguing questions relate to how this happens and what this might mean for the development of adult identity.

Such questions resonate with findings from the Edinburgh Study of Youth Transitions and Crime which suggest the potential for entrapment in criminal justice processes and the tendency of official agencies – in this instance police, social care and the children's hearing system – to recycle the 'usual suspects' (McAra and McVie, 2005; 2007). Furthermore, 'the deeper the usual suspects penetrated the system, the more likely it was that their pattern of desistance from serious offending was *inhibited*' (McAra and McVie, 2012, 9, emphasis in original). These are points that I return to later. At this stage it is important only to note the possible effects of labelling and being designated as a 'problem' in educational, care or criminal justice settings upon maturation and identities-in-formation.

## Self-identity in development

Cognitive abilities are not the only aspect of personal development in adolescence of interest. However, they are significant for the 'identity work' that young people engage in and the narratives of self they create, whether constructed (or co-constructed) in interactions or through reflecting on experiences and biography. Psychological research has found that young people are increasingly able to make sense of life experiences, to evaluate their significance and to identify connections and themes during their teenage years. The growing skills in autobiographical reasoning (Habermas and Bluck, 2000) enable the individual to build a relatively stable sense of self, identifying personal traits, qualities and motivations that are consistent over time. These skills also allow him or her to explain apparent discrepancies or discontinuities without losing coherence (McAdams and McLean, 2013). Yet there are huge variations in how young people undertake the developmental task of constructing an adult identity and the timing of different elements. Moreover, in the current social context the process has even been characterised as 'inventing adulthood' (Henderson et al, 2007), reflecting the uncertainty and indeterminacy of present-day transitions.

While many of the discussions in this book centre around the various qualitative approaches that might be used to uncover the creation of narrative, it is helpful to consider the findings from the sorts of empirical studies cited in this and in the previous section. I have certainly found them useful in grounding a sense of how narrative abilities develop over time both in terms of skills and in terms of cultural competence (Fivush et al, 2011). By the latter, I mean access to shared stories, archetypes and understandings of how to present narratives to different audiences and for different purposes (McAdams, 1993), which are patently not available in equal measure to all young people. Family and other social relationships may encourage such learning, for example though conversations that explore explanations and evaluations of experiences (McAdams and McLean, 2013). And their wider social environment may provide young people with shared images, life scripts and master narratives that they can use in their efforts to understand and articulate their experiences and what they mean for self (Fivush et al, 2011). Yet this is not the case for all young people, some of whom have social, psychological and physical worlds existing within strikingly narrow parameters and providing a much thinner range of identity resources for them to draw upon.

Of course, life courses are affected by many different events that may have significance in objective reality, but perhaps even more so in what they subjectively mean to the individual. Such 'critical moments' – events seen as having important consequences for life and identity (Thomson et al, 2002) – may become embedded into the narratives of young lives as 'self-defining memories' (Fivush et al, 2011). Relatedly, research by Pasupathi et al (2007) explored the developmental implications of what they term 'self-event relations' or the types of links narrators make between life experiences and identity. The links they label as explanatory or dismissal both reinforce an existing sense of self. In the first case this is typified by the narrator affirming consistency between the event and self-concept. In the second case the narrator would dismiss it as atypical, a 'not like me event' and so reject it from his or her life story (Pasupathi et al, 2007). Imagine a young man involved in a fight: he might later relate a story of this incident in which it is portrayed as consistent with his values and ways of being, concerned with standing up for himself and 'taking no nonsense'; or he might describe it as out of character, not like his normal peaceable self, and therefore of no consequence for his sense of self.

Other self-event relations are associated with change rather than continuity (Pasupathi et al, 2007). Life events may improve a young person's self-concept, perhaps following a significant achievement or 'lucky break'. However, other experiences – chronic illness, accident, loss – are likely to be detrimental rather than self-enhancing where feelings of powerlessness, inadequacy or distress are internalised. These kinds of experiences feature disproportionately in the life histories of young people with the most troubling behaviours, who may struggle to find the support and resources that could enable them to turn their suffering into stories of survival or redemption (McAdams and McLean, 2013).

Finally, Pasupathi et al (2007) identify a 'reveal' connection where an experience discloses something to the narrator that was previously unknown or unacknowledged (perhaps acting as the kind of 'epiphany' referred to in desistance literature (for example, Denzin, 1987)). At the very least this is likely to prompt a reworking of 'self' to integrate the newly revealed element of identity – sexual orientation, for example. But in other cases, new knowledge may result in a real fracturing of the sense of self. As an illustration, Halsey and Deegan describe how one participant in their research was told by an uncle that the man who had brought him up was not his biological father, commenting that 'the news about his "father" literally shook his world and it took Billy many years to recover from it' (2015, 36).

This naturally leads us on to the question of external conditions and individual agency, acknowledging that young people are increasingly recognised as acting upon as well as reacting to the circumstances in which they find themselves. They also exercise agency in the ways they interpret and derive meaning from life events and circumstances. Here the work of psychologist Michael Ungar seems to me deeply insightful. Drawing on McAdams (1993) and his own clinical practice, he argues that 'a youth's identity is the culmination of the story the young person tells about his "self" or her "self" in relationship with others' (Ungar, 2004, 200). Being officially categorised as problematic or risky may become negatively absorbed into an identity-in-formation, but may also be resisted by young people in a struggle to define themselves rather than being defined by others, effectively to take back discursive power (Ungar, 2001; see also France et al, 2012). Their efforts to do so may involve behaviours that could be seen as antisocial or self-destructive by conventional standards. However, he argues that by listening to young people's accounts, we can better understand the benefits that they perceive and what drives them:

> When high-status and socially acceptable self-constructions are under-resourced, or unavailable, teens turn instead to dangerous, deviant, delinquent and disordered behaviours. Although these may appear to be undesirable, they are frequently successful at maintaining for the youth a healthy self-definition as an empowered, attached and accepted individual in a limited range of interactional spheres. (Ungar, 2004, 179)

Arguably Ungar (2004) overstates his case and the examples he uses to illustrate his argument should be treated with some caution as they are composite case studies based on his clients (contrasting sharply with the methodological rigour of other studies cited in this chapter). His remarks also refer to a particularly troubled population of adolescents with long-term involvement in clinical practice. Nevertheless, his thesis gives pause for thought about how young people see their needs and the best (or most achievable) routes to meeting them in challenging circumstances. This is reflected in Kate Brown's exploration of the 'vulnerability–transgression nexus', where, in the face of profound disadvantage and difficulties, 'transgressive behaviours such as criminal activities, antisocial behaviour or what young people call "attitude", could be viewed as important "identity work" to preserve dignity and self-worth or a strategy for mitigating against social marginalisation'

(2015, 180). Elsewhere such behaviours are conceptualised by Monica Barry (2006, drawing on Bourdieu, 1986) as a search for social capital at a stage of life where durable and legitimate forms of capital are not accessible for many young people. The challenge for research is how to interrogate the complexities of identity, individual agency and social relations as they are experienced by young people in their mid-teen years, rather than, as in Barry's (2006) case, looking back at that phase of life.

## Subjective selves

So far I have argued that evidence of growing cognitive skills and abilities in autobiographical reasoning, for example, sheds important light on adolescent development, but this accounts for only part of what is happening as young people form social identities and more definite self-concepts in their mid-teens. Focusing on biographical narratives as a mechanism for constructing identity runs the risk of over-emphasising rational thought processes and the practice of reflexivity that Giddens (1991) suggests contribute to the youthful 'project of self'. Social, emotional and other aspects of development also exert their influences. In any case, willingness and capacity to engage in conscious reflexive processes may depend on personal characteristics and context as well as age. McLeod (2003), for example, found that attempts to encourage reflexivity within interviews in a longitudinal study worked 'better' with middle-class young women than working-class or minority ethnic boys. (Although even here it was double-edged in terms of young women's heightened levels of self-awareness and self-scrutiny.)

Research also suggests that social identities develop in specific social, spatial and institutional contexts, and are affected by the dynamics between the different actors in these spheres, including figures of authority, peers and local communities (McAra and McVie, 2012: France et al, 2012). There is, then, a ring of truth about Jenkins' (2006) proposition that social identity is a process, not a fixed point, that is at the same time interior (subjective) and exterior in the sense of engaging in relationships with the outside world. So the way that we feel about ourselves is affected by our interactions with others, how we are treated and, for example, the sorts of official recognition that are given or withheld. By extension, these feelings may become absorbed into the mood, tone and substance of our self-stories and the meanings we derive from our social relations and encounters. Young people relate to schools and other institutions by necessity not choice, and are possibly geographically restricted to neighbourhoods or estates. So this may have especial significance for them, because the possibilities of removing themselves from situations of conflict, blame or disapproval which are having a negative impact on their self-identity, are so much more limited.

With this in mind, I have started to consider how young people develop and use non-biographical forms of narrative to contribute to self-identity (and in some situations affirm key identifications). These may take the form of 'small stories' (Bamberg, 2004; Bamberg and Georgakopoulou, 2008) revealed in everyday conversations and interactions. Such stories could be part of deliberate efforts at self-presentation, but not always. Focusing on oral narratives presents problems in research, not least because collection and interpretation of data is complicated by the need to take account of how the setting and the investigator him- or herself might influence the story told (or co-created within a group) (Reissman, 2008). However, narrative must be understood as an inherently social artefact. Within their social interactions, young people exploit narratives as devices to define themselves and their relationships. These narratives may be partial, fragmentary or possibly contradictory, yet those very qualities could represent their utility for identities that are to different degrees 'works in progress' and so highly contingent. This suggests that there is merit in trying to capture young people's 'small stories' and descriptions of self, and the discourses in which they locate them. In the interests of reliability, this is best done over a period of time. Researchers could even draw on ethnographic approaches, whether within institutional settings such as schools, or, in contrast, in the spaces where young people spend unstructured time (Heath et al, 2009). Conventional narrative interviews have been adapted for young participants in any case (see Henderson et al, 2007; Ross et al, 2009, for examples). However, finding ways to explore the dynamics of identity-in-action could be especially valuable, if methodologically challenging.

Kevin McDonald's (1999) three-year study of young adults in the Australian state of Victoria is a fascinating attempt to do this. He adapted a mode of investigation pioneered by the French sociologist, Alain Touraine, for the study of social movements, and drew on Touraine's concept of the 'sociology of action' and François Dubet's later 'sociology of experience'. McDonald's interest is in the subjective experience of his young participants and the ways that 'they confront an increasingly urgent imperative of constructing and mobilising an identity to navigate a social world defined in terms of uncertainty and communication' (1999, 11) and no longer structured by social institutions and norms. Ultimately his analysis does not have the same level of authenticity as the research data he presents, but the extracts from transcripts of meetings with groups of young people are striking. The most powerful are the words of young people from 'Westview', an area of extreme urban poverty and stigmatisation. The variations and the conflicts in what they say suggest that these young people have a fragile and often threatened sense of self. They are at one and the same time proud of their community, fearful of its disintegration and aware that they are affected by its reputation:

Cindy:          *I did a traineeship at the Ministry of Housing. They're mostly old ladies [who work] there. They say 'Where do you live?' and you say 'Westview'. They go, 'Western suburbs!' It's like, 'Oh, no! You come from the bad side.' Everything…it's as soon as you mention the western suburbs, it's like, oh…!'*

Jane (researcher): *Is that an experience that you others have had?*

All:            *Yeah!*

In part, this stigma can be controlled by making light of it, managing it through humour:

*We tease each other, when we're in a group. [We say] you're from the western suburbs. What would you know?* (Elsa)

Managing the two dimensions of this identity is a recurring question among the research groups:

Cindy:          *I love it, I really do. I wouldn't go and live on the other side. No way!*

Elsa:           *I can go places here, there are things to do.*

Cindy:          *But when my kids grow up, they'll probably hate me.* (McDonald, 1999, 24)

The group affiliations and identifications are particularly illuminating: the young people defined themselves against the residents of the wealthier suburbs on the 'other side', against the younger people in their own community whom they saw as not respecting community norms, and against recent immigrants. The young men, in particular, also positioned themselves in opposition to the police.

What McDonald suggests is that these young people's experiences of selfhood are peculiarly individualised in the absence of work and structured transitions to adulthood. Interestingly, the research design involved the young people identifying and then meeting with key actors who might have influence in their social world. The encounter with local politicians is particularly instructive. The two older working-class men (the current and former mayor) encourage the young men to connect with the local political system when they want action or improvements, rather than working through their youth worker for individualised solutions. This suggestion is ultimately resisted – clearly the youth worker, Rod, is safer and, in any case, the sense of solidarity on the basis of common class experience is difficult for this group to grasp. While McDonald's claim that his research explores 'the end of the working-class experience' is rather grand, he does expose the difficulties of building positive adult identities from experiences of marginality and exclusion. I come back to this theme later in the chapter.

## Agentic selves

Studies of younger people, their identities and behaviours also reveal their concerns about threats, vulnerabilities and the extent to which they themselves can act in response to these. And responses are very situation specific, contingent on both immediate circumstances and the wider social context. This latter determines at the very least the access to financial support, training opportunities and educational expectations that bear down on young people. In contrast to McDonald's focus on extreme subjectivity, France et al's (2012) analysis combines Bourdieu's ideas of social capital with the concepts of 'nested ecology'. This involves social systems operating at different levels upon the individual, from intimate micro-systems such as the family to large societal structures (Bronfenbrenner, 1979). They use this framework to provide a more detailed analysis of the interplay of structure and agency for their young participants (aged 11–18 years). Place continues to be important in defining young people's experiences. (In this instance there are four research sites in the study, each located in poor neighbourhoods.) The authors comment that

> Young people's explication of their experience in the neighbourhoods, peer groups and the areas in which they live, challenges simplistic notions of delinquent

youth offending being driven by 'rational choice'. Their depictions of offences generally do not indicate that they are looking for trouble or to cause trouble or harm. Rather, more often, offending is a re-categorisation of behaviours and activities very differently conceived. (France et al, 2012, 59)

Putting aside the issue of young people and adults framing behaviour differently, it is pertinent to question how intentional young people's involvement in offending really is. France et al (2012) show that in many instances 'things just happen', and so how easy it is to cross a line in environments where opportunities to get into trouble are plentiful (and environments that are arguably over-regulated to boot). The dynamics they outline in their research could be likened to Matza's (1964) classic description of 'drift', suggesting that there is a degree of purpose in young people's behaviours but not necessarily a commitment to deviance. However, France et al (2012) look elsewhere for help in understanding the ways that young people act and their social relations. They again turn to Bourdieu, this time to his notion of habitus, or 'systems of durable, transposable dispositions' (1977, 72) developed from past experience and cultural context. Through this lens we can better appreciate how young people's social practices might originate from deeply embedded behaviours, beliefs and ways of being. These are in turn shaped by the experience of material conditions and structures, such as the physical space, economy and culture of their local community. This suggests that, while young people's narratives, for example, might offer reasons for what they do, their choices from a range of possible actions may not be the product of reasoning or strategy, but are much more subjective in origin.

Bourdieu (1977; 1990) proposes, of course, that all human actors draw upon the habitus of their environment in ways that establish habitual actions and routines so that everyday practices and social relations do not demand constant conscious decision-making. Habitus is by definition embodied, not an abstraction, and in that sense is expressed in the physical here and now through tastes, preferences and actions with capacity for self-reproduction. Thus, the more that something is done in a particular way, the more that becomes the way that it is done (and therefore will tend to be done in the future). This runs deeper than social or cultural learning. Bourdieu suggests that habitus becomes part of each individual's internalised way of understanding and responding to the external world, and is therefore an integral part of the individual's perception and self-perception.

Interacting with specific social environments or 'fields', this enables the individual to develop a 'feel for the game' (Bourdieu, 1998) – for example, being able to anticipate and live up to the behaviours and mores of the street gang (see Harding, 2014, for an illustration).

So what might this mean for young people? In particular, what might it mean as they approach the transition to adulthood? As argued earlier, during the maturation process, young people typically increase their abilities to distance themselves from immediate experience and to consider different perspectives. In narrative terms, this implies greater capacity to review and make sense of previous life experiences. Young people also become more able to look ahead and to plan further into the future. Staying with the notion of habitus, this suggests that future selves are not pre-determined, but that what young people may envisage for their future may be circumscribed by beliefs and expectations about what is possible, attainable or appropriate. For example, in certain parts of the inner city, the height of aspiration may be the power and reputation associated with gang membership (Harding, 2014). Similarly, in areas characterised by disengagement from formal education, young people may believe that 'university is not for the likes of me'. This does seem to chime with evidence from research (see, for example, MacDonald and Marsh, 2005; Henderson et al, 2007).

Habitus as an explanatory construct, however, underplays the potential of individual agency, particularly in terms of deliberate efforts to change patterns of behaviour and the peer relationships involved. The conscious attempts to reinvent selves explored in the adult desistance literature frequently seem to imply a break from the social and cultural environments surrounding drug use, for example, and in many instances a 'knifing off' of past friendship groups or routines (Laub and Sampson, 2003). That may denote the individual reacting where he or she perceives that his or her new concerns and commitments are incompatible with the possible future versions of self supported by his or her existing habitus. According to Vaughan (2007), individuals exercise agency in their internal conversations, emotional re-appraisals and deliberations about actions, as well as in the actions themselves. Bourdieu, however, does not allow for such reflexivity. Elsewhere, King (2014) points to the role of agency in the early stages of desistance in facing the uncertainties of transition. What are the implications for young people who may be negotiating transitions to adulthood and transitions out of youthful criminality at the same time? Furthermore, in answering this question, I wanted to look at what research tells us might affect these transitions, in terms of both personal capacities and external conditions.

## Desistance in transition?

Until recently the transition to adulthood has received relatively little criminological attention which is surprising given the enduring recognition of the age–crime curve and the tendency for most young people to 'grow out of crime'. However, it must be of interest in the light of present-day transitions which are becoming longer and almost certainly less predictable for most young people (Furlong and Cartmel, 2007; Jones, 2009). Barry (2006) identifies the period of youth as a 'liminal' phase, when social roles and relationships are in flux between the social world of the child and that of the adult. Intriguingly, Healy (2010) also refers to the anthropologist, Victor Turner's (1970) ideas of liminality in her desistance study with Irish probationers. She describes this middle period between separation from previous roles and aggregation into new roles as 'characterised by introspection, ambiguity and social withdrawal, but it is also a time of "fruitful darkness" when personal transformation and growth can occur' (Healy, 2010, 35).

Although Healy's concern is the early stage of transition to a non-offending identity, the qualities she highlights are also pertinent to late adolescence. King (2014), again writing about early stages of desistance, talks about the agency that individuals might use in making preparing and planning for 'desistance journeys', referring to this as 'a time where individuals may reflexively consider their social contexts and the goals that they want to realise within them' (2014, 67). This may also apply to young people as they approach adulthood with opportunities and possibilities that transition opens up for them, as well as new risks and threats. However, as argued earlier, the ability to stand back from experience and to weigh up different perspectives and future possibilities varies according to age and from one young person to another. Capacity for acting in a purposeful and agentic way, as opposed to merely acting, varies too.

Seeking to understand the development and use of agency, I returned to the work of Emirbayer and Mische (1998) who argue that it can be viewed as having three dimensions. Although these can be separated out for analysis, in practice the three dimensions tend to work together, with one or another dominating at any given time. Emirbayer and Mische represent this as a 'chordal triad of agency' which is deeply embedded in a temporal world of social engagement, relating to past, future and present. They further suggest that

> The ways in which people understand their own relationship to the past, future and present *make a difference*

to their actions; changing conceptions of agentic possibility in relation to structural contexts profoundly influence how actors in different periods and places see their worlds as more or less responsive to human imagination, purpose and effort. (1998, 973, emphasis in original)

This is interesting in relation to young people as they typically become more skilled and sophisticated in determining actions based on experience and habit, as well as views and aspirations for the future. Developing abilities to interpret and to create narrative meaning from past events creates potential for continuing to build on existing experiences or purposefully changing course. Young people may also begin to create more complex visions of self, projecting further into their future and imagining alternative possibilities. And these may engage powerful emotions such as hope, fear and desire, as well as rational expectation.

It is the third element, which the authors term *practical evaluative*, which I feel is most significant here. This denotes an important range of cognitive, moral and practical capacities which typically grow during the mid-teens and early adulthood through experience and social relations. While the practical evaluative dimension exists within its immediate context, Emirbayer and Mische (1998) suggest that individuals draw on their past experience to understand their present situation, to recognise what may be problematic or unresolved, and to identify the nature or character of the 'problem'. Aspects of agency are also apparent in terms of deliberating over possible courses of action, making decisions and then executing or taking action. Again, this is not distinct from the temporal order, because

> [a]ctors are always living simultaneously in the past, future and present...they continuously engage patterns and repertoires from the past, project hypothetical pathways forward in time, and adjust their actions to the exigencies of emerging situations. (1998, 1012)

And neither is it distinct from the structural circumstances in which the individual finds him- or herself, as these affect the situations and problems that might arise – victimisation on the street, for example, or homelessness – as well as the extent of opportunities, networks and resources to assist resolution.

We should perhaps be wary of indicating too close a similarity in the experiences of transition to a non-offending identity and young people's transitions to adulthood. Nevertheless, it is important to note the vulnerability and the ambiguity that characterises both and may affect the way individuals act and their orientations to agency. Young people look to the professionals and to the agencies with which they are involved for advice, support and opportunities. Interestingly, King (2014) in examining the probation service's role in facilitating change, found that probation officers encouraged future orientated or *projective* agency through identifying goals and objectives to work towards, and by encouraging motivation, self-confidence and alternative self-identities. However, officers failed to capitalise on the potential for enhancing offenders' *practical evaluative* orientations to agency, particularly in terms of making decisions about and taking practical steps to move forward. This then limited the possibilities of 'doing things differently', leaving the would-be-desister acting *iteratively* (Emirbayer and Mische, 1998) by falling back onto past patterns of behaviours. And it may be that the forms of help and intervention available to young people – from social care, youthwork, Connexions – have been similarly lacking in efforts to assist their transitions and the formation of adult identities through strengthening the practical–evaluative aspects of agency.

Yet adulthood is perhaps a status rather than a destination, which involves feeling oneself to be adult and being recognised as such by others. Although the normative timetable for crossing the threshold – employment, financial independence, leaving home – is less clear for young people today (Jones, 2009), the transition is still associated with responsibility and autonomy. In most cases, the transition is also characterised by a move away from delinquency, which at low levels is normalised among young people but becomes less age-appropriate over the life course. So how might continued offending affect the transition to adulthood and recognition as being adult? Or does the effect work in the opposite direction, with delayed transitions having an impact upon the 'normal' process of withdrawing from delinquency?

These questions have been explored by Massoglia and Uggen (2010) who note, first, that entanglement in criminal justice processes in themselves can disrupt transitions, affecting relationships, employment prospects and accommodation. With the US currently imposing unprecedented levels of sanctions and incarceration on young people, the wider societal effect on delayed adolescence should not be discounted. However, they are more interested in the way that young people feel about themselves and the way they are viewed by others when their transgressions are in the public domain. Speaking from a symbolic interactionist perspective, they contend that

> [T]he appraisals of significant others play a large part in determining how people come to see themselves...we suggest that those who persist in delinquency will be less likely to be seen as adults by their reference group (others' appraisals), more likely to perceive that others see them as less than adults (reflected appraisals) and thus more likely to understand themselves as less than adult (self-appraisals). (Massoglia and Uggen, 2010, 550)

Data from the Youth Development Study (Massoglia and Uggen, 2010) sample interviewed for the last time in their late 20s, largely confirms their hypotheses, which includes the proposition that 'individuals will feel less like adults while engaged in delinquent activities and more like adults when engaged in conforming activities' (Massoglia and Uggen, 2010, 554). They measured this in terms of subjective views and behaviours (such as acting as 'designated driver'). Interestingly, they asked their participants about voting and other indicators of civic responsibility, which were positively associated with adulthood and 'feeling adult', unlike illegal or unethical behaviours. In general, continued delinquency was experienced as a marker of non-adult status (and counterintuitively, it appears that petty criminality has much the same effect as serious offending). Participants who had been arrested in the previous three years reported less progress against traditional indicators of adulthood – employment, financial independence and so on – and also tended to see themselves as 'less like an adult'. Those participants who described themselves at the time of interview as involved in less delinquency than they had been five years previously, were more likely to view themselves as adult. The authors note that 'subjective desistance' appears to be a strong predictor of 'subjective adulthood', further suggesting that

> [M]ovement away from delinquency is a distinct dimension of the transition to adulthood. With the unique and perhaps expected exception of parenthood, those who fail to desist generally fail to attain the markers of adulthood in a timely fashion and are not accorded adult status by others. Internalising these appraisals, they come to see themselves as less than adults. (Massoglia and Uggen, 2010, 571)

On a related note, Graham and Bowling (1995) found that desistance and transition to adulthood seem more closely associated for young women than for young men, at least up to the age of 25. The 'growing up' effect is illustrated by participants in Barry's (2006) research, some of whom clearly evidenced increasing awareness that continued offending was incompatible with adult status and achieving personal goals. Earlier in life, a desired lifestyle may have involved excitement and risk-taking, but here, as in other research (for example, Shapland and Bottoms, 2011), her participants express strikingly normative aspirations for family, employment and secure homes:

> "I've got away from all the bad things in life...I can't be bothered with all that...I am just getting too old for it. I am just not wanting to roll around the streets fighting and things like that. It's embarrassing...I am not wanting that kind of life anymore. I want to get a house and get settled down." (Carol, 29, cited in Barry, 2006, 116)

## Difficult transitions

These transitions, of course, take place in specific social, spatial and temporal contexts. While the responsibilities of parenthood may be significant for both young women and – perhaps less immediately – for young men (Graham and Bowling, 1995), the effects of the economy, local labour markets and ways of spending leisure time play equally important parts. These affect not only the environment and the habitus in which transitions are taking place, but also resources, networks and opportunities available to young people (Henderson et al, 2007). More immediately, young people grow up in families (or alternative care settings) and engage with social organisations such as schools. From their unique social contexts young people derive what Raffo and Reeves (2000) characterise as 'individualised systems of social capital'. Recognising that these may be weak, strong, changing (in a positive or negative direction) or fluid helps us understand the differences in what young people are able to draw upon as would-be-adults (and would-be-desisters). And it also suggests that these differences are not fixed because capital may be gained or lost over time.

The situationally specific way that different elements of young people's lives develop and intertwine in transition, is most powerfully evoked by Robert MacDonald and colleagues at the University of Teesside. *Disconnected youth?* (MacDonald and Marsh, 2005) and associated studies are not focused on crime, but the research was located in one of the most deprived areas of the country suffering from the loss of heavy industry and the plentiful employment that it previously provided. Inevitably, then, the stories that young people contributed touch upon their engagement or otherwise with school, connection to a precarious labour market and, for many, youthful involvement in delinquent activities.

Similar to France et al (2012), street-based leisure was the norm for most of these young people throughout adolescence and the mid-teen years. With little money to spend on alternative pursuits and limited mobility, 'hanging around' with friends provided young people with a social outlet, a way of relieving boredom and access to drink and recreational drugs (MacDonald and Marsh, 2005). However, widening the debate about transitional markers to include other facets such as 'leisure careers', MacDonald and Shildrick (2007) describe the majority of their participants moving on to mainstream commercial venues when they became old enough and had the money to frequent the pubs and clubs in the town centre. This tended to coincide with starting work and exploring larger, more diverse social networks. However, sadly, a minority of young people – predominantly male – were unable to make those transitions and remained physically and socially constrained in their locality.

For most of their participants, involvement in street-based leisure was unproblematic, except where continued commitment to 'street corner society' coincided with frequent absences from school and the development of oppositional identities (MacDonald and Marsh, 2005; MacDonald, 2006). The other contextually specific impact on continued offending was heroin which had flooded Teesside in the 1990s around the time fieldwork was conducted. Although affecting only a small number of the young people in the research, the downward spiral – or 'corkscrew heroin careers' – they described are dramatic, narrowing the perimeters of their social worlds and prospects. Mixing with other drug using peers may have provided some bonding capital and networks of sorts, but they were detrimentally affected by 'allegiances and associations [that] reinforced transition pathways, narrative possibilities and social identities, progressively "knifing off" limited legitimate social and economic opportunities and non-criminal identities' (MacDonald et al, 2011, 141).

The transitions of the young people in the Teesside studies were made more difficult by the insecure jobs available in that specific local economy and the prevailing ambivalence about education (at least during compulsory schooling). While all the young people had these conditions in common, some were faced with additional complications due to personal histories or individual circumstances – health, family, poor housing and so on. Nevertheless, most wanted, and managed to achieve, adulthood and viewed their youthful behaviours as belonging to that particular period of life. Overall, even those enmeshed in offending appear surprisingly conformist in their views of morality and social norms, a finding that is far from unique (see Shapland and Bottoms, 2011). However, both here among dependent drug-users (MacDonald and Marsh, 2005), and among the sample of recidivist offenders followed in the Sheffield desistance study, altered perspectives and more mature moral sensibilities were not necessarily enough in themselves to bring about sustained behavioural change. It is only too easy to resort to well-established behaviours (forms of *iterative* agency) in the face of practical 'obstacles' and given the emotional attractions that offending may still hold. Indeed, it is very much 'easier to form sincere intentions to change than it is actually to alter patterns of behaviour' (Bottoms and Shapland, 2011, 66)

The twists and turns of long offending trajectories and the difficulties of achieving primary, never mind secondary, desistance (Maruna and Farrall, 2004) are powerfully captured in Halsey and Deegan's (2015) study in South Australia. They present detailed narratives of 12 young men collected over almost a decade, starting at the age of 15 or 16, when each had already served a period in juvenile detention. It is clear to see from these narratives the growing sense of perspective and shifting life priorities over the years, even though these are often not reflected in long-term moves away from offending. The authors engage in a complex analysis of the challenges for these young men in making such moves and why the progress of several gets roughly 'on track' while others experience 'recurring breakdown' or 'major derailments' in their life course (Halsey and Deegan, 2015).

There are three points I wish to draw from Halsey and Deegan's analysis. First, almost without exception these young men had experienced significant disruption, loss or abuse in their early lives that affected their later capacities and resilience in the face of difficulties. Consequently, their transitions to adulthood were exceptionally tough experiences, in the main without consistent family involvement and interspersed with periods in custody. These institutions also failed to provide appropriate care and support, most particularly once the young men entered more adult prison environments at the age of 18.

Second, Halsey and Deegan highlight how early life experiences in family, school and so on, had resulted in these young men having 'a deep and abiding sense of being *jilted* or disrespected at a young age' (2015, 204, emphasis in original). Crime, then, becomes a means of seeking dignity and self-respect in the face of repeated humiliation and poor reputation. In Ungar's (2004) terms, acting out may be a way of seeking power and perhaps resisting the negative labels applied by family, schools and others such as the criminal justice system. The conundrum, of course, is then the challenge of trying to move on at a later stage and build a future as an adult that is less destructive and more self-enhancing.

Third, criminal justice interventions in these young men's lives were largely unconstructive and failed to engage with the very real psychological, social and practical difficulties that they faced and the milieu in which they survived. Court decisions and parole supervision were particular points where understanding and discretion could have been extended. In practice this was rare, with the emphasis of parole clearly on monitoring rather than helping. Moreover, the interface between prisons and services in the community was too often poor, hardly assisting integration into the community.

The net result was a series of obstacles for these young men in leaving their 'offenderhood' behind, although they each in their individual way reached a stage where they realised the futility of continued criminality. And their struggles were often exacerbated by social and criminal justice processes, which seem to allow little leeway for relapse in desistance journeys and to continue affirming criminal identities in court reports and other records. Thus the authors suggest that

> After all, everyone mucks up some time, especially as a kid. But when one's offending starts to span well beyond teenage years – or becomes extremely serious in those years – it becomes increasingly hard to rebuild the reservoir of goodwill and respect that most 'normal' citizens enjoy. This in part accounts for why the secondary stage of desistance has proved so difficult to attain for the majority of young men in our research. That stage is not just about the development of internal scripts – the story built and rehearsed from within about past, present and future. Rather, it is equally about how others with standing interpret such stories and about the stories these others invest in and put into wider circulation on behalf of would-be desisters. (Halsey and Deegan, 2015).

## Brief notes on generativity

It is only too easy to dwell on the problems that young people might encounter in their growing up, and the many snares they could fall into, especially if they start their journeys badly prepared and ill-equipped. Extending the metaphor somewhat, to focus only on the difficulties that young people have in pulling themselves out of the pit of 'degenerative' lifestyles deflects attention from enablers and generative possibilities. Although generativity is considered in more depth in Chapter Ten, I want to address it here in relation to young people, specifically because it is not a quality generally associated with this age group (see McAdams, 1993, for a fuller discussion of generativity within the life-course).

Generativity has been defined as

> The concern for and commitment to promoting the next generation, manifested through parenting, teaching, mentoring, and generating products and outcomes that aim to benefit youth and foster the development and well-being of individuals and social systems that will outlive the self. (McAdams and de St Aubin, 1998, xx, cited in Maruna, 2001, 99)

Thus, young people may more often be the beneficiaries of other people's generative activities than acting in purposefully generative ways themselves. The types of generativity discussed in the desistance literature – volunteering, working in a caring capacity, community activity – would not be easy or obvious options for young adults moving towards desistance. However, if generativity is viewed in its widest sense as linked to reciprocity in relationships and caring for others, it surely has relevance.

Halsey and Deegan argue that generativity can be conceived as 'the desire and/or capacity to care for self, other and future in meaningful, non-violent and enduring fashion' (2015, 6). This helps us think through how the concept might apply to young people, particularly as it emphasises a projective dimension as well as a focus on present activities. Young people's preparations and plans for parenthood can therefore be seen as generative, and certainly a change in what might have been their central concerns or aims in life hitherto. Such preparation and plans embody hope – an essential element in motivating and sustaining change. It is important, too, for young people to have opportunities to connect to others in a variety of other ways, even within environments such as prisons that might seem at first blush to hold little promise – showing new arrivals 'the ropes', helping with writing letters and other practical tasks, offering emotional support, for example. These benefit not only the recipient but also the giver, encouraging a positive sense of self-worth and responsibility (doubly powerful when recognised by others). While different from the development of ambitions for future work and family, everyday transactions and roles can add to a real shift in self-perception that can bolster a growing sense of adulthood.

Although her research involved only 40 young adults, Barry (2007) found that the desisters in her sample were more likely to have opportunities for responsibility and generativity than those who persisted in offending. Roles that involve caring and giving attention to others – partners, parents or children – are perhaps more available to young women (Barry, 2007), and they are more likely to maintain their commitment to parenting after the breakdown of a relationship. Nevertheless, assuming parental responsibility is pivotal for some young men in their decisions to stop offending, while others are able to demonstrate care and responsiveness to the needs of others in their relationships with partners or family (McIvor et al, 2004).

However, being able to develop life projects that are generative rather than stagnative requires robust systems of social support (Halsey and Deegan, 2015). Those individuals who are most damaged and hurt are not likely to be able to show care for others (or self-care) unless they have experienced care themselves. In an ideal world, support should be offered at an early stage to families under stress, but there are opportunities even later on to offer helpful services and relationships. Young people under supervision or released from prison should have access to appropriate accommodation, meaningful employment and, if needed, support for mental ill health or problematic substance use. Prolonged involvement with the criminal justice system can curtail possibilities for positive progress in each of these areas, with knock-on effects for transition to adulthood and moves towards desistance. It is surely time for a more understanding and less punitive approach to young offenders – and across the board to all young people growing up in adversity – to help them take steps towards successful (adult) lives.

## Conclusion

In essence this chapter sets out to capture my explorations and reflections at the early stage of doctoral study. The nature of self and identity – especially identity at critical stages of development – is complex and contested. Even within the chapters of this book, the transformations that take place in the processes of desistance and recovery are framed in different ways, reflecting the authors' understandings of identity construction and change.

Following McAdams (1993), I view identity as intrinsically tied up with narratives of self. The telling of self-stories allows each of us to cognitively filter and to attribute value and emotional import to the variety of our inter-related life experiences and events. Narratives may be entirely private, but they are also often created in social interactions and for many different purposes (and here I perhaps do part company with McAdams). Whether we are inwardly reflecting or talking to others about ourselves or our lives, our narratives are constitutive of our self-concept. It is now widely recognised that we have seen a 'narrative turn' in qualitative research. More recently research has also taken a distinct 'biographical turn' which has spawned a growing number of studies that see individuals as 'creators of meanings which form the basis of their everyday lives. Individuals act according to meanings through which they make sense of social experience' (Roberts, 2002, 6). Narrative methodologies have lent themselves to exploring the lived social experience and the events that resonate with individuals across their life course.

I have argued that the capacity for meaning-making and a sense of individual biography grows during the teenage and early adult years. This implies that young people develop not only their understandings and presentations of their personal pasts, but also imaginative projections of their futures. The question answered only partially so far by research is how young people exercise agency in their narrative constructions of identity. The elements of this appear to be: first, the internal processes of making sense of and evaluating experiences and opportunities (and here young people may be equipped to greater or lesser extents); second, the encouragement, connections and knowledge that might be available in each young person's social world *and which he or she sees as accessible*; and third, the role of individual choice and determination. This is precisely where I am locating my doctoral studies, exploring with a small group of young people their self-perceptions and self-constructions.

The social reality, however, is that extended biographical self-presentation is rare for young people in their mid-teen years. That means that research must look at the varied contexts in which young people tell their self-stories and develop themes. As narratives are often developed in dialogue or conversation, this brings the role of audience into the frame. The impact of acceptance, challenge or indifference varies according to the listener's position of power relative to the narrator and the dynamic of the relationship: a young person is likely to react differently to an expression of disapproval from a social worker than from a younger friend. Jenkins (1996) stresses the dual importance of psychological and social processes, arguing that identity is formed through a constant dialectic between internal and external definitions of self. Following this line, therefore,

> What people think about us is no less important than what we think about ourselves. It is not enough to assert an identity. That identity must also be validated (or not) by those with whom we have dealings. *Social identity is never unilateral.* (Jenkins, 1996, 21, emphasis in original)

Viewing identity as socially constructed leads researchers to look at the impacts on that identity of social classifications (such as gender, class and place of origin) and identifications. The qualities that families, schools and others attribute to young people on the basis of these – achieving, competent, adventurous – may encourage positive aspirations. But other types of attributions limit possibilities and future expectations – failing in education, emotionally unstable, behaviourally difficult, hyperactive – and may trail a young person throughout early life. My interest is in the latter and, specifically, how individual young people manage to construct positive identities from difficult circumstances and unpromising sources of social capital. Within that, I want to explore the ways that each recognises and works with (or against) being designated in some way as 'troubled or troublesome'.

Visual, mobile and creative methodologies may be helpful for capturing young people's 'big' and 'small stories' (see Robinson, 2015). However, investigating change over time requires sustained longitudinal research designs. Studies such as *Inventing adulthoods* (Henderson et al, 2007) and *Disconnected youth?* (MacDonald and Marsh, 2005) are insightful about identities in transition, but have a relatively small number of participants who are heavily criminally involved. Granted, the Teesside studies are specifically interested in young people's experience of growing up on the margins of society with poor economic prospects. Nevertheless, their observations on trajectories of offending and desistance are side-notes to their main findings. Other research projects revisiting participants over a period of time have focused on an age range starting from the late teenage years (for example, the Sheffield desistance study (Bottoms and Shapland, 2011)). This leaves a dearth of qualitative studies in criminology that follow young people through adolescence into early adulthood. Halsey and Deegan's (2015) research with a small group of very active offenders is a notable – and extremely powerful – exception.

It is only too common to find chapters and articles concluding by saying that more research is needed. Yet in this area it truly is. Looking around the question of young people and 'growing out of crime', there are many studies from across the disciplines that shed some light, but as yet, none that really illuminate the common aspects of identity change for young would-be adults and would-be desisters. If change is driven by psychosocial development and maturation, we surely need to understand more fully the interaction of individual self-perceptions, social practices and the roles that young people are allowed and enabled to take up. The nub of the problem may indeed lie in situations that prevent young people – whether actively or by default – from trying out adult-like roles or taking on responsibilities. If 'being adult' presupposes feelings of mastery and competence *that are recognised by others*, young people need exposure to new experiences and social relations that help shape positive identities. As researchers we must also listen to young people to better appreciate how they can use challenges, risks and life events as opportunities for growth and resilience.

## References

Bamberg, M, 2004, Talk, small stories and adolescent identities, *Human Development* 47, 366–9

Bamberg, M, Georgakopoulou, A, 2008, Small stories as a new perspective in narrative and identity analysis, *Text and Talk: An Interdisciplinary Journal of Language, Discourse Communication Studies* 28, 3, 377–96

Barry, M, 2006, *Youth offending in transition: The search for social recognition*, Abingdon: Routledge

Barry, M, 2007, The transitional pathways of young female offenders, in R Sheehan, G McIvor, C Trotter (eds) *What works with women offenders*, pp 23–39, Cullompton: Willan

Bottoms, A, Shapland, J, 2011, Steps towards desistance among male young adult recidivists, in S Farrall, R Sparks, S Maruna, M Hough (eds) *Escape routes: Contemporary perspectives on life after offending*, pp 43–80, Abingdon: Routledge

Bourdieu, P, 1977, *Outline of the theory of practice*, Cambridge: Cambridge University Press

Bourdieu, P, 1986, The forms of capital, in JG Richardson (ed) *Handbook of theory and research for the sociology of education*, Westport, CT: Greenwood Press

Bourdieu, P, 1990, *The logic of practice*, Stanford, CA: Stanford University Press

Bourdieu, P, 1998, *Practical reason*, Stanford, CA: Stanford University Press

Bronfenbrenner, U, 1979, *The ecology of human development: Experiments by nature and design*, Maidenhead: Open University Press

Brown, K, 2015, *Vulnerability and young people: Care and social control in policy and practice*, Bristol: Policy Press

Cauffman, E, Steinberg, L, 2000, (Im)maturity of judgment in adolescence: Why adolescents may be less culpable than adults, *Behavioural Sciences and the Law* 18, 743–60

Denzin, N, 1987, *The recovering alcoholic*, London: Sage

Emirbayer, M, Mische, A, 1998, What is agency?, *American Journal of Sociology* 103, 4, 962–1023

Fivush, R, Habermas, T, Walters, TEA, Zaman, W, 2011, The making of autobiographical memory: Intersections of culture, narratives and identity, *International Journal of Psychology* 48, 5, 321–45

France, A, Bottrell, D, Armstrong, D, 2012, *A political ecology of youth and crime*, New York: Palgrave Macmillan

Furlong, A, Cartmel, F, 2007, *Young people and social change: New perspectives* (2nd edn), Maidenhead: Open University Press

Giddens, A, 1991, *Modernity and self-identity: Self and society in the late modern age*, Cambridge: Polity Press

Giordano, PC, Cernkovich, SA, Rudolphe, JL, 2002, Gender, crime and desistance: Towards a theory of cognitive transformation, *American Journal of Sociology* 107, 4, 990–1064

Giordano, P, Schroeder, RD, Cernkovitch, SA, 2007, Emotions and crime over the life-course: A neo-Meadian perspective on criminal continuity and change, *American Journal of Sociology* 112, 6, 1603–61

Graham, J, Bowling, B, 1995, Young people and crime, *Home Office Research Study* 145, London: Home Office Research and Statistics Department

Habermas, T, Bluck, S, 2000, Getting a life: The emergence of the life story in adolescence, *Psychological Bulletin* 126, 5, 748–69

Halsey, M, Deegan, S, 2015, *Young offenders: Crime, prison and struggles for desistance*, Basingstoke: Palgrave Macmillan

Harding, S, 2014, *The street casino: Survival in violent street gangs*, Bristol: Policy Press

Healy, D, 2010, *The dynamics of desistance: Charting pathways through change*, Abingdon: Routledge

Heath, S, Brooks, R, Cleaver, E, Ireland, E, 2009, *Researching young people's lives*, London: Sage

Henderson, S, Holland, J, McGrellis, S, Sharpe, S, Thomson, R, 2007, *Inventing adulthoods: A biographical approach to youth transitions*, London: Sage

Jenkins, R, 2006, *Social identity*, London: Routledge

Jones, G, 2009, *Youth*, Cambridge: Polity Press

King, S, 2014, *Desistance transitions and the impact of probation*, Abingdon: Routledge

Laub, J, Sampson, R, 2003, *Shared beginnings, divergent lives*, London: Harvard University Press

McAdams, DP, 1993, *The stories we live by*, New York: William Morrow

McAdams, DP, de St Aubin, E, 1998, Introduction, DP McAdams, E de St Aubin (eds) *Generativity and adult development: How and why we care for the next generation*, pp xix–xxiv, Washington DC: American Psychological Association

McAdams, DP, McLean, K, 2013, Narrative identity, *Current Directions in Psychological Science* 22, 3, 235–8

McAra, L, McVie, S, 2005, The usual suspects? Street-life, young people and the police, *Criminal Justice* 5, 1, 5–36

McAra, L, McVie, S, 2007, The impact of system contact on patterns of desistence from offending, *European Journal of Criminology* 4, 3, 315–45

McAra, L, McVie, S, 2012, Negotiated order: The groundwork for a theory of offending pathways, *Criminology and Criminal Justice* 12, 4, 347–75

MacDonald, R, 2006, Social exclusion, youth transitions and criminal careers: Five critical reflections on risk, *The Australian and New Zealand Journal of Criminology* 39, 3, 371–83

MacDonald, R, Marsh, J, 2005, *Disconnected youth? Growing up in Britain's poor neighbourhoods*, Basingstoke: Palgrave Macmillan

MacDonald, R, Shildrick, T, 2007, Street corner society: Leisure careers, youth (sub) culture and social exclusion, *Leisure Studies* 26, 3, 339-355

MacDonald, R, Webster, C, Shildrick, T, Simpson, M, 2011, Paths of exclusion, inclusion and desistence, in S Farrall, R Sparks, S Maruna, M Hough (eds) *Escape routes: Contemporary perspectives on life after offending*, pp 135–57, Abingdon: Routledge

McDonald, K, 1999, *Struggles for subjectivity: Identity, action and youth experience*, Cambridge: Cambridge University Press

McIvor, G, Murray, C, Jamieson, J , 2004, Desistance from crime: Is it different for women and girls?, in S Maruna, R Immarigeon (eds) *After crime and punishment: Pathways to offender reintegration*, pp 181–97, Cullompton: Willan

McLeod, J, 2003, Why we interview now – reflexivity and perspective in a longitudinal study, *International Journal of Social Research Methodology* 6, 3, 201–11

McVie, S, 2004, Patterns of deviance underlying the age-crime curve: the long term evidence, Paper for the British Society of Criminology Conference, Portsmouth

Maruna, S, 2001, *Making good: How ex-convicts reform and rebuild their lives*, Washington DC: American Psychological Association

Maruna, S, Farrall, S, 2004, Desistance from crime: A theoretical reformulation, *Kolner Zeitschrift fur Soziologie and Sozialpsychologie*, 43, 171–94

Massoglia, M, Uggen, C, 2010, Settling down and aging out: Towards an interactionist theory of desistance and the transition to adulthood, *American Journal of Sociology* 116, 2, 543–82

Matza, D, 1964, *Delinquency and drift*, New York: Wiley

Moffitt, T, 1993, Adolescent-limited and life-course-persistent anti-social behaviour: A developmental taxonomy, *Psychological Review* 100, 4, 674–701

Mulvey, E, Steinberg, L, Piquero, AR, Besana, M, Fagan, J, Schubert, C, Cauffman, 2010, Trajectories of desistance and continuity in anti-social behaviour following court adjudication among serious adolescent offenders, *Development and Psychopathology* 22, 2, 453–75

Pasupathi, M, Mansour, E, Brubaker, JR, 2007, Developing a life story: Constructing relations between self and experience in autobiographical narratives, *Human Development* 50, 85–110

Prior, D, Farrow, Kathryn, K, Hughes, N, Kelly, G, Manders, G, White, S, Wilkinson, B, 2011, *Maturity, young adults and criminal justice: A literature review*, Birmingham: University of Birmingham

Raffo, C, Reeves, M, 2000, Youth transitions and social exclusion: Developments in social capital theory, *Journal of Youth Studies* 3, 2, 147-166

Reissman, CK, 2008, *Narrative methods for the human sciences*, London: Sage

Roberts, B, 2002, *Biographical research*, Maidenhead: Open University Press

Robinson, A, 2015, Life stories in development: Thoughts on narrative methods with young people, *British Journal of Community Justice* 13, 2, 59-77

Ross, N, Renold, E, Holland, S, Hillman, A, 2009, Moving stories: Using mobile methods to explore the everyday lives of young people in care, *Qualitative Research* 9, 5, 605–23

Shapland, J, Bottoms, A, 2011, Reflections on social values, offending and desistance among young adult recidivists, *Punishment and Society* 13, 3, 256–82

Steinberg, L, Cauffman, E, 1996, Maturity of judgement in adolescence: Psycho-social factors in adolescent decision-making, *Law and Human Behaviour* 20, 249–72

Steinberg, L, Cauffman, E, Monahan, KC, 2015, *Psychosocial maturity and desistance from crime in a sample of serious juvenile offenders*, Laurel, MD: US Dept of Justice, Office of Juvenile Justice and Delinquency Prevention

Thomson, R, Bell, R, Holland, J, Henderson, S, McGrellis, S, Sharpe, S, 2002, Critical moments: Choice, chance and opportunity in young people's narratives of transition, *Sociology* 36, 2, 335–54

Turner, V, 1970, *The forests of the symbolic: Aspects of the Ndembu ritual*, London: Cornell University Press

Ungar, M, 2001, The social construction of resilience among 'problem' youth in out-of-home placement: A study of health-enhancing deviance, *Child and Youth Care Forum* 30, 3, 137–54

Ungar, M, 2004, *Nurturing hidden resilience in troubled youth*, Toronto: University of Toronto Press

Ungar, M (ed), 2012, *The social ecology of resilience: A handbook of theory and practice*, New York: Springer

Vaughan, B, 2007, The internal narrative of desistance, *British Journal of Criminology* 47, 3, 23–39

# Different pathways for different journeys: ethnicity, identity transition and desistance

*Adam Calverley*

## Introduction

Identity transition is integral to our comprehension of desistance from crime at both a definitional and theoretical level. As the phenomena whereby individuals who have been actively engaged in crime reduce or curtail their offending behaviour it involves, at its most basic, a binary shift from the status of one identity, 'an offender', to that of another identity, that of 'non-offender'. This conceptualisation, albeit crude and simplistic, conveys the essence of what desistance is and is understood to mean. The processes involved in both desistance and identity transitions are, of course, much more complicated than this. Determining the identification of one's own identity and the labelling of others' identities is a subjective, as opposed to an objective, consideration. This subjectivity has implications for the measurement of desistance and its operationalisation that raises questions of typology and timing: for example, 'under what circumstances can someone be considered a "desister" or to have successfully desisted?'; 'when does an offender become a "non"-offender?'; 'is the identity of non-offender acquired easily or is it subsumed under the more problematic identity of ex-offender?' (Farrall and Calverley, 2006; Maruna, 2001; Kazemian, 2007).

As well as comprising a description of what desistance entails, by bridging both the social and the personal, identity also provides an explanatory framework for how desistance takes place. Making a (or *the*) transition from offending to non-offending identity is one of the key processes associated with desistance. Research has identified that this can involve a number of psychological and psycho-social processes that take place within the 'internal' world of the desister in relation to events outside. For example, faced with the dilemma of incoherency in their narrative identity and reconciling their past lives as active offenders with their future desires to avoid offending, successful desisters in Maruna's (2001) sample underwent a process of re-biographing where they rewrote the story of their lives using a 'redemption script' that cast themselves as essentially good people. Others have framed this transition to a desisting identity as being a slowly unfolding and ordered process of events. Vaughan (2006) theorises that desisters engage in an 'internal conversation' during which they weigh up the pros and cons of desisting as they go through separate phases of discernment, deliberation and dedication. Similarly, Giordano et al (2002) argue that the decision to stop offending is a conscious but sequential process wherein desisters undergo a cognitive re-evaluation of their lives, identifying a 'blueprint' for a future self which serves as a roadmap and motivating factor to continue with their efforts to desist. Alternatively, the internal process whereby individuals decide to stop may be an unconscious one resulting from the psychic motivation of desisters to invest in available discourses that will enable the construction of a protective self-identity that will minimise anxiety (Gadd, 2006; Gadd and Farrall, 2004). What all these processes allow is for reflection and reflexivity on the part of the desister about who they are and their place in the world, and also for desisters to make sense of their past offending self (who they were), and their present and future non-offending selves (Bottoms, 2006, 270–1).

Identity, therefore, provides a useful theoretical framework that bridges both the social – how individuals are seen by others – and the personal – how individuals see themselves. The transition from one set of personal and social identities associated with involvement in crime to another set of personal and social identities associated with having successfully left crime behind, means that desistance entails an existential re-construction of the self. The meanings individuals give to their lives are affected by their actions, the events in their lives, the meanings and emotions they ascribe to these events, and the meanings ascribed to them and their actions by others with whom they have relationships in the social world (Farrall, 2005; Paternoster and Bushway, 2009; Weaver, 2016). This means that the identities that characterise desisters' inner worlds are ultimately dependent on what identities are available for them to transition into within the social structural and cultural context that they inhabit, the means and mechanisms through which they are able to do this and their ability and willingness to do so. It is significant that the principal external factors that research has identified as supporting desistance, such as work, marriage, parenthood and maturation (see Laub and Sampson, 2001; Farrall, 2002), all involve new roles and expectations of normative behaviour, and are all associated with the adoption of accompanying prosocial identities such as 'provider', 'husband', 'father', 'responsible citizen'. Desistance, therefore, does not simply involve the (re)-construction of a single, unitary identity of non-offender, but inevitably entails the assumption of a wide range of supportive, multiple, constitutive identities. As has already been highlighted by Hamilton (Chapter One, this volume), the continuous nature of identity construction, its fluidity and reflexivity mean that there is, of course, nothing fixed or foregone about the forms these identities will take. Their accessibility is dependent on desisters' cultural repertoires in terms of what is desirable and expected of them, their relationships with others, their socio-economic position and resources available to them. Consequently, it is reasonable to assume that differences in cultural and structural position affect how processes associated with desistance 'play out'.

That desistance involves the interaction of structural and agentic factors has been well rehearsed elsewhere (Farrall and Bowling, 1999; Farrall and Calverley, 2006; Farrall et al, 2011; Weaver, 2016). However, it is worth reiterating that how desisters interpret and navigate the structural opportunities and impediments that chart their journey towards desistance will affect their identity. Farrall et al (2010, 553), in their discussion of how Bourdieu's and Mouzelis' theories can inform our understanding of desistance, demonstrate its relevance:

> persistent offenders who have decided to try to desist can strive to achieve that desistance through situating themselves in relation to the structures surrounding them, adjusting their self-perception along the way (see Farrall, 2005). Because, for Mouzelis, structures are not just simply institutional arrangements (such as the eligibility and priority rules for social housing in a given local area) but also *patterned sets of relationships in particular contexts* (which might include relationship structures based on racism or on hostility to sex offenders), the desistance-related struggles of the actor might very well occur in relation to patterns of informal behaviour and accepted moral views, as well as in relation to the formal institutions of the state, the employment market, etc. (my emphasis)

What the above analysis suggests is that, where significant differences in the 'patterned sets of relationships in particular contexts' are known to exist, such as around differences indexed by ethnicity, the ways that these impact upon processes of desistance are worthy of further investigation. The issue of how these ethnic differences affect the structural context in which processes of desistance operate and how this, in turn, affects the 'desistance-related struggles of the actor' in question, may have a number of implications for identity change: first, the forms of prosocial identities available to individuals through which to support their desistance may vary by ethnicity; second, the availability of capital, be it economic or social, held within these patterned relationships may be ethnically structured; third, differing norms, values and expectations held by others within their communities may affect the character and direction of desistance; and fourth, differences may exist between ethnic groups in terms of how and when identity change is supported and confirmed. There exists, therefore, a strong *prima facia* case for investigating how differences between ethnic groups may affect desistance and associated identity transformation.

## Review of ethnicity and desistance literature

Given the strong case for studying desistance and ethnicity outlined above, it is somewhat surprising that it has received relatively little research attention to date (see Calverley, 2013; Glynn, 2014), with what exists either comprising small-scale qualitative research or being based in the USA. In fact, there is a notable absence of any large-scale long-term longitudinal studies that have exclusively charted, examined and provided a wider comparative analysis of criminal careers among offenders of different ethnic groups. While some research studies that have addressed this issue found few differences in desistance outcomes between ethnic groups (Piquero et al, 2002; Hughes, 1997; 1998), others have confirmed that structural and cultural variations by ethnicity do produce differential effects. This includes studies that have found poorer levels of success among minority ethnic offenders in avoiding further offending compared with white offenders, and attributed this to their disadvantageous socio-economic location (Baskin and Somers, 1998; Reisig et al, 2007). Other studies have identified ethnic differences in engagement with social institutions as responsible for producing differences in offending behaviour. Rand (1987) found marriage and military service had a less positive associative effect on desistance for non-white people. Craig and Connell (2015, 344) found the reverse, that military service had 'a transformative effect' for non-white people, increasing their likelihood of desisting whereas it had the opposite effect for white people. Nielsen (1999) found marriage to be associated with a reduction in drunkenness among white people and Hispanic people but this was not applicable to black people. Chu and Sung (2008) reported that religious involvement had a positive effect on recovery from substance misuse for black but not for white people. These studies – along with others not focused on ethnic differences, such as Savolainen's (2009) research in Finland and Godfrey et al's (2007) study of criminal careers of men in the nineteenth century – underline the importance of appreciating how wider social processes, such as marriage and co-habitation, operate within different cultural (and historical) contexts, and that these have implications for desistance

Research has also identified how the significance of cultural attitudes towards desisters held by their immediate community shapes the pathways and the availability of socially approved and endorsed roles through which to exit their criminal pasts. For example, the two communities of US immigrants (Italians and Poles) in Finestone's (1967) study had very different attitudes towards returning prisoners, the role of the family in assisting in their rehabilitation, and the extent to which they were willing to work with community workers to achieve this. This, in turn, had an impact on the roles ex-offenders from these communities adopted to secure their reintegration. Other studies have identified that support, encouragement and empathy from one's immediate community and peers is crucial to supporting desistance among minority ethnic offenders who have experienced major social marginalisation resulting from processes of historic and ongoing racism and exclusion. In the case of Aboriginal gang members in Canada who wanted to stop offending (Deane et al, 2007; Bracken et al, 2009) this involved a specialised tailored intervention. This not only gave an opportunity to gain skills via a community-based training programme but also, through the reacquisition of cultural traditions, acknowledged their biography and the structural constraints of their position, and re-engaged them with traditional prosocial values of community and reciprocity that supported the development of a non-offending identity that recognised that they were an 'an Aboriginal person'. This awareness of wider history and exclusion allowed them to depersonalise problems and see them as wider problems of colonialism and racism, while the reacquisition of cultural traditions re-enforced their 'essentially good' self, and provided a symbolic restoration and 'healing' for some of the harm done to them. The implications of this research suggests that, to overcome the impeding effects of racism and discrimination, desistance for some minority groups may need to be supported via 'awareness programmes'.

On the other hand, Sullivan's ethnographic study into the lived desistance experiences of male Aboriginal serial offenders in New South Wales, Australia, suggests that, rather than being a 'lost' identity requiring reclamation, 'the Aboriginality of the participants...was never in doubt' (2012, 69) with 'Aboriginal repeat offenders [being] Aboriginal first and offenders second' (Sullivan, 2012, 269) and the cultural values and socialisation associated with 'Aboriginality' serving to frame both their offending and their desistance. The desistance 'projects' described by men in Sullivan's investigation did not envision the ambitious vocational aspirations of participants in Maruna's study (2001) – or even fairly ordinary aspirations involving basic employment. Residing in poor rural communities with few employment opportunities, and already stigmatised and 'othered' owing to the racism of non-Aboriginal society, meant that 'breadwinning' (Sullivan, 2012, 288) was arguably not a realistic option. Instead, participants were much more likely to envision their desistance around 'cultural schemas' such as partnership and parenthood, providing support and bolstering motivation. Aboriginal self-identity, Sullivan argues, must be seen within the cultural context of Aboriginal sociality and its values of relatedness – commitment to kin and ethics of generosity and sharing – and, somewhat contradictory to the value of autonomy – 'a person's right to be themselves' (Macdonald, cited in Sullivan, 2012, 275), which meant not condemning those in their community who were in 'trouble with the law' as criminals. The process of reformulating their identity as part of their desistance requires a re-definition of relatedness whereby they remain independent but are still supporting their kin. This took the form of improvised modification of existing social relationships (pp 289–90) rather than 'knifing off' previous relationships or establishment of new relationships, and generativity through community projects working with other offenders or small-scale paid employment which allowed them to 'help their community' and connect with their Aboriginal identity at the same time.

Glynn's (2014) research into the challenges facing black men from the UK and USA in trying to desist raises a number of salient issues concerning the intersectionality between identity, race and/or ethnicity and desistance. That the experience of well documented racism and discrimination, both throughout the criminal justice system and in wider society (Phillips and Bowling, 2012), might have potentially detrimental effects for successful desistance of different ethnic groups, seems an obvious point. How it affects desisters' identities, however, has still to be explored fully. Glynn (2014, 58–79) argues that understanding black men's desistance necessitates an appreciation of the way that racialisation and criminalisation affects it, and that this, in turn, has implications for the construction of a racialised identity. He cites the existence of significant 'barriers' to desistance in the form of systemic racial bias and structural impediments and, within the context of masculinity, in the form of 'father absence', 'fatherhood', 'hyper-masculinity' and criminogenic pressures of gangs and 'the street'. His participants reported a 'racialised' identity that was fully aware of the inequity and injustice of 'the system'. However, the failure of criminal justice practice to acknowledge these processes and of mainstream criminology to privilege the 'voices' of experience of desisting black men themselves, and the insights that they offer, means that this identity is not validated and is rendered invisible. Glynn contends that the deployment of critical race theory is required as an intellectual framework through which to learn more about black men's desistance, allowing them to tell their 'stories' and to construct a counter-narrative 'that questions and challenges official discourse' and, in doing so, he asserts, aids the construction of a narrative that 'fashion[s] a new identity and develop[s] a more "pro-social" life' (Glynn, 2014, 130).

In sum, the above research literature raises a number of relevant points for considering the different ways that ethnicity may affect desisters' identities, the forms these take and the processes through which they are constructed. It highlights how ethnic differences in structure and culture may affect processes associated with desistance and outcomes. The attitudinal responses (of their community and wider society) towards desisting offenders shape their desistance strategies, available prosocial identities through which to exit crime, and desisters' 'awareness' of their identity and possible need for specialised interventions to support these processes. It also raises the need to consider not only how ethnic differences produce variation in individuals' desisting identities, but also how these intersect with other identities and social processes such as gender and racism. The rest of this chapter will explore these themes in further detail: revisiting the findings of my doctoral research. Following a brief outline of its methodology, it will demonstrate the ways that processes of desistance vary and coalesce around ethnicity, and the consequences this has for the availability, accessibility and types or forms of prosocial identity that could be utilised to support desisters' efforts to stop offending.

## Research study and methodology

The results discussed herein are taken from my doctoral research (Calverley, 2009; Calverley, 2013[1]) where I investigated the experience of desistance among men from three of the UK's largest minority ethnic groups: 'Indians', 'Bangladeshis'[2] and 'black and dual heritage'. This relied on interviews with 33 male probationers who were desisting or who had desisted from crime, recruited from London Probation Area offices. Of these 33, 8 were Indian, 11 Bangladeshi and 14 either black or dual heritage.[3] To be included in the study, a probationer needed to be from one of these groups, have at least three previous convictions (not exclusively for motoring offences); have grown up or spent a significant part of their life in the UK; and, in the assessment of probation staff, to have stopped offending, or at least shown evidence of making significant progress toward desistance. In-depth semi-structured interviews asked participants about their experiences of stopping offending, past lives, current life circumstances and future plans.

These three ethnic groups were selected as they occupy different positions in terms of their social and economic statuses. National census data (ONS, 2006) and other research reveal[4] that: compared with the national average and with other ethnic groups, Indians in the United Kingdom have higher levels of employment, home ownership and educational attainment; Bangladeshis are the most mono-religious of all ethnic groups, for whom the practice of marriage is almost universal (Coleman, 2006), often arranged in conjunction with their parents (Beishon et al, 1998, 50–1) and they have high rates of unemployment (Piggott, 2004, 35) and the highest number of households with dependent children (Connolly and Raha, 2006); black Caribbean households, on the other hand, are much more likely to be smaller, characterised by a low rate of marriage and high rate of cohabitation, divorce and lone parenthood (Berthoud, 2000, 1), boys have low levels of attainment at school, experience high levels of school exclusion (DfES, 2006, 87) and, as men, also have higher levels of unemployment (Bradford and Forsyth, 2006, 122). Therefore, these three ethnic groups allow for the exploration of how wider differences in social, economic and cultural formations impress upon processes of desistance. They 'stand in'[5] for cultural variation since each has subtly differentiated values, aspirations, cultural arrangements and expectations and is differently placed from each of the others in socio-economic terms.

### Indian desisting identities: work, family, ambitious aspirations

Indian desisters arguably occupied a much more favourable economically and socially resourced position than the Bangladeshi and black and dual heritage men in the sample. Their accounts revealed that, although they may have been involved in crime, this was in stark contrast to other members of their family (such as their parents, siblings or wider family) who had achieved success either through self-employment or becoming professionally qualified. These family members often provided access to local employment opportunities in one of two ways: either working for family businesses themselves, or by using personal contacts and networks to find them work in other businesses. In fact, all Indian desisters revealed that previously there had been at least one occasion when they had secured employment through these means so that, despite possessing few basic educational qualifications similar to the Bangladeshi and black and dual heritage interviewees, they had all managed to acquire a history of employment and to bypass the two-fold discrimination they faced as ex-offenders and ethnic minorities. Critically, despite having let down their family on previous occasions by losing their jobs through offending or drug use, access to employment through these social networks remained open to them; and, at the time of interview, they had either taken advantage of this opportunity or were aware that there still existed a possibility that they could do so. As a result, the option of building a non-offending identity around work presented Indian desisters with a reachable 'hook for change' upon which, if they so wished, they could envision a non-criminal replacement 'self' which would be acceptable both to their family and to themselves. Their family supported the construction of this new prosocial identity, in part, because they were often involved in facilitating opportunities to make these changes.

The above support is indicative of a key feature associated with Indian desisters' families of origin – a willingness to intervene in their lives with the hope of re-directing them away from crime. This included the provision of financial resources such as accommodation. For five out of the eight Indian desisters in the sample, the parental home was still offered to them as a place to live in spite of their previous failures to uphold promises to avoid offending and having been excluded and made homeless on other, previous, occasions. It was also evident in cases where their families made significant financial investment to bring an end their addiction to heroin by sending them to drug rehabilitation clinics in India. However, the motivation behind this interventionist disposition arguably owed as much to control as it did to care, being informed by cultural pressures to maintain status within wider familial and community networks and to minimise the shame associated with their errant son's offending that prompted intervention to try and reform them together with, of course, a genuine desire to help them.

The cultural context of Indian desisters was also defined by high aspirations and expectations imposed upon them by their families of what they were expected to be achieving. Indeed dramatic deviation from this journey of respectable achievement due to repeated re-offending prompted the adoption of a counter-factual narrative to account for their absence while in prison:

> *Parents have to lie to other people and say, 'My son ain't a junkie. My son is doing quite well. He's working this place or this place.' For example, when I was in prison on my third sentence one of my aunties asked my Mum, 'Where's Parminder? Where is he?' And my mum would have to lie and say, 'Oh, he got a job in Spain. He's working out in Spain for a couple of weeks and then he's going to Scotland.' So they'd have to lie. You understand? Just to cover my back so it's not embarrassing for the family.* (Parminder)

The idea behind this was that, by presenting an acceptable image of success to the outside world, they could in the meantime assist their sons to get their lives 'back on track' and return to normality without having to acknowledge publicly that there had been a problem. This strategy comprised a shared project for both Indian desisters and their families to work towards and provided a mutual shared interest that the former be assisted with their desistance efforts and moved into pre-imagined respectable prosocial identities as soon as possible. Interestingly, previously these efforts at intervention had repeatedly failed to secure permanent desistance. This was because, even with the best intentions of their families, success was ultimately dependent on the commitment and agency of individuals beyond the pressures of their family. In this context the pressure provided by the family had little success in fast-tracking permanent desistance. Significantly, however, despite these failures the cultural pressures that gave rise to these forms of intervention remain, which meant that the requirement that the transition to desired prescribed prosocial identities be supported and made available continues to be offered. These opportunities could be acted upon in the future if Indian desisters sought to utilise them.

Furthermore, there is evidence that Indian desisters were aware of their families' expectations for them and that this was responsible for creating a recognition that they should re-orient themselves and 'make something of their life':

> *I think now [my Dad] just expects from me to just get into a job, because he wants me to take over the payments for the houses. He wants to put the houses in my name now. He says, 'Look, you know, it's time now. Look, you're old enough. Take the houses.*

*They are yours anyway. They are yours and your brother's. I bought them for you two…are you trying to tell me you can buy a house?' I say 'no'. Obviously I can't put twenty or thirty grand down for a deposit for a house and afford to pay a mortgage, because I can't. So my dad has done that for us.* (Gurpreet)

The high expectations of their families, combined with the availability of resources, provided Indian desisters with scripted 'exit roles' (Rumgay, 2004) to move into and a 'blueprint' of expected behaviour (Giordano et al, 2002), that, if they applied themselves, they could achieve. The incentive to do so was also, arguably, reinforced by the fact that many of them had siblings or cousins who had fulfilled their families' expectations:

*I would hope one day to have my own business. I want to try doing plumbing, bricklaying or something…My little brother, he is, like, going to go into architecture and what not so I want to try and go into business with him…My cousin…is making shit loads of money. My uncle has got his own business. He buys and sells pubs. My dad is into property. So, like, financial support is there. I just have to get into something and prove, like, that I can do something. That's not a problem.* (Gurpreet)

In contrast to the participants from the other two ethnic groups, their descriptions of where they saw themselves in the future – as well-paid businessmen, owning their own business and owning property – were more ambitious. Acting upon their families' wishes also enabled Indian desisters to send a message that they shared their families' values of work and 'self-improvement'. This gave the outward appearance that they were willing to live within these values. While Indians reported low levels of religiosity, family gatherings such as weddings provided a public forum where family members certified the authenticity of their desistance efforts (Maruna, 2001; 2011). Therefore, Indian desisters were able to construct a prosocial identity around work and, in most cases family, provided they were willing to work within their families' expectations, take advantage of their resources and demonstrate their commitment.

## Bangladeshi desisting identities: forgiveness, family and religion

Bangladeshi desisters in my sample occupied a weak socio-economic position. The majority lived with their parents in overcrowded public sector accommodation. They were unemployed at the time of interview, had little previous work history and, apart from brief and unsuccessful periods doing low-skilled jobs in 'Indian' restaurants obtained via family contacts, had low levels of social capital through which to access secure meaningful employment. Their families had access to fewer economic resources than the families of Indian desisters with only one case reporting that his family was able to afford the cost of sending him to drug rehabilitation abroad.[6] However, the negative effects of what would appear to be a hostile desistance environment were mitigated by the sympathetic cultural context that they inhabited. In fact, what marked the Bangladeshis out was that their desistance rarely involved reconstructing a new self-identity centred on employment (Meisenhelder, 1977; Mischkowitz, 1994; Farrall, 2002) nor was it reliant on the structured routines work provided as has been identified by studies involving mainly white offenders (Shover, 1983; Warr, 1998). Instead they were able to reconstruct a non-offending identity around their family, framed by their families' support and expectations and the beliefs, values and expectations of their religion.

Bangladeshi desisters' parents often played a crucial role in enabling their desistance, primarily because they were willing to become actively involved in their lives. As with Indian desisters' families, the reputational damage resulting from their son's offending meant the pressures of shame from others in the local community provided a vested interest in reforming their behaviour. However, their willingness to offer support also reflected wider Islamic belief that, as parents, they had a duty to offer forgiveness for what their sons had done and to promise acceptance back into the family. The message this sent to desisters, by making it clear that their futures would not be defined by their past involvement in offending, was instrumental in the embryonic construction of a non-offending identity. For Kabir, a telephone conversation with his parents in prison helped him envision a future away from crime, and their assurances provided certainty which engendered hope, a resource that he could draw upon for motivation:

> *Well, the support, like, you see, like, I used to speak to my mum, my missus on the phone when I was in prison. I used to speak to her all the time. She'd say to me 'Alright, listen, this is what you need to do, this is what you need', she was just telling me things…That's the support I used to get from my missus on the phone when I was in prison. That support I'm getting now, what kind of support? Well basically [pause] it's just [pause] it's just that love there is. You get me? That's the support I'm getting from*

*the whole family, kind of thing. When it started it's just the day I came home, they all came around and asked me 'How was this?', 'How was that?' and where this lot's been and 'What have you been doing?'...You do need family support. That's what basically built up myself again; that relationship on the phone; speaking to them on the phone; and I knew that I was going to come back and stay with them again. Things like that. (Kabir)*

Actions such as this generated awareness among Bangladeshi desisters that, if they so wished, and took the necessary actions, they could build a non-offending future self-identity around their family.

For Bangladeshi desisters, taking up the roles and responsibilities of fathers, partners and husbands that were expected of them consolidated their desistance. Initially marriage did not act as an effective mechanism for impeding offending, as their spouses, whom they married in Bangladesh, knew few people and were not in employment so were in a weak position to exert influence over their husbands' behaviour.[7] However, what had previously been a weakness of marriage as a mechanism for supporting desistance, which is that their spouses were isolated and could not easily withdraw from the relationship, became an advantage; there was a guarantee that someone would be waiting for them after release from prison. Likewise, the cultural practices surrounding marriage provided a context which helped bolster and focus the desistance efforts of Bangladeshi desisters who were not married. Not only did they share their families' expectations that they should get married – and soon – and that the appropriate means of organising this would be 'an arranged marriage' involving an 'amicable negotiation' between respective parties, children and elders of both families (Berthoud, 2000, 19), but also the fact that their reputational capital in their 'marriage market' had already been depleted by their previous offending, and would deplete further if they offended again, all provided strong incentives for collaborative cooperation between Bangladeshi desisters and their families so that further offending could be avoided. After Bangladeshi desisters assumed their expected roles within the family and carried out their responsibilities, family members offered recognition and validation of their efforts. In this way, they acted as important agents of (re)certification (Maruna, 2001; 2011), as the following extract demonstrates:

*Basically, the way that I'm getting support from my family, yeah, it's, like, when I look at my kids, yeah, they're just too happy to see me, like. See my brother, yeah, he's told me when he used to see my daughter and he used to see my son looking at other people's fathers and that and they're, like, depressed kind of thing, but, where I've come back now my brother sees, like, walking with them, walking my daughter and my son, yeah, it's like: 'I can see the change in your daughter and your son, the expressions on their faces. They're happier and more cheerful and that.' I can understand that…I didn't have no communication whatsoever [before], but now it's just like everything has just, like, hit me at one go and I can't really explain it, how everyone's just talking to me. Because they can see the change in me, like the person I was from before, like, it's not the same person. He's changing himself. That's where they're seeing me like, 'Yeah, fair enough, he's changing himself' so they're just talking to me more. That's the support I'm getting at the moment: the talking support.* (Kabir)

As well as structuring a new sense of identity, the adoption of expected roles and familial responsibilities helped to structure Bangladeshi desisters' time in more productive ways, through childcare and running errands for family members. This helped support their policy of isolating themselves from potentially tempting situations which could trigger their reoffending.

Bangladeshi desisters were much more likely than their Indian and black and dual heritage counterparts to report that a (re)engagement with religion had helped them to desist (six out of eleven Bangladeshis, compared with one black/dual heritage interviewee and none of the Indians). Five of the Bangladeshi desisters reported that their spiritual transformation began in prison, where it was initially sought as a means to structure their time (Meisenhelder, 1985) but later exposed them to co-prisoners or clerics who were already committed to strict religious observance and who had an interest in informing them about Islam. These interactions proffered Bangladeshis an image of a future self, centred on being a 'good Muslim', that they could act upon. As with Christianity for Giordano et al's sample, Islam helped Bangladeshi desisters 'provide entree to or solidify [their] position with pro-social others' (2008, 118). Their (re)engagement with Islam allowed them to socialise with other religious friends and reconnect with 'good friends' with whom they had previously lost contact due to their involvement in crime. This helped to communicate to others in the wider community, as well as to their family and their friends themselves, the sincerity of their desire to change. By re-embracing Islam, many Bangladeshi desisters were able to choose another easily accessible prosocial identity that allowed the emergence of what they felt to be their 'true' self.

These desisters typically cited that they had been exposed to religion as children (this is found among desisters of other religions too – see Giordano et al, 2008) but had not taken it seriously. It was only now as adults that they had come to appreciate its significance and to realise that they were privileged and appreciated its value. This enabled them to see their adoption of Islam as returning to their true course while at the same time forming a key part of how they saw themselves in the future. Thus, it was simultaneously compatible with their past and future sense of self. This new value system (with its inter-connected familial and religious components) allowed Bangladeshi desisters to take comfort in 'realistic' aspirations based on continuing to support their family by staying away from offending, hopefully finding work and living a 'normal' life away from offending. These aspirations were relatively modest in their scale, at least compared with the financial ambitions of Indian desisters and the professional and 'generative' ambitions of the black and dual heritage desisters discussed below.

## Black and dual heritage desisters: independent, isolated, self-directed

Black and dual heritage desisters inhabited a comparatively adverse social context for enabling desistance. Their families and social networks offered fewer resources that could be drawn upon to assist their efforts to find work and structure their time constructively, and less support and encouragement to direct them away from offending. Unlike Indian and Bangladeshi desisters who were densely bonded within family networks, the relationships which black and dual heritage desisters had with their families were often damaged or non-existent. This meant that they had lower levels of social capital impeding access to work opportunities in the community (Farrall, 2004). Even where they did have relatives in employment, they were still disadvantaged because, unlike the businesses where Indians found work, the jobs they worked in, typically in the public sector, did not allow for the allocation of employment opportunities on the basis of trust and word-of-mouth. Consequently, their families of origin were not resourced to facilitate easy provision of a prosocial identity based around work

Ethnic differences in household structures and family formation produced very different contexts in which their involvement in offending and their desistance operated. Unlike Bangladeshi participants, who, following the arrest and discovery of their drug-misuse and the deterioration of their lifestyle into greater involvement in offending, stayed within the family home, such behaviour among the black and dual heritage cases prompted separation from their partners. There was no cultural expectation that they should remain together, neither was there an economic need since, during their offending, they were out of work and incapable of fulfilling the role of family provider. There was, though, a shared cultural viewpoint that a 'responsible father' should be a 'provider' who shows their children care and love. However, where this found expression varied from being within the family home, as with Bangladeshi desisters, to regularly seeing their children for visits, as with black and dual heritage desisters. For the latter, being estranged from their former partners meant that adopting or re-establishing the role of father could be difficult. Yet it still functioned as a mechanism that encouraged desistance as the promise of visits and seeing their children regularly provided the incentive to desist. Presenting themselves as a respectable father to their ex-partners was essentially a 'constitutive identity' that had to be worked on and maintained through positive behavioural change (Rhodes, 2008). Staying away from trouble with the law, avoiding drugs and making efforts to secure a job all constituted evidence to their ex-partner that they were successfully making changes which would, hopefully, secure access to their children. In contrast, for Bangladeshis the idea that they would occupy the role of father and would see their children was a given, as it was expected that they would live with their families. The closer contact and access Bangladeshis had with their children meant that it was arguably easier for them to fit into a prosocial identity around being a parent that supported their desistance and was more easily recognised and certified than the one that black and dual heritage fathers endeavoured to construct.

Faced with fewer immediately accessible prosocial identities through which to desist, black and dual heritage participants were compelled to fall back on their own resources to initiate strategies that would secure desistance by minimising risks and embarking on a self-directed project that would enable the construction of a viable, established and visible non-offending identity. In response to external pressures that could threaten their desistance they pursued a number of 'knifing off strategies' (Sampson and Laub, 1993; Maruna and Roy, 2007). First, and at its most extreme, this involved physically removing themselves entirely from the local neighbourhood because the risks it posed were incompatible with successful desistance. A second and more commonly used approach was to isolate themselves by staying at home and avoiding friends in order to avoid temptation and hope that enough time would eventually pass that such opportunities would no longer present themselves, what Shapland and Bottoms (2011) refer to as 'diachronic self-control'. A third available strategy was regularly attending the gym. Aside from 'using up' significant amounts of time, this gave them a motivational project of self-change, both physical and mental, to focus on and provided a means through which to develop an alternative prosocial identity around exercise (Meek, 2013), as the following quote illustrates:

> I use the gym. I use it maybe three, four times a week. Because it just helps. I like looking healthy and it makes me feel good and it helps me stay focused...I wasn't doing these things before anyway... All these things are things that I've implemented that I enjoy doing and are good for me, basically. So, it's just like changing the bad for the good. (Linton)

While all these strategies, however, successfully guarded against the encroachment of a return to offending and so enabled the protection of their self-identity as non-offenders, the extent of their transformation and its nature remain secretive. Coupled with fewer proximate 'agents of certification' (Maruna, 2001) owing to their less densely bonded social networks, this meant that they were less successful in communicating to others that they were engaged in change and reform. Countering this invisibility, therefore, required independent initiation and achievement of plans to improve themselves and their environment that demonstrated the validity of their change to a non-offender identity through 'pro-social accomplishments' (Maruna and Roy, 2007, 116) such as securing training and educational qualifications, taking part in voluntary organisations, and helping others, particularly expressing a 'generative' concern for the younger generation. This was evident in the aspirational desire voiced by some black and dual heritage desisters, similar to desisters in other studies (Maruna, 2001; Visher and Travis, 2003), to build the prosocial identity of 'a professional ex', using the insight of their experience to help others avoid offending:

> I think what kids want. I'll tell you what I really want to be. What I really wanted. Because I've been in care, right, it's, like, when it comes to people with pain, like trouble, or problems, people from similar backgrounds to me, I can relate to these people. This is what I realised. Yeah? They can sit down. They can talk to me... like these people actually relate to me because I've been through the same struggle that they're going through now. So, yeah, I really want to do something like help people. (Joseph)

Interestingly, this desire was almost completely absent among the desisters from the two South Asian ethnic groups. This is probably because there were other prosocial identities available to them. Compared with being accepted and validated by one's family, becoming a professional ex is not an easy transition (Farrall et al, 2014), and sustaining it is much more dependent on individual motivation. Like finding legitimate work, it still relies on the goodwill of others and requires social capital and experience. Proof of one's success in this field is a more gradual, slower process. Initial recognition from figures in authority is dependent on accessing voluntary work, while establishing the professional identity is dependent on long-term performance.

For black and dual heritage men in my sample, their structural position and its associated cultural context meant that their desistance was a much more isolated experience and they faced fewer easily accessible 'hooks for change' and obvious 'blueprints' for future noncriminal selves (Giordano et al, 2002). Whereas for Indian and Bangladeshi desisters re-constructing non-offending self-identity was very much a collective process achieved through a range of easily accessible and *pre-determined* supportive associated prosocial identities, for black and dual heritage desisters, this same process was much more individualistic. The availability of desistance-supportive prosocial identities needed to be determined by independent strategies and actions to ensure access and availability. At the same time, for black and dual heritage desisters, the security of this non-offending identity was more vulnerable to threats of derailment (such as friends and associates who were still involved in crime) and without the protection afforded Indian and Bangladeshi desisters by greater familial and community support.

## Ethnicity, masculinity and desisting identities

As well as influencing the types of prosocial identities that might be pursued to support their desistance, there was also evidence that ethnic differences in the cultural and structural context helped shape the availability of different forms of masculine identity that desisters sought to establish, both personal and social. Research has found establishing and constructing a cohesive and coherent male identity to be a requirement of desistance (Carlsson, 2013). This process should not be seen as taking place as separate from, and alongside, the process of managing the shift in identity from offender to ex-offender, but as integral to it. Desistance for the men in my sample was dependent on the availability of accessible male identities with which they could identify and which they could secure for themselves. In turn, desisters' assumptions about gender roles and masculinities and what it meant to them to be a 'proper' man were indexed by ethnicity.

My research indicated that the desisters in my sample of the same ethnicity typically shared normative assumptions about how they should or should not behave as men. This consequently had implications for their desistance. These assumptions are influenced by what Bourdieu calls their 'habitus' or 'durable individual dispositions arising out of the prevailing culture' (cited in Bottoms et al, 2004, 273–4) which are ethnically variant, influenced as they are by differing the cultural norms, expectations, practices and aspirations outlined in the previous section. For example, black and Bangladeshi desisters shared similar ideas about what being a 'good father' should look like, namely spending time with their children and providing and protecting for them and avoiding further offending. However, their different socio-cultural and structural context meant that the processes through which they built this desired prosocial identity differed and they faced very different challenges. Bangladeshi desisters shared the assumptions of their families and others in their community that their futures would, or rather should, involve them taking up roles within their family around marriage and parenthood. This involved being a 'good son' to their parents and a good supportive 'husband' to their wives through running errands for family that helped structure their time. By helping with daily childcare they were also able to build an identity around being a 'good' father to their children. There was a mutual expectation (including among those who were not married) that, as men they should marry, and that this was the best institutional arrangement for parenting children. These roles were also shaped by (re)-engagement with religion and the adoption of values of duty, responsibility and reciprocity that closely align with the prosocial identity of being 'a good Muslim'. Therefore, for Bangladeshi desisters, the 'blueprint' for a desistance supportive masculine identity is co-constructed and more rigorously prescribed than it was for the black and dual heritage desisters.

For the latter, there was not the same notion that being a 'good father' necessitated them being married or living with the mother of their children, nor that they were expected to marry their partners. Their 'blueprint' for 'being a man' entailed the successful maintenance of self-directed strategies to manage risks to their desistance, avoid further offending and the pursuit of self-improvement through the gym and educational training so as to demonstrate to others, such as the mothers of their children, that they had independently reformed themselves and had become someone their children and the next generation could look up to and learn from. The virtues of the desistance supportive masculinity identity that they sought to construct – resourcefulness, independence and strong willpower – were integral to their desistance self-project's success. Communicating this wider message of achievement and their successful identity transformation provided the means and motivational goal to desist.

For the Indian desisters, on the other hand, the construction of an appropriate masculine identity that helped to support their desistance must be seen within the strongly maintained kinship networks characteristic of British Indian families with their tradition of generational reverence for elders and cultural expectations of obligations and duty (Berthoud and Beishon, 1997; Beishon et al, 1998). By accepting and taking advantage of the enduring opportunities for employment provided by their family and community they were able to 'retro-fit' their identity back into social roles of expected appropriate behaviour and be the kind of 'men' that their families' hoped they would be, while allowing for them to develop ambitious aspirations as a means of building a male identity around financial 'success' in business. Moving into these roles was dependent on their own agency in terms of recognising the value and legitimacy of opportunities available for them to pursue, and provided a generative means for them to 'give something back' to their families for their help.

My findings therefore indicate that ethnic differences in social context did affect the range of masculine identities available to desisters to aid their shift from an offending to a non-offending identity. It also suggests, from a psychosocial perspective (Gadd and Farrall, 2004) that, while all three ethnic groups' masculine identities underwent similar process of formation, there were ethnic differences in the character and typology of their masculine identities. As men they made decisions to consciously or unconsciously invest in discursive positions situated within range of social discourses that supported the formation of a coherent and protective masculine self-identity. These gendered discourses – be they religious (Bangladeshi), based on 'middle-class' aspirational values of success (Indian), or generativity and self-reliance (black and dual heritage) – also varied by ethnicity.

## Racism, identity and desistance

What then of the influence of racism and racial discrimination? Given their significance as structural factors affecting criminal justice outcomes (Tonry, 1997) and in processes of criminalisation (Hall et al, 1978), it is reasonable to assume that it affords a potential shared experience for participants across all three ethnic groups and one that sits in contrast to the experience of white desisters. Its impact upon the character and direction of their desistance and the effects it has for their identity is worthy of further consideration. It is therefore worth noting that experiences of racism and discrimination were an identifiable presence in the biographic accounts of interviewees from all three groups in the study, at least in terms of their early lives, their adolescence, and during periods when they were engaged in offending. For example, negative experiences of school were reported across the sample and included being expelled for poor behaviour to incidents of direct racism ranging from racist name calling to persistent racist bullying by fellow pupils. Significantly, some participants viewed these events as 'turning points' (Sampson and Laub, 1993) in their lives contributing to their initial or further involvement in offending, be it through marking the beginning of long-term absence from school due to truanting or provoking a violent retaliation which resulted in their formal exclusion from school. Thus, the effects of racism played a formative role upon the initial criminal careers of sample members.

The effects of racism upon desistance, however, produced two divergent sets of experiences. On the one hand, for black and dual heritage desisters, there was evidence that racism had an impact on their lives in ways that could potentially disrupt their desistance. For example, they were more likely to complain about harassment and being repeatedly stopped and searched by the police (nine out of fourteen) than Indian (two out of eight) or Bangladeshi interviewees (one out of eleven). As well as being unpleasant in itself, the experience of stops and searches by the police provided black and dual heritage desisters with an unwelcome reminder of how they were still viewed by others, as the following quote conveys:

> I got stopped outside the ice rink not so long ago and the detective said to me… 'Oh yeah'…they stopped me whatever, and questioned me, asked me where I was going, took my details, and everything and turned around and said to me, 'Oh yeah, don't worry Mr [ ], you'll soon be back in our good books when you're back to crime and back in prison.' And I was just, I was actually shocked that they could actually say that and I took their numbers and I was going to report it, but I thought there is no point; what's it going to achieve?…It's just going to piss them off and make them want to get me. (Stephen)

The failure to successfully communicate the authenticity of their commitment to change underlines the vulnerabilities of the much more independent desistance strategy pursued by black and dual heritage desisters. The unwelcome stigma and shame associated with being unwarrantedly stopped and searched produced frustration that their newly formulated non-offending identity was not given duly deserved recognition, potentially undermining desisters' motivation and, with it, the possibility of success. It is also reasonable to infer the presence of racism among prospective employers. This may be viewed as indirectly impeding their desistance as it represented a further difficulty which black and dual heritage desisters needed to overcome to secure employment. In doing so, it removes them from the possibility of accessing this opportunity and the associated support it has the potential to bring to their desistance. On the other hand, the more interventionist collective collaborations between desisters and their family and community associated with Indian and Bangladeshi desistance provided greater assistance in sheltering them from the deleterious effects that racism might have on their desistance. For example, access to greater resources of family level social capital among Indian desisters ensured that they had an opportunity to by-pass the discriminatory hurdles of the job market; and the availability of prosocial religious friends and engagement with family roles and responsibilities helped structure Bangladeshi desisters' day-to-day routines in a way that re-affirmed their prosocial identity (Farrall et al, 2014) and reduced exposure to previous criminal peers or surveillance by the police stop and search tactics.

The apparent lesser impact of processes of direct racism upon Indian and Bangladeshi desisters should not be misunderstood as claiming that racism played no role in structuring the social and economic context where their desistance took place. On the contrary, not only did direct experiences of racism characterise their biographic accounts of their lives to date, they also played an indirect role in influencing the conditions under which desistance occurred. For instance, high levels of self-employment among UK Indians, and the greater access to levels of economic capital which this provided to Indian desisters, cannot be divorced from the effects of racism. As Ballard (1999) argues, the high levels of self-employment among Indian communities are not only reflective of entrepreneurial aspirational values and community resourcefulness, but must also be viewed partly as a response to barriers placed in their way by white racism in the employment market. Similarly, the high levels of religiosity present among the social networks of Bangladeshi desisters have to be seen in part as a response to racism because of the feelings of security and empowerment religion can provide against exclusionary effects of racism (Garbin, 2008).

A noteworthy absence from my study's findings was the existence of an explicitly 'racialised' identity within interviewees' narrative accounts. They did not report that their desistance involved establishing a reflexive appreciation of the role of wider historical and social processes upon their current structural position within society or the reclamation of a 'lost' cultural identity as reported by desisting Aboriginal gang members in Canada (Bracken et al, 2009; Deane et al, 2007). Neither were there any reported examples that their desistance necessitated a desire to 'give voice' to their silenced frustrations with the racialised processes of criminalisation and experiences of racism and discrimination within the justice system and so be allowed the opportunity to construct a counter-narrative by employing a critical race theory perspective to explore their own understandings of their desistance (Glynn, 2014). In sum, there was little exemplar evidence from the minority ethnic offenders in my sample that the development of their desistance was contingent upon a process of identity transformation entailing the establishment of a politically self-aware racial identity.

This finding may in part be a result of positional dynamics of the interview process itself, perhaps reflective of research participants being more reluctant to disclose to me, as a white researcher, the significance of their racial identity as they would to a black researcher. Indeed Glynn (2014) makes a good case for the advantages provided by his 'insider researcher' perspective interviewing fellow black men in his research study in terms of establishing trust and insight not available to 'outsider' researchers. However, I should reiterate that my positionality did not preclude building rapport and trust or my research participants from disclosing close and personal details of other aspects of their past and present lives and current efforts to desist or discussion of their ethnic identity. All were asked questions of 'how would you describe your ethnic identity?' and follow up questions on a 'time where you've felt strongly about this identity' and asked about their experiences of the criminal justice system (see Calverley, 2013, 199). In other words, there was ample opportunity to discuss the importance of a racialised identity to their desistance; its lack of presence probably reflects reality to desisters in my sample. The overwhelming majority of respondents' self-defined ethnicities fell under 'national' typology with black respondents describing themselves as 'black', 'black British' or 'British (13 of 14); Bangladheshi desisters self-identifying as 'British Asian', 'British Bangladeshi' or 'Bengali' (11 of 11); and the Indian desisters described their ethnicity as 'British Asian', 'British Indian' or 'Indian'. Their ethnic identity was viewed in positive terms, as the following responses reveal:

*African Caribbean. We all originated from Africa though.* [AC: What does that mean to you?] *Well, I don't know. It just means we're free now, innit. I don't know any other way to see that. I'm always proud of my identity. I don't. I just see us all as equal, but I'm not pissed that I'm black or I don't wish that I was white or anything.* (Joseph)

*I'm Bangladeshi. British Bangladeshi. Yeah, I'm okay, after all, it's who I am, what I am.* (Syed)

*I'm Indian, innit. I'm from Britain. I was born here this is my home, but my parents are from India.* [AC: What does that mean to you, being Indian?] *It's good. I feel safe with it.* (Manmohan)

In all cases, their ethnic identity was an aspect of their overall identity but, unlike the Aboriginal desisters in Sullivan's research (it did not constitute) their 'master identity'. Even for the two cases who did mention a politically aware African-centric identity (Leonard, Linton) the construction of this identity long preceded their desistance while in prison or school and, although valued, did not form an integral guiding component of their desistance strategy. Furthermore, as both were experiencing difficulties in securing reliable contract work as a rehabilitation worker (Leonard) or work at all (Linton), its efficacy at overcoming structural impediment such as lack of job opportunities was still limited. Interestingly, in both cases they learnt auto-didactically rather than through formalised institutionalised settings, which is perhaps reflective of the independence characteristic of other aspects of their desistance project generally.

All of this indicates that the development of a politically racially aware identity is neither inherent to the evolution of minority ethnic offenders' desistance nor a pre-requisite for its success. It is ultimately favoured by structured institutional arrangements and 'supportive patterned relationships' being established to support its development rather than being an inevitable feature of their desistance endeavour. This holds lessons for the design and implementation of specially designed interventions that may seek to cater for the desistance needs of specific ethnic groups through the development of a 'positive' politically aware racial identity informed by critical race theory perspectives (Glynn, 2014; Williams, 2006; Durrance and Williams, 2003). These hold open the promise of making black and dual heritage offenders' desistance journeys less isolated, but they need to be aware that the establishment of a politically self-aware racial identity provides *one* example of a viable desistance supportive identity, and in relation to other prosocial identities around work, family, masculinity and generativity, it may not be the most important (nor perceived by desisters as the most important). The success of these programmes is ultimately dependent on supporting a whole range of processes associated with desistance, ethnically defined as they are, not in isolation but in conjunction with assisting in the construction of a supportive, secure, non-offending identity that takes into account the social context which the desisters inhabit and allows them to navigate impediments and make use of available resources and support.

## Conclusion

Having made the rationale for why desistance might vary by ethnicity, its implications for identity, and reviewed the lessons from the literature, this chapter went on to examine how ethnic differences in the structural and cultural context between the ethnic groups in my research produced differences in terms not only in how their desistance 'played out' but affected the availability and forms of prosocial identity through which offenders of different ethnicities sought to exit crime. Desisters identities were dependent on the culturally formed expectations, norms and values of their family and community and their access to resources; their desistance strategies were formed in response to these. They were also intrinsically tied up with other aligned identities of masculinity and shaped by processes of racism and discrimination. Thus, for Indian desisters, the construction of a masculine prosocial identity involved less concentration on a journey away from crime and the construction of a newly formulated identity, but was rather a desistance journey characterised by 'a return to expected behaviour' (Shapland and Bottoms, 2011), similar to what Goodwin (Chapter Four) refers to as reclaiming a 'lost' identity. The same is true of the Bangladeshi desisters' identity change. For the black and dual heritage desisters, construction of an appropriate masculine and desistance supportive identity was much more of a pioneering venture requiring independent strategies of resourcefulness and self-improvement to manufacture their own access to viable supportive non-offending desistance identities. If criminal justice interventions and policy are to better cater for the desistance needs of minority ethnic offenders they need to adopt an appreciative and reflective approach to help support the transition to already available prosocial desistance identities, to provide arrangements for certifying and confirming their validity and, where necessary, to create and provide appropriate social capital in the form of developing social support networks and resources to counter isolation and maintain motivation.

## Notes

[1]   See Calverley (2013, 37–54) for more detailed discussion of methodology.

[2]   I appreciate that, to a certain extent, Indian and Bangladeshi people share a South Asian ethnicity and could be argued to fit within the label of 'nationalities', rather than ethnicities; however, as the respondents were drawn from two separate geographical locales, occupied different socio-economic positions and their families and communities represented different cultural and institutional practices, such as religion – in other words precisely the important variables that I was arguing that ethnicity indexed – it makes sense to treat these two groups as two separate ethnicities.

[3]   This last group was the most heterogeneous. It included five probationers of mixed African Caribbean and white British parentage, seven of black African Caribbean heritage, and two of black African heritage. Despite this variance they have been grouped together because they had grown up and spent their lives in similar geographic areas, and in terms of relevant cultural and structural variables, such as religion, family structure, experiences of the employment, education, the criminal justice system, their experiences were largely indistinguishable from one another.

[4]   Again see Calverley (2013) for much more detailed discussion.

[5]   I am grateful to Stephen Farrall for this suggested phrase.

[6]   Others in the sample reported that their families wish they could do this but were prohibited by cost.

[7]   Compare Godfrey et al (2007), whose research investigating criminal careers of men in Victorian England attributed the weak effect of marriage on curtailing offending to the comparatively weaker position of women to exert influence during an era of greater gender inequality.

## References

Ballard, R, 1999, *Upward mobility: The socio-economic and educational achievements of Britain's visible minorities*, paper commissioned by Commission for the Future of Multi-Ethnic Britain, http://www.casas.org.uk/papers/pdfpapers/mobility%202.pdf

Baskin, D, Sommers, I, 1998, *Casualties of community disorder: Female violent offenders*, Oxford: Westview Press

Beishon, S, Modood, T, Virdee, S, 1998, *Ethnic minority families*, London: Policy Studies Institute

Berthoud, R, 2000, *Family formation in multi-cultural Britain: Three patterns of diversity*, Institute for Social and Economic Research Working Paper 2000-34, Essex: University of Essex

Berthoud, R, Beishon, S, 1997, People, families and households, in T Modood, R Berthoud, J Lakey, J Nazroo, P Smith, S Virdee, S Beishon (eds) *Ethnic minorities in Britain: Diversity and disadvantage*, pp 18-59, London: Policy Studies Institute

Bottoms, A, 2006, Desistance, social bonds and human agency, in P-O Wikstrom, R Sampson (eds) *The explanation of crime*, Cambridge: Cambridge University Press

Bottoms, A, Shapland, J, Costello, A, Holmes, D, Muir, G, 2004, Towards desistance: Theoretical underpinnings for an empirical study, *Howard Journal of Criminal Justice* 43, 4, 373–4

Bracken, D, Deane, L, Morrisette, L, 2009, Desistance and social marginalization: The case of Canadian Aboriginal offenders, *Theoretical Criminology* 13, 1, 61–78

Bradford, B, Forsyth, F, 2006, Employment and labour market participation, in J Dobbs, H Green, L Zealey (eds) *FOCUS ON: Ethnicity and Religion*, Office of National Statistics, pp 111-149, Basingstoke: Palgrave Macmillan

Calverley, A, 2009, *An exploratory investigation into the processes of desistance amongst minority ethnic offenders*, PhD thesis, Keele: Keele University

Calverley, A, 2013, *Cultures of desistance*, London: Routledge

Carlsson, C, 2013, *Criminology* 51, 3, 661–93

Chu, DC, Sung, HE, 2008, Racial differences in desistance from substance abuse, *International Journal of Offender Therapy and Comparative Criminology* 53, 6, 696–716

Coleman, D, 2006, Immigration and ethnic change in low fertility countries: A third demographic transition, *Population and Development Review* 32, 3, 401–44

Connolly, H, Raha, S, 2006, Households and families, in J Dobbs, H Green, L Zealey (eds) *Focus on: Ethnicity and religion*, pp 83–110, Office of National Statistics, Palgrave: Macmillan

Craig, J, Connell, N, 2015, The all-volunteer force and crime: THE effects of military participation on offending behaviour, *The Armed Forces and Society* 41, 2, 329–351

Deane, L, Bracken, D, Morrissette, L, 2007, Desistance within an urban aboriginal gang, *Probation Journal* 54, 2, 125–41

DfES (Department for Education and Skills), 2006, *Ethnicity and education: The evidence on minority ethnic pupils aged 5–16*, Research Topic Paper (2006 edn), London: DfES

Durrance, P, Williams, P, 2003, Broadening the agenda around what works for black and Asian offenders, *Probation Journal* 50, 3, 211–24

Farrall, S, 2002, *Rethinking what works with offenders*, Cullompton: Willan

Farrall, S, 2004, Social capital and offender reintegration: Making probation desistance focussed, in S Maruna, R Immarigeon (eds) *After crime and punishment: Ex-offender reintegration and desistance from crime*, pp 57–82, Cullompton, Devon: Willan Publishing

Farrall, S, 2005, On the existential aspects of desistance from crime, *Symbolic Interaction* 28, 3, 367–86

Farrall, S, Bowling, B, 1999, Structuration, human development and desistance from crime, *British Journal of Criminology* 39, 2, 253–68

Farrall, S, Calverley, A, 2006, *Understanding desistance from crime*, London: Open University Press

Farrall, S, Bottoms, A, Shapland, J, 2010, Social structures and desistance from crime, *European Journal of Criminology* 7, 6, 546–69

Farrall, S, Sharpe, G, Hunter, B, Calverley, A, 2011, Theorizing structural and individual-level processes in desistance and persistence: Outlining an integrated perspective, *Australian and New Zealand Journal of Criminology* 44, 2, 218–34

Farrall, S, Hunter, B, Sharpe, G, Calverley, A, 2014, *Criminal careers in transition*, Oxford: Oxford University Press

Finestone, H, 1967, Reform and recidivism amongst Italian and Polish criminal offenders, *American Journal of Sociology* 72, 6, 575–88

Gadd, D, 2006, The role of recognition in the desistance process: A case of analysis of a former far-right activist, *Theoretical Criminology* 10, 2, 179–202, doi: 10.1177/1362480606063138

Gadd, D, Farrall, S, 2004, Criminal careers, desistance and subjectivity, *Theoretical Criminology* 8, 2, 123–55

Garbin, D, 2008, A diasporic sense of place: Dynamics of spatialization and political fields among Bangladeshi Muslims in Britain, in MP Smith, J Eade (eds) *Transnational ties: Cities, identities and migrations*, New Brunswick and London: Transaction Publishers

Giordano, PC, Cernkovich, SA, Rudolph, JL, 2002, Gender, crime and desistance: Toward a theory of cognitive transformation, *American Journal of Sociology* 107, 4, 990–1064

Giordano, P, Longmore, MA, Schroeder, RD, Sefferin, PM, 2008, A life course perspective on spirituality and desistance from crime, *Criminology* 46, 1, 99–132

Glynn, M, 2014, *Black men, invisibility and desistance from crime*, London: Routledge

Godfrey, B, Cox, D, Farrall, S, 2007, *Criminal lives*, Oxford: Oxford University Press

Hall, S, Critcher, C, Jefferson, T, Clarke, J, Roberts, B, 1978, *Policing the crisis: Mugging, the state and law and order*, London: Macmillan

Hughes, M, 1997, An exploratory study of young adult black and Latino males and the factors facilitating their decisions to make positive behavioural changes, *Smith College Studies in Social Work* 67, 3, 401–14

Hughes, M, 1998, Turning points in the lives of young inner-city men forgoing destructive criminal behaviours: A qualitative study, *Social Work Research* 22 3, 143–51

Kazemian, L, 2007, Desistance from crime: Theoretical, empirical, methodological, and policy considerations, *Journal of Contemporary Criminal Justice* 23, 1, 5–27

Laub, JH, Sampson, RJ, 2001, Understanding desistance from crime, in MH Tonry, N Norris (eds) *Crime and Justice: An Annual Review of Research* 28, 1–78, Chicago, IL: University of Chicago Press

Maruna, S, 2001, *Making good: How ex-convicts reform and rebuild their lives*, Washington, DC: American Psychological Association Books

Maruna, S, 2011, Reentry as a rite of passage, *Punishment and Society* 13, 1, 3–27

Maruna, S, Roy, K, 2007, Amputation or reconstruction? Notes on the concept of 'knifing off' and desistance from crime, *Journal of Contemporary Criminal Justice* 23, 1, 104–24

Meek, R, 2014, *Sport in prison: Exploring the role of physical activity in correctional settings*, London: Routledge

Meisenhelder, T, 1977, An exploratory study of exiting from criminal careers, *Criminology* 15, 3, 319–34

Meisenhelder, T, 1985, An essay on time and the phenomenology of imprisonment, *Deviant Behaviour* 6, 39–56

Mischkowitz, R, 1994, Desistance from a delinquent way of life?, in EGM Weitekamp, HJ Kerner (eds) *Cross-national longitudinal research on human development and criminal behaviour*, Kluwer: Academic Publishers

Nielsen, A, 1999, Testing Sampson and Laub's life course theory, *Deviant Behaviour* 20, 2, 129–51

ONS (Office for National Statistics), 2006, Focus on Ethnicity & Identity, 21 February, http://web.ons.gov.uk/ons/rel/ethnicity/focus-on-ethnicity-and-identity/focus-on-ethnicity-and-identity summary-report/index.html

Paternoster, R, Bushway, S, 2009, Desistance and the 'feared self': toward an identity theory of criminal desistance, *Journal of Criminal Law and Criminology* 99, 4, 1103–56

Phillips, C, Bowling, B, 2012, Ethnicities, racism, crime and criminal justice, in M Maguire, R Morgan, R Reiner (eds) *The Oxford handbook of criminology (5th edn)*, Oxford: Oxford University Press

Piggott, G, 2004, Census profiles: Bangladeshis in London, *Data Management and Analysis Group (DMAG) Briefing*, London: DMAG, Greater London Authority

Piquero, AR, MacDonald, JM, Parker, KE, 2002, Race, local life circumstances, and criminal activity, *Social Science Quarterly* 83, 3, 654–70

Rand, A, 1987, Transitional life events and desistance from delinquency and crime, in ME Wolfgang, TP Thornberry, RM Figlio (eds) *From boy to man, from delinquency to crime*, Chicago, IL: University of Chicago Press

Reisig, MD, Michael, D, Bales, WD, Hay, C, Wang Xia, 2007, The effect of racial inequality on black male recidivism, *Justice Quarterly* 24, 3, 408–34

Rhodes, J, 2008, Ex-offenders, social ties and the routes into employment, *Internet Journal of Criminology*, www.internetjournalofcriminology. com/Rhodes%20-%20Ex-offenders%20and%20Employment.pdf

Rumgay, J, 2004, Scripts for safer survival: Pathways out of female crime, *The Howard Journal of Criminal Justice*, 43, 4, 405–419

Sampson, RJ, Laub, JH, 1993, *Crime in the making: Pathways and turning points through life*, London: Harvard University Press

Savolainen, J, 2009, Work, family and criminal desistance: Adult social bonds in a Nordic welfare state, *British Journal of Criminology* 49, 3, 285–304

Shapland, J, Bottoms, A, 2011, Reflections on social values, offending and desistance among young adult recidivists, *Punishment and Society* 13, 3, 256–82

Shover, N, 1983, The later stages of ordinary property offender careers, *Social Problems* 31, 2, 208–18

Sullivan, K, 2012, *Motivating and maintaining desistance from crime: Male Aboriginal serial offenders' experience of 'going good'*, PhD thesis, Canberra: Australian National University

Tonry, M (ed), 1997, Ethnicity, crime, and immigration: Comparative and cross-national perspectives, *Crime and Justice: A Review of the Research* 21, 1–30, London: University of Chicago Press

Vaughan, B, 2006, Internal narrative of desistance, *British Journal of Criminology* 47, 3, 390–404

Visher, C, Travis, J, 2003, Transitions from prison to community: Understanding individual pathways, *Annual Review of Sociology* 29, 89–113

Warr, M, 1998, Life-course transitions and desistance from crime, *Criminology* 36, 2, 183–215

Weaver, B, 2016, *Offending and desistance: The importance of social relations*, Abingdon: Routledge

Williams, P, 2006, Designing and delivering programmes for minority ethnic offenders, in S Lewis, P Raynor, DE Smith, A Wardak (eds) *Race and probation*, pp 145–63, Cullompton: Willan Publishing

# Fear and loathing in the community: sexual offenders and desistance in a climate of risk and 'extreme othering'

*Jacky Burrows*

Perhaps more than any other 'type' of offender, those who have committed sexual offences have been systematically vilified, demonised and ostracised from mainstream society. As will be seen, sexual offenders are routinely perceived as an homogenous group that is especially risky and dangerous and wholly outside the acceptable limits of diversity in humanity. This is particularly so for those labelled as 'deniers' (that is, those who categorically maintain their innocence). For once, the public, the media, the government, and indeed, large numbers of professionals seem to be in agreement that this group of individuals should not be entitled to the same dignity and rights afforded to everyone else, with the almost unquestioned assumption that this 'othering' is entirely right and proper. It is perhaps for these reasons that the literature regarding sex offender desistance is considerably less developed than others. Moves are being made to address this (for example, Farmer et al, 2015), but a number of the challenges sexual offenders face are arguably particular to the nature of their conviction and the literature particularly struggles to separate desistance discussions from the justice system. This chapter, therefore, contains more discussion on the barriers to desistance than others in this volume. Indeed at this stage of debate and research it could be argued that exploring the implications of this unparalleled and deeply entrenched negative culture remains valid. For example, Hudson's (2013) analysis of sex offender identity suggests that their self-perception is very much based on public misconceptions. This chapter also makes some preliminary observations about other relevant issues that are arguably particularly notable for sexual offenders: the role of shame, the role of distortion and denial, the gendered nature of sexual offending and the possibilities for desistance, and the significance of previous victimisation, with an overall aim of identifying a way forward.

It should be noted that one issue that has particularly featured in risk debates when it comes to sexual offending, especially in comparison to other offenders, is that of age (Fazel et al, 2006). This is clearly also a feature of the ontogenetic desistance paradigm and there is therefore valuable in considering this in both theoretical and empirical terms; however, given present constraints and strong coverage of the current literature elsewhere (see for example, Laws and Ward, 2011), this issue is not considered within the scope of the present chapter. It is interesting, however, to see that Laws and Ward (2011) conclude that sexual offenders, like most offenders, desist without formal psychological intervention.

## Sex offenders in the justice system: evidence, ethics and errors

Following the implementation of the 'What Works' agenda during the 1990s, the approach to sexual offending in the UK and elsewhere, became very much one of risk assessment and risk management (Kemshall, 2001). Implemented as part of this was a medical model of intervention involving identifying what was 'wrong' with the offender, such as poor empathy or social skills, and 'correcting' it, often through group work programmes (see, for example, Andrews and Bonta, 1998; McGuire, 1995). The 'RNR' model, in which responding to an offender's 'risk', (criminogenic) 'needs', and 'responsivity' became essential intervention criteria, became standard for most offence-focused work including that with sexual offenders (Andrews and Bonta, 1998). While celebrated as being evidence-based and demonstrably more effective than previous approaches, this approach was also (among other issues) criticised for its failure to recognise and respond to offenders as individuals and for being part of a shift in criminal justice culture to one of accountability and risk aversion which, in some cases, may actually increase risk (Kemshall, 1998; Tuddenham, 2000; Lacombe, 2008; Laws and Ward, 2011; Brayford and Deering, 2013; Vanstone, 2013; Weaver and Barry, 2014). Accountability is not in itself a negative concept, the resulting obsession with being able to quantify the progress of any given individual was highly intolerant of 'softer' forms of progress and created a tick-box culture (Fitzgibbon, 2011).

The apex of risk aversion appears to have passed (in part due to academic critique and discussion of defensible rather than defensive decisions, for example, Kemshall, 1998). However, the social and political context surrounding sexual offending is arguably still one of a 'risk society' imposing a level of punitiveness that is based on moral panic further exacerbated by the media, for example, coverage of contemporary events such as the large-scale UK abuse investigation, Operation Yew Tree (see Beck, 1992; Cowburn and Dominelli, 2001; Lacombe, 2008; Laws and Ward; 2011; Wilson, 2011; Grey and Watt, 2013; Vanguard, 2013; Brayford and Deering, 2013; Hudson, 2013; Stevens, 2013; Kemshall and McCartan, 2014; Weaver, 2014). Overall, the general belief is that sex offenders can never change and are undeserving of reintegration, and there remains a great deal of professional anxiety about giving much room for any offender to recidivate, let alone a sexual offender (Laws and Ward, 2011). In practice, this has translated into a reliance on actuarial risk assessment tools, the physical separation of sex offenders in the prison population, often difficult parole processes, austere public protection arrangements, particularly stringent licence conditions, and sex offender registration and notification. This is accompanied with government rhetoric and criminal justice practice involving a range of negative labels, such as 'high risk', 'dangerous', or 'sex offender'. Less formally, 'normal' prisoners may adopt terms such as 'nonce', 'kiddie fiddler', 'beast', or 'bacon' to refer to those convicted of sexual offences. Among the public and media, they are emotively labelled 'pervert', 'paedo', or simply 'evil', with those who work with them sometimes also acquiring similarly unhelpful labels such as 'paedo-pals' (Cowburn and Dominelli, 2001; Roberts, 2006; Stevens, 2013; Brayford and Deering, 2013).

Although some of these developments can be supported empirically and, indeed, morally, some cannot. Particularly noteworthy are concerns about the public's inflated ideas of recidivism and the ultimate value of controlling risk management strategies, both in terms of actually managing any risk and in ethical terms given it is argued that sexual offenders are often denied the basics needed to live decent lives (Farmer and Mann, 2010; Laws and Ward, 2011). It is of course not the aim to minimise the harm that can be caused by sexual offending, rather it is to stress the intensely inaccurate public view of risk and the resultant fear and vilification as a context for offenders trying to establish new lives for themselves. As will be seen, this context is at least partially replicated by the professionals working in the field. The author judges that these beliefs, attitudes and processes constitute the 'extreme othering' of those who have committed sexual offences.

## Sexual offending and the discovery of desistance

As previously noted, while the desistance literature has generally established itself firmly in criminological dialogues, the desistance literature that specifically relates to sexual offending is generally more recent and far more limited. The little which does exist remains rather tentative and often, even when seeking to describe the lived experience of desistance, 1) relies on applying broader desistance findings to the population, 2) seeks to integrate desistance into existing criminal justice practice or considers it in a specifically justice system-based context, or 3) in some cases focuses on desistance more as an outcome than a process (see for example, Kruttschnitt et al, 2000; Laws and Ward, 2011; Gobbels et al, 2012; Reeves, 2013; Weaver and Barry, 2014; Farmer et al, 2015).

These issues are not entirely negative in that the individualised nature of desistance and the varied nature of sexual offending means that sexual offenders should not necessarily be seen as a discrete group from this perspective, and the discussion at least has pragmatic value, for example, in assisting criminal justice practitioners to shift their practice. However, it means that little has been done to understand desistance in its own right, offering the offenders themselves limited voice, particularly in terms of lived experience outside of the justice system. Although this trend could be explained in a number of ways, for example, that the literature on sexual offending and desistance is simply lagging behind or that those who are writing about it have very clear positive intentions about instigating structural change or simply have pragmatic issues about accessing participants, it could also be suggested that there appears to be an unwritten rule whereby sex offenders hold a special status in which they may only ever be discussed within some context of risk and justice. In some ways, therefore, the academic world could be seen as adding to the already substantial othering of sexual offenders.

The approach here, therefore, will be to identify the main features of desistance, and discuss them with reference to sexual offending. Initially this will include a heavy emphasis on the impact of the justice system, but it will then continue to consider some of the features of sexual offending that have thus far received little attention in the literature, such as the gendered nature of such offending. Although through necessity this is somewhat speculative, it is hoped that it will form the basis of further debate and research.

As is generally the case, Maruna (2001) discusses desistance as both an outcome and process, with the emphasis on the latter. This process is recognised as being diverse and non-linear and may involve offenders trying out new identities or having setbacks (see for example, Laws and Ward, 2011). The literature talks in terms of identity shift although the language and nature of this varies. For example, in some cases individuals may establish new identities, and in others rediscover their previous self (Maruna, 2001; Weaver and Barry, 2014). Maruna (2001) further argues that narrative theory is useful in helping to explain this, and that desisters need a coherent self-story to move through issues such as stigma and shame. Such narratives tend to include individuals understanding their criminal pasts and being able to imagine change, the necessity of opportunities for change, and references to hope, agency, social relatedness and access to resources (Maruna, 2001; McNeill et al, 2012; Weaver and Barry, 2014; Weaver, 2014). Desistance, therefore, requires both social and psychological capital (Laws and Ward, 2011).

Maruna (2001) also talks in terms of 'condemnation scripts' (a 'doomed to deviance' way of thinking in persisting offenders) and 'redemption scripts', finding that, while offenders can feel powerless to change for a variety of reasons, the 'voice/s' of that condemnation tended to come from external, societal sources, leaving offenders lacking agency. The redemption script crucially starts with 'establishing the goodness and conventionality of the narrator – a victim of society' and involves:

1. 'an establishment of the core beliefs that characterize the person's "true self"';
2. 'an optimistic perception (some might say useful illusion) of personal control over one's destiny';
3. 'the desire to be productive and give something back to society, particularly the next generation'. (Maruna, 2001, 87–8)

Maruna (2001) further notes that it is far from shocking that so many offenders are reconvicted. He describes the situation for recidivist offenders as akin to a brick wall on account of background factors, such as lack of legitimate opportunities, and those more related to the individual, such as their motivation, a sentiment still echoed ten years on by Laws and Ward (2011). Given the extreme othering resulting from social stigma and risk aversion, this 'brick wall' is arguably particularly tall, wide and troublesome for those convicted of sexual offences. For example, desistance is regarded as an often messy process but sexual offenders are trying to function in societal structures (both formal and informal) with very little tolerance of error (see for example, Maruna, 2001; Gobbels et al, 2012). Offenders are likely to have lost key identities they may have had as 'parent', 'partner', or 'employee' as a result of their conviction, increasing the likelihood of feelings of 'identity nakedness' (Lofland, 1969, cited in Maruna, 2001), and are perhaps now also understanding, and possibly internalising, society's judgement of them based on their offence rather than their character (see for example, Tewksbury, 2005; Hudson, 2013). For those who complete a prison sentence and are released into the community, the range of requirements they are subjected to such as licence conditions, sex offender registration and notification procedures, can infiltrate almost every part of their lives, especially if 'high risk' (although it should be noted that the assumption that this will always have a negative impact on desistance is not always borne out (Weaver, 2014; Farmer et al, 2015)). Seemingly simple hobbies can be off limits, however, if a potential risk is perceived such as the presence of children, another sexual offender currently attending, or an opportunity to gain a position of trust is identified, thus restricting the development of social capital and a meaningful life. Even the more therapeutic elements of an offender's sentence can inhibit identity change. For example, Lacombe (2008) argues that therapy operating in a risk society results in risk constructing the identity of the sex offender. Others have observed that the narrow focus of some treatment gives key messages that sex offenders are labelled as sex-obsessed and risky, compromising offender narratives and reducing moral agency (Lacombe, 2008; Waldram, 2010; Stevens, 2013). Maruna's (2001) participants were aided by understanding the difference between their behaviour and their character. Being 'permitted' to do this is a luxury that society, and indeed some practice, simply does not afford sexual offenders.

One useful study that explicitly sought offenders' views on desistance in relation to the justice system is Weaver and Barry (2014). They found that there may be parts of the justice system that are experienced as beneficial, such as some access to opportunities and resources with scope for bolstering psychological and social capital, and a gradual reduction in restrictions or the presence of professional support being seen as reinforcing change in some cases. However, it seems that sexual offenders generally experience the system as being controlling at the expense of being change-promoting (Weaver and Barry, 2014). The authors specifically noted that licence conditions were especially restrictive and sometimes left the individual feeling embittered, and that restrictions often directly inhibited change, for example, by limiting employment opportunities (even beyond what would reasonably be expected to manage risk). The use of Approved Premises was deemed to particularly decrease opportunity and access to social capital and increase negative emotion, thus arguably decreasing psychological capital. Given that the offenders largely endorsed the idea that control needed to come from within, this was felt to be particularly unhelpful. Some of these phenomena could be regarded 'collateral consequences' or 'invisible punishments' in that they are not the intended consequence of the measure but nonetheless increase social stigmatisation and create problems in creating social capital (Tewksbury, 2005; Laws and Ward, 2011). These barriers to desistance will now be considered in greater depth.

Goffman (1963, 9) defines stigma as 'the situation of the individual who is disqualified from full social acceptance'. As discussed, for many people, sexual offenders do not qualify for even the most basic social regard. Madden (2008) observes, for example, that stigma is fuelled by labelling and stereotyping, even when the label is wrongly applied. This has on occasion proved fatal, for example, in the British case of Bijan Ebrahimi who was killed by neighbours who wrongly thought that he was a paedophile (Morris, 2015). However, as noted, extensive labelling and stereotypical, if inaccurate, social attitudes can be an everyday issue for those legitimately convicted of sexual offences.

Goffman (1963) regards relationships (as opposed to attributes) as central to stigma and talks in terms of social identity, noting that 'membership' of a particular group increases the chance of meeting and forming relationships with others in the same group. Best (Chapter Eight, this volume) discusses change as a social process, with people's sense of self very much coming from their social networks. In the case of sexual offenders, the combination of feeling stigmatised by mainstream society ('normals') and having their social contact restricted by the system, limits the opportunity to form positive relationships. Conversely, given that they are often only imprisoned with other sexual offenders and perhaps being released to Approved Premises where a number of other residents are also sexual offenders (arguably, even with the best intentions, a form of othering within othering), this increases the chance that any relationships they do form will be of the sort that brings a corresponding level of anxiety from the authorities. After all, if one sex offender is scary, then two must be doubly so. The system tends not to acknowledge how it encourages these problems, let alone to consider that in some cases there may, for example, actually be some value in sexual offenders supporting each other; however, the potential impact on an individual's social capital and therefore on their capacity for change is clear.

Related to this last point, Maruna (2001) describes how desisters in his sample often reworked their past in order to turn it into something good, for example, extracting the full 'learning' from it and channelling it into some form of 'generativity'. Given the intense social stigma against sexual offenders, any such reworking is likely to be especially challenging and any opportunities for generativity much more limited. In talking about offenders in general, Maruna (2001, 117) quotes Sir Stephen Tumin, 'I have always been rather against the idea of prisoners becoming professional former prisoners.' Although not impossible, the idea that someone convicted of sexual offences may attempt to put something back into society is likely to be met with cynicism if not outright concerns about risk, with their motives constantly questioned and any sense of legitimacy denied them.

While falling short of the extreme labels that wider society may offer, the messages given by the justice system to sexual offenders is that they are inherently risky, cannot be trusted, and cannot change, arguably the epitome of the voice of condemnation. After all, when it comes to sex offenders, if the penal system gives messages of hope and of the possibility of a non-criminal identity, then it surely cannot possibly be 'properly' punishing its offenders. The risk, therefore, is that, while sexual offenders might have multiple identities, the label of 'sex offender' may become their master status that is, it dominates their lives and stays with them in perpetuity (Hudson, 2013; Becker, 1963, cited in Hudson, 2013; Blagden et al, 2011). It is again argued that, while this is true of the 'offender' label, it is even more the case for those convicted of sexual offences, and thus particularly increases social exclusion and reduces access to social capital (Hattery and Smith, 2010).

## Shame

The idea of shame features in both the sexual offending literature and the desistance literature (see for example, Maruna, 2001; O'Ciardha and Gannon; 2011; Miller, 2012). Maruna (2001) links shame with identity and guilt with behaviour, observing that shame can be useful in some situations but, in more entrenched cases, it can be particularly problematic. This appears to be because, if shame is associated with identity, then it is also regarded as much more difficult to change than guilt. This is particularly important for the next section on denial and distortion. Additionally, Goodwin (Chapter Four, this volume) discusses confidence as an essential part of desistance among her female participants. She notes some gender in the literature but, given that her understanding of confidence is almost the exact opposite of the shame that sexual offenders may particularly feel and it is argued that many sexual offenders suffer from low self-esteem, further research to consider the importance of this feature in relation to those convicted of sexual offences may be of use (Marshall et al, 2009). This may particularly be the case in the current climate, as for many people, a confident, hopeful sex offender, particularly one who does not self-identify as a sex offender, is a rather alarming concept. Therefore, research which may give practitioners 'permission' to encourage this might be particularly valuable.

## Denial and distortion

Much of the 'What Works' approach focuses on challenging offender distortion and denial, particularly for sexual offenders (Maruna and Mann, 2006; Howitt and Sheldon, 2007; Strickland, 2008; Barriga et al, 2008; Van Vugt et al, 2011). These two notions are nominally distinct but are regularly either partially or wholly conflated with each other and a number of other commonly used intervention targets, for example, thinking errors, minimisations, neutralisations and offence-supportive attitudes (see Marshall, 2004; Maruna and Mann, 2006; Yates, 2009; O'Ciardha and Gannon, 2011). In this context, it is perhaps best to see distortion as any part of someone's thinking that is apparently supportive of their sexual offending, and denial as being either categorical (the individual entirely denies the offence) or partial, perhaps as part of a 'continuum of denial' (for example, an individual may minimise or deny an element of the offence such as any planning, impact on the victim, or that it is morally wrong) (Hollin et al, 2010; Nunes and Jung, 2012; Blagden et al, 2013). The issue of distortion is problematic enough in itself given that: first, there are questions over the timing of its use and therefore whether it is linked to offending; second, the weak evidence base for it being an appropriate intervention target; and third, the much stronger evidence that it is actually both normal and healthy. However, denial is arguably even more troubling given that it can essentially prevent access to rehabilitation opportunities and potentially, therefore, release from prison, especially as there appear to be a number of systemic and practitioner-level misconceptions around this issue (Brown, 2005; Hanson and Morton Bourgon, 2005; Maruna and Mann, 2006; Nunes et al, 2007; Yates, 2009; Marshall et al, 2011; Blagden et al, 2011; Evans, 2011; Ware and Mann, 2012; Bullock and Condry, 2013). As will be seen, however, both concepts are also particularly important in desistance terms.

Societal and system expectations are that offenders will take responsibility for their offences. Given estimates that there is some degree of denial in between 50 and 98 per cent of sexual offenders and categorical denial in 30–35 per cent of sexual offenders, these individuals are routinely particularly judged on their failure to do this. In turn this has often resulted in the perception of their risk being elevated (Yates, 2009; Barbaree, 1991, cited in Blagden et al 2011; 2013; 2014). This judgement is not logical when considering what is known about memory and the likely consequences of sexual offenders fully admitting their offences (for example in both the prison system and their families) but, more than this, the empirical findings do not *tend* to support the idea that denial predicts recidivism. Indeed, quite to the contrary, it can be seen as demonstrating recognition of accepted social values and as potentially very important in desistance, with the system-based obsession with responsibility potentially being harmful (Rogers and Dickey, 1991; Lord and Wilmot, 2004; Maruna, 2004; Maruna and Mann, 2006; Appleton, 2010; Marshall et al, 2011; O'Ciardha and Gannon, 2011; Blagden et al, 2011; Miller, 2012; Ware and Mann, 2012; O'Ciardha and Gannon, 2011).

It has, for example, been shown that people who take full responsibility for their mistakes risk depression, shame and reduced self-esteem which therefore decreases their psychological capital and inhibits change (Kelly, 2000; Maruna and Mann, 2006; Marshall et al, 2011). The value of distortion and denial comes from increasing an individual's degree of agency by creating a sense of control over similar future events and helping to construct a 'desirable identity'. When considering identity, distorted thinking and denial can be seen as an offender's attempt to manage shame, de-label, avoid a doomed to deviance script, and especially to provide both physical and psychological protection against the sex offender label becoming their master status (O'Ciardha and Gannon, 2011; Miller, 2012; Hudson, 2013). Maruna (2004) describes how 'distortion' can assist in developing narrative identity, for example, finding that positive events tend to be explained through more internal, stable and global causes and negative events through more external, unstable and specific causes ('That was just a phase I was going through' or 'That wasn't the "real me", it just happened'). It thus serves as a 'useful illusion' (Maruna, 2001, 88). It is therefore unfortunate, if understandable, that the emphasis on offender responsibility and risk remains such a focal point for society and criminal justice practitioners, even when those practitioners are aware of the empirical research (Maruna and Mann, 2006; Ware and Mann, 2012; Blagden et al, 2013).

## A gendered approach to desistance: male sexual offenders

With the majority of perpetrators of sexual offending being male and the majority of victims being female, few would argue against the idea that sexual offending is a gendered phenomenon (see for example Cowburn and Dominelli, 2001; Wykes and Welsh, 2009). The relevance of gender identity in sex offender desistance, however, has received little attention.

The importance of gender identity in more general offending and desistance processes has been touched upon elsewhere in this volume. For example, Hamilton (Chapter Two, this volume) asserts that the primary emotion of masculinity is fear (of sexuality, emotion, other men, and in particular of failing to meet standard societal criteria of the 'real man'). She further argues that the adaption to this fear contributed to an individual's offending in a number of cases, also including shame and self-esteem as relevant factors, and noting that shame in men often relates to the 'hegemonic ideal' and how they perceive they meet the 'real man' standard. This is arguably, therefore, applicable to male sexual offenders. For example, Stevens (2013) observes that, even in more supportive environments that deliberately seek to challenge hyper-masculinity such as in therapeutic communities, part of the issue with 'othering' is of sex offenders not being seen as 'real men'. Sykes (1958, cited in Stevens, 2013) also describes the emasculating impact of prison, for example, through lack of opportunities for sexual contact with women and loss of autonomy. By extension, it can be hypothesised that this is a possibility for sexual offenders, both inside and outside of prison, if their relationships and freedoms continue to be so tightly controlled, thus affecting their narratives, psychological capital, and possible identity change. Given society's particular view of paedophiles, having a sexual attraction to children may also have an impact on whether they regard their offending as an integral part of their identity and the extent to which an individual sees themselves as a 'real man'. This may result in the need to establish a new identity rather than re-establish a previous one.

Among Hamilton's participants, desistance often started with something that triggered their acknowledgement of and appreciation of their emotions and recognition of their 'false self' (Chapter Two, this volume). If sexual offending is largely construed as a gendered offence, a 'false self' in this case could perhaps be conceived as a hegemonic mask in that it may hide male vulnerability under the façade of a forced 'masculine' identity, or as an inappropriate adaptation to recognising a failure to achieve this. As noted by a number of authors, any consideration of these possibilities by offenders risks 'identity nakedness' which is unlikely to helped by hyper-masculine institutions such as prisons (Lofland,1969, cited in Maruna, 2001).

It therefore seems likely that gender identity may be particularly important for at least some sexual offenders and that there may be a number of quite substantial barriers to their resolving this. Of course, the main way forward is to undertake research on these specific issues, ideally considering some of the variation in desistance in relation to the heterogeneity of male sexual offending. There is reason to think, however, that once again, a shift in societal attitudes would be of particular value. Cowburn and Dominelli (2001) argue that the persistent societal notions of dangerousness regarding some sexual offenders have been rooted in hegemonic masculinity in that it enables men to re-establish their identities as protectors of the weak, perhaps in the form of vigilantism or more formal roles. This led to the gender-based othering of male sexual offenders by separating them from 'normal', 'good' men. However, they also argue that the media obsession with the paedophile, a genderless term, means that the importance of gender is often overlooked. Given that the evidence indicates this othering is a false male dichotomy (Cowburn and Dominelli, 2001 offer an overview), it is possible to suggest that a more nuanced societal understanding of gender may be useful in both preventing sexual offending and supporting desistance.

## A gendered approach to desistance: female sexual offenders

As a distinct minority, female sexual offenders are in general grossly under-researched. The research that has been undertaken is often plagued with gender-normed assumptions, including those that relate to the social construction of women (for example as carers) and feminine sexual scripts (for example, women as passive sexual beings) (Ford, 2006; Brayford and Roberts, 2012; Hayes and Carpenter, 2013). The implication of some of this research is that society is unwilling to identify women as sexual offenders; however, once identified there is an odd mix of continued denial and double deviancy in relation to female sexual offenders (Deering and Mellor, 2009; Embray and Lyons, 2012; Hassett-Walker et al, 2014).

Female sexual offenders should also be regarded as a heterogeneous group with a wide range of motivations including, for example, gender-contrary notions such as sexual attraction to children and instrumental goals such as making money (Cortoni, 2010). However, some of the more consistent trends are that the gender-specific features of female sexual offending include the role of previous abuse (domestic abuse may be more pertinent), and the role of a (usually male) co-perpetrator (Nathan and Ward, 2002; Vandiver, 2006; Gannon et al, 2008; Cortoni, 2010; Brayford and Roberts, 2012).

In discussing more general female desistance, Goodwin (2014) notes that, while a positive relationship often features in male desistance, this is not the case for female offenders, and in fact relationships can often be negative. Goodwin notes that relationships that are balanced in terms of power and understanding can be positive. Given the role other people appear to play in female sexual offending, there is reason to think that this may also hold true for female sexual offenders. However, like their male counterparts, female sexual offenders often find that their relationships are to some extent controlled by the authorities, further limiting the likelihood that they will find a suitable partner. Women may also particularly feel that their identity as a parent or potential parent has been taken away from them via the restrictions imposed, perhaps forcing them to define themselves in other ways. More positively, being able to 'blame' a co-perpetrator may limit self-blame and help women to entertain the idea of a 'good' possible future self.

It seems likely that the desistance pathways for female sexual offenders will also be varied although, clearly, further research is also needed in this area. They may particularly need to be creative in the opportunities they create to redefine themselves, however they may also find that society's sexism and inability to accept the idea of female sexual offenders in some cases may work for them.

## Previous victimisation

Although contentious, there is some consistent evidence that previous victimisation can play a part in the development of sexually abusive behaviour (for example, DeLisi et al, 2014). The likely role of previous abuse in female sexual offending has already been mentioned. A history of abuse may, therefore, be one possible variable in desistance narratives. Goodwin (Chapter Four, this volume) notes that regardless of gender, for those who have experienced more substantial victimisation, there could be low confidence that affects identity. The commonly felt stigma of being a victim of abuse is well documented and often argued to be worse for male victims who, again, may include hegemonic masculinity-based explanations in their accounts, for example, feeling that they are seen as less than 'real men' as the result of their abuse (Holmes et al, 1997). This may thus be internalised, which has an impact on identity transformation. Regarding oneself as a victim has traditionally been seen as an excuse that helps the individual to avoid taking responsibility but, as previously noted, being allowed to do so may help to establish 'the goodness and conventionality of the narrator' (Maruna, 2001, 87), and from there create some optimism for a possible, good future self.

Again, this may offer interesting lines of research and it does not seem unreasonable to suggest that the age at which the abuse took place may make a difference as to whether individuals seek to re-establish a previous identity or establish a new one. It also seems that society's attitudes, even towards victims, are once again entirely unhelpful in the formation of successful identities.

## Conclusions and possible ways forward

Society is failing these men and women and is therefore failing itself. Although understandable, the continued focus on balancing risk with other more forward looking approaches (for example, Weaver, 2014) may slow greater advances. The greatest necessity therefore is one of structural culture shifts that put an end to such extreme othering. It is recognised however that progress is likely to be slow. A three-pronged attack is therefore necessary: (1) continued engagement in discussion that is both risk- and desistance-focused, (2) the emergence of desistance studies without a specific justice focus, and (3) concerted efforts to better inform societal attitudes.

To assist this, research may focus on the heterogeneity of sexual offending and desistance, the role of gender identity in sexual offender desistance, and the impact of previous vicitimisation and sexual attraction to children on desistance. However, at this stage, particularly open methods of inquiry which focus on the lived experience of desistance are likely to yield the most meaningful findings and identify further avenues to pursue. Such research would hopefully include individuals who have desisted without formal intervention. It may also be of interest to engage with those people with problematic sexual interests who have not offended, for example, considering the impact of stigma in these cases, and to consider the scope to which former sexual offenders can assist those attempting to desist. In order to potentially appease some sceptics, such research could include social desirability measures but it would somewhat undermine the offender 'voice'.

In terms of the justice system, there are likely to be varying degrees of balance and compromise. Better practice in the immediate future is likely to continue to operate in a culture with risk as its lead priority, but will also hopefully include further development of the strengths-based Good Lives Model as a more desistance-focused approach, an increased use of redemption rituals such as re-entry courts, continued involvement with Circles of Support and Accountability, and more creative ideas such as the use of the arts or Communities of Enquiry[1] (Maruna, 2001; Laws and Ward, 2011; Kemshall and McCartan, 2014; Bilby, 2014). Through these and other developments, the justice system may therefore steadily do more to change its message of hope and increase opportunities for change, even if it does not give up its language of risk. Within the confines of their role, practitioner attitudes could also shift a little more. For example, Laws and Ward (2011) and Gobbels, Ward and Willis (2012) make note of the Pygmalion effect in which the high expectations of others aid positive outcomes and practitioners could recognise progress more effectively. It is likely that within this process of balance and compromise there will need to be a concerted effort not to let understandings of desistance become diluted beyond recognition. For example, anecdotal evidence from colleagues suggests that some practitioners have begun to equate desistance with the Good Lives Model or think that they are 'doing desistance' merely by making small changes to their practice. This comment does not serve to judge practitioners nor to suggest that these changes are not important. It seeks only to impress the importance of not losing sight of what is really important when it comes to desistance.

It would seem that in many ways sexual offenders need more space in which to desist though, of course, the flip side of this is giving them more space to recidivate. It has been seen that practice can move away from more extreme risk aversion as long as justice practitioners are given 'permission' to do so but, while false positive predictions of recidivism are often deemed acceptable, false negative predications in a risk society are most certainly not. This 'permission' therefore needs to come from governmental policy and endorsed practice guidance. Maruna (2001, 164–5) raises the idea of 'rebiographing as policy' and states that, without this permission to 'legally move on from the past', offenders will always be othered. Given society's inability to separate behaviour from the individual and its view that 'once a sex offender, always a sex offender', it does not seem likely that governments will find it easy to make such changes. The concerns of extreme othering when it comes to sexual offenders appear justified.

Kemshall and McCartan (2014) discuss ways of progressing societal attitudes and increasing trust in the system, for example, using a public health model, the media, and 'public criminology'. It would certainly seem that there is an argument for academics taking responsibility for changes in public views through engaging directly with them. There has been some recent media consideration that may result in dialogue and a more nuanced view of sexual offenders. For example, the advert for the German Dunkelfeld prevention project attempts to reduce society's othering on the basis of a sexual interest in children while stressing an individual's responsibility for their behaviour (Don't Offend, 2013). In the UK, a recent TV documentary featured a man who was worried about his attraction to children but did not want to commit an offence (Press Association, 2014).

Maruna (2001) believes that society 'others' sexual offenders in order to assuage the guilt of having had some role in creating 'them'. It is incredibly unlikely that there is much that can be done that will rapidly change this. Realistically, it may be wiser to approach such a challenge as a gradual process in which academics and informed practitioners and media representatives scaffold changes in public opinion, gently moving them towards a more accurate, nuanced, tolerant stance. This will mean balance and compromise in the meantime, but this is time that can be spent further researching desistance from sexually abusive behaviour. It would be satisfying to think that at some stage, the risk from others towards those who have committed sexual offences may diminish enough that sexual offenders can become more visible and have a voice of their own. Ultimately, it is hoped that sexual offenders will be freed from the fetters of extreme othering and shed their damning master status to become ex-offenders. Crucially, for this to happen, both society and the system must be to be able to recognise this as a credible possibility.

## Note

[1] This idea came about through discussion with Andrew Fowler, a colleague at Sheffield Hallam University, based on his communications with the Society for the Advancement of Philosophical Enquiry and Reflection in Education (SAPERE).

## References

Andrews, DA, Bonta, J, 1998, *The psychology of criminal conduct*, Cincinnati, OH: Anderson Publishing

Appleton, CA, 2010, *Life after life imprisonment*, Oxford: Oxford University Press

Barriga, AQ, Hawkins, MA, Camelia, CRT, 2008, Specificity of cognitive distortions to antisocial behaviours, *Criminal Behaviour and Mental Health* 18, 104–16

Beck, U, 1992, *Risk society: Towards a new modernity*, London: SAGE

Bilby, C, 2014, Creativity and rehabilitation: What else might work in changing sex offenders' behaviour?, in K McCarten (ed) *Responding to sexual offending: Perceptions, risk management and public protection*, pp 189–205, Basingstoke: Palgrave Macmillan

Blagden, NJ, Winder, B, Thorne K, Gregson, M, 2011, 'No-one in the world would ever wanna speak to me again': An interpretative phenomenological analysis into convicted sexual offenders' accounts and experiences of maintaining and leaving denial, *Psychology, Crime and Law* 17, 563–85

Blagden, N, Winder, B, Gregson, M, Thorne, K, 2013, Working with denial in convicted sexual offenders: A qualitative analysis of treatment professionals' views and experiences and their implications for practice, *International Journal of Offender Therapy and Comparative Criminology* 57, 332–55

Blagden, N, Winder, B, Gregson, M, Thorne, K, 2014, Making sense of denial in sexual offenders: A qualitative phenonemological and repertory grid analysis, *Journal of Interpersonal Violence* 29, 1698–731

Brayford, J, Deering, J, 2013, Media influences on public perceptions of sex offenders, in J Brayford, F Cowe, J Deering (eds) *Sex offenders: Punish, help, change or control?*, pp 52–68, New York: Routledge

Brayford, J, Roberts, S, 2012, Female sexual offending, in J Brayford, F Cowe, J Deering (eds) *Sex offenders: Punish, help, change or control? Theory, policy and practice explored*, Abingdon: Routledge

Brown, S, 2005, *Treating sex offenders*, Cullompton: Willan

Bullock, K, Condry, R, 2013, Responding to denial, minimization and blame in correctional settings: The 'real world' implications of offender neutralizations, *European Journal of Criminology* 10, 572–90

Cortoni, F, 2010, Female sexual offenders: A special subgroup, in K Harrison (ed) *Managing high risk sex offenders in the community*, Cullompton: Willan

Cowburn, M, Dominelli, L, 2001, Masking hegemonic masculinity: Reconstructing the paedophile as the dangerous stranger, *British Journal of Social Work* 31, 399–415

Deering, R, Mellor, D, 2009, Sentencing of male and female child sex offenders: Australian study, *Australian Study, Psychiatry, Psychology and Law* 16, 394–412

DeLisi, M, Kosloski, AE, Vaughn, MG, Caudill, JW, Trulson, CR, 2014, Does childhood sexual abuse victimization translate into juvenile sexual offending? New evidence, *Violence and victims* 29, 4, 620–35

Don't Offend, 2013, video, www.youtube.com/watch?v=ck3uOCyWB50

Embray, R, Lyons, PM, 2012, Sex-based sentencing: Sentencing discrepancies between male and female sex offenders, *Feminist Criminology* 7, 146–62

Evans, M, 2011, The dilemma of maintaining innocence, http://insidetime.org/download/publications/Maintaining%20Innocence-updated-PRT.pdf

Farmer, M, Mann, R, 2010, High-risk sex offenders: Issues of policy, in K Harrison (ed) *Managing high-risk sex offenders in the community*, pp 18–38, Cullompton: Willan

Farmer, M, McAlinden, A, Maruna, S, 2015, Understanding desistance from sexual offending: A thematic review of research findings, *Probation Journal* 62, 320–35

Fazel, S, Sjostedt, G, Langstrom, H, Grann, M, 2006, Risk factors for criminal recidivism in older sexual offenders, *Sex Abuse* 18, 159–67

Fitzgibbon, W, 2011, In the eye of the storm: The implications of the Munro Child Protection Review for the future of probation, *Probation Journal* 59, 7–22

Ford, H, 2006, *Women who sexually abuse children*, Chichester: Wiley

Gannon, TA, Rose, MR, Ward, T, 2008, A descriptive model of the offense process for female sexual offenders, *Sexual Abuse: A Journal of Research and Treatment* 20, 352–74

Gobbels, S, Ward, T, Willis, GM, 2012, An integrative theory of desistance from sex offending, *Aggression and Violent Behavior* 17, 453–62

Goffman, E, 1963, *Stigma: Notes on the management of spoiled identities*, London: Penguin

Goodwin, S, 2014, Relatively supported? Desisting women and relational influences, in J Shapland, J de Maillard, S Farrall, A Groenemeyer, P Ponsaers (eds) *Desistance, social order and responses to crime*, GERN Research Paper Series 2, pp 13–28, Antwerpen: Maklu.

Grey, D, Watt, P, 2013, *Giving victims a voice: Joint report into sexual allegations made against Jimmy Savile*, www.nspcc.org.uk/globalassets/documents/research-reports/yewtree-report-giving-victims-voice-jimmy-savile.pdf

Hanson, RK, Morton Bourgon, KE, 2005, The characteristics of persistent sexual offenders, A meta-analysis of recidivism studies, *Journal of Consulting and Clinical Psychology* 73, 1154–63

Hassett-Walker, C, Lateano, T Di Benedetto, M, 2014, Do female sex offenders receive preferential treatment in criminal charging and sentencing?, *Justice System Journal* 35, 62–86

Hattery, A, Smith, E, 2010, *Prisoner reentry and social capital: The long road to reintegration*, Plymouth: Lexington

Hayes, S, Carpenter, B, 2013, Social moralities and discursive constructions of female sex offenders, *Sexualities* 16, 159–79

Hollin, CR, Hatcher, RM, Palmer, EJ, 2010, Sexual offences against adults, in F Brookman, M McGuire, H Pierpoint, T Bennett (eds) *Handbook on crime*, pp 505–24, Cullompton: Willan

Holmes, GR, Offen, L, Waller, G, 1997, See no evil, hear no evil, speak no evil: Why do relatively few male victims of childhood sexual abuse receive help for abuse-related issues in adulthood?, *Clinical Psychology Review* 17, 69–88

Howitt, D, Sheldon, K, 2007, The role of cognitive distortions in paedophilic offending: Internet and contact offenders compared, *Psychology, Crime and Law* 13, 469–86

Hudson, K, 2013, Sex offenders' identities and identity management, in J Brayford, F Cowe, J Deering (eds) *Sex offenders: Punish, help, change or control?*, pp 71–89, New York: Routledge

Kelly, AE, 2000, Helping construct desirable identities: A self-presentational view of psychotherapy, *Psychological Bulletin* 126, 475–94

Kemshall, H, 1998, Defensible decisions for risk: Or 'it's the doers wot get the blame', *Probation Journal* 45, 67–72

Kemshall, H, 2001, *Risk assessment and management of known sexual and violent offenders: A review of current issues*, Police Research Series Paper 140, http://webarchive.nationalarchives.gov.uk/20110218135832/http:/rds.homeoffice.gov.uk/rds/prgpdfs/prs140.pdf

Kemshall, H, McCartan, K, 2014, Managing sex offenders in the UK: Challenges for policy and practice, in K McCarten (ed) *Responding to sexual offending: Perceptions, risk management and public protection*, pp 207–26, Basingstoke: Palgrave Macmillan

Kruttschnitt, C, Uggen, C, Shelton, C, 2000, Predictors of desistance among sex offenders: the interaction of formal and informal social controls, *Justice Quarterly* 17, 61–87

Lacombe, D, 2008, Consumed with sex: the treatment of sex offenders in risk society, *British Journal of Criminology* 48, 55–74

Laws, R, Ward, T, 2011, *Desistance from sex offending: Alternatives to throwing away the keys*, New York: Guilford Press

Lord, A, Wilmott, P, 2004, The process of overcoming denial in sexual offenders, *Journal of Sexual Aggression* 10, 51–61

McGuire, J (ed) 1995, *What works: Reducing reoffending. Guidelines from research and practice*, Wiley: Chichester

McNeill, F, Farrall, S, Lightowler, C, Maruna, S, 2012, *How and why people stop offending: Discovering desistance*, Glasgow: Institute for Research and Innovation in Social Services (IRISS), University of Glasgow

Madden, S, 2008, *The labelling of sex offenders: The unintended consequences of the best intentioned public policies*, Plymouth: University Press of America

Marshall, WL, 2004, Adult sexual offenders against women, in C Hollin (ed) *The essential handbook of offender assessment and treatment*, pp 147–62, Chichester: Wiley

Marshall, WL, Marshall, LE, Serran, GA, O'Brien, MD, 2009, Self-esteem, shame, cognitive distortions and empathy in sexual offenders: Their integration and treatment implications, *Psychology, Crime and Law* 15, 217–34

Marshall, WL, Marshall, LE, Kingston, DA, 2011, Are the cognitive distortions of child molesters in need of treatment?, *Journal of Sexual Aggression* 17, 118–29

Maruna, S, 2001, *Making good: How ex-convicts reform and rebuild their lives*, Washington, DC: American Psychological Association

Maruna, S, 2004, Desistance from crime and explanatory style: A new direction in the psychology of reform, *Journal of Contemporary Criminal Justice* 20, 184–200

Maruna, S, Mann, RE, 2006, A fundamental attribution error? Rethinking cognitive distortions, *Legal and Criminological Psychology* 11, 155–77

Miller, S, 2012, *Management of sexual offenders: Understanding non-engagement in offender behaviour programmes*, Edinburgh: Scottish Prison Service (SPS)

Morris, B, 2015, *PCs deny ignoring appeals of man killed in Bristol vigilante attack*, www.theguardian.com/uk-news/2015/dec/02/pcs-deny-ignoring-appeals-of-man-killed-in-bristol-vigilante-attack

Nathan, P, Ward, T, 2002, Female sex offenders: Clinical and demographic features, *The Journal of Sexual Aggression* 8, 5–21

Nunes, KL, Jung, S, 2012, Are cognitive distortions associated with denial and minimisation among sex offenders?, *Sex Abuse* 25, 166–88

Nunes, KL, Hanson, RK, Firestone, P, Moulden, HM, Greenberg, DM, Bradford, JM, 2007, Denial predicts recidivism for some offenders, *Sex Abuse* 19, 91–105

O'Ciardha, C, Gannon, TA, 2011, The cognitive distortions of child molesters are in need of treatment, *Journal of Sexual Aggression* 17, 130–41

Press Association, 2014, *Channel 4 film features paedophile confessing attraction to children,* www.theguardian.com/media/2014/nov/24/channel-4-documentary-paedophile

Rehabilitation Services Group, Maruna, S, 2010, *Understanding desistance from crime,* www.safeground.org.uk/wp-content/uploads/Desistance-Fact-Sheet.pdf

Roberts, Y, 2006, *They're not monsters,* www.theguardian.com/news/2006/jul/11/crime

Rogers, R, Dickey, R, 1991, Denial and minimization among sex offenders: A review of competing models of deception, *Annals of Sex Research* 4, 49–63

Reeves, C, 2013, 'The others': Sex offenders' social identities in probation approved premises, *The Howard Journal* 52, 383–98

Stevens, A, 2013, *Offender rehabilitation and therapeutic communities: Enabling change the TC way,* New York: Routledge

Strickland, SM, 2008, Female sex offenders: Exploring issues of personality, trauma, and cognitive distortions, *Journal of Interpersonal Violence* 23, 474–89

Tewksbury, R, 2005, Collateral consequences of sex offender registration, *Journal of Contemporary Criminal Justice* 21, 67–81

Tuddenham, R, 2000, Beyond defensible decision-making: Towards reflexive assessment of risk and dangerousness, *Probation Journal* 47, 173–83

Vandiver, DM, 2006, Female sex offenders: A comparison of solo offenders and co-offenders, *Violence and Victims* 23, 339–54

Vanstone, M, 2013, From minority interest to accredited programmes, in J Brayford, F Cowe, J Deering (eds) *Sex offenders: Punish, help, change or control?,* pp 34–51, New York: Routledge

Van Vugt, E, Hendriks, J, Stams, G, Van Exter, F, Bijleveld, C, Van der Laan, P, Asscher, J, 2011, Moral judgment, cognitive distortions and implicit theories in young sex offenders, *Journal of Forensic Psychiatry and Psychology* 22, 603–19

Waldram, JB, 2010, Moral agency, cognitive distortion, and narrative strategy in the rehabilitation of sexual offenders, *Ethos* 38, 251–74

Ware, J, Mann, R, 2012, How should 'acceptance of responsibility' be addressed in sexual offending treatment programs?, *Aggression and Violent Behavior* 17, 279–88

Weaver, B, 2014, Control or change? Developing dialogues between desistance research and public protection practices, *Probation Journal* 61, 8–26

173

Weaver, B, Barry, M, 2014, Risky business? Desistance from sexual offending, in K McCarten (ed) *Responding to sexual offending: Perceptions, risk management and public protection*, pp 153–69, Basingstoke: Palgrave Macmillan

Wilson, C, 2011, Managing the problem: Working with people convicted of sexual offences, in S Hanvey, T Philpot, C Wilson (eds) *A community-based approach to the reduction of sexual reoffending: Circles of support and accountability*, London: Jessica Kingsley

Wykes, M, Welsh, K, 2009, *Violence, gender and justice*, London: SAGE

Yates, PM, 2009, Is sexual offender denial related to sex offender risk and recidivism? A review and treatment implications, *Psychology, Crime and Law* 15, 183–99

# EIGHT

# Social identity, social networks and social capital in desistance and recovery

*David Best*

## Introduction

The purpose of this chapter is to introduce the concepts and principles of social identity theory to a criminology audience and to apply it to the model of desistance from offending concurrent with recovery from substance use problems. The empirical examples used to illustrate this come from a study of alcohol and drug workers who are in recovery from their own addiction, with the sub-sample used for the current analysis restricted to those who also have a history of criminal involvement. The chapter starts with an overview of the relationship between recovery, desistance and the role that identity change is understood to have played in each of these processes.

## Recovery, desistance and identity

While definitions have been highly contentious around subjective versus objective criteria, there have been two consensus groups convened that have attempted to create shared definitions. The Betty Ford Institute Consensus Panel defines recovery from substance dependence as a 'voluntarily maintained lifestyle characterised by sobriety, personal health and citizenship' (2007, 222). This position is consistent with the UK Drug Policy Commission statement on recovery as 'voluntarily sustained control over substance use which maximises health and wellbeing and participation in the rights, roles and responsibilities of society' (2008, 6). The contrasting view is outlined in Valentine's (2011) statement 'you are in recovery if you say you are' (p 264), which emphasises the importance of the subjective experience of change.

One of the core concepts in recovery has been the idea of recovery capital (Granfield and Cloud, 2001), with Best and Laudet (2010) developing this concept to suggest that it consists of three components – personal, social and community capital. The possibility that recovery capital may have a negative as well as a positive side was explored by Cloud and Granfield (2009). Stigma and exclusion may well be key aspects of negative recovery capital that block sustained recovery from addiction and/or desistance from offending. Cloud and Granfield argued that one of the primary negative recovery capital factors was a history of criminal justice involvement (along with a history of mental health problems) and, further, that those addicts with significant criminal justice histories had a much more demanding and complex pathway to recovery.

In contrast, the definition of desistance has been less contentious politically, although it has been subject to considerable academic debate. Desistance has been described as a process involving 'the long term abstinence from criminal behaviour among those for whom offending had become a pattern of behaviour' (McNeill et al, 2012, 3). However, akin to recovery from substance addiction, McNeill and colleagues argued that desistance is a two-stage process (Maruna and Farrall, 2004), with the first involving the termination of the offending behaviour, and the second the much more prolonged and complex process of discovering, defining and socially negotiating a new way of life and a new identity. Indeed, more recently, McNeill (2014) has introduced the concept of 'tertiary desistance' to describe a sense of belonging to a community, arguing that desistance requires not only a change in identity, but also the corroboration of that new identity within a (moral) community. In both recovery and desistance there is recognition that this is not a linear process, and that there will be occasions of relapse and slips that may occur within the larger change trajectory. There are considerable overlaps in the perception that this is a process that occurs in a range of social contexts and that markers of change involve engagement in meaningful relationships, meaningful activities and community engagement. However, central to this process is the idea that the identity of the desister is not that of the offender, and, moreover, that the process of defining and refining a new identity and negotiating its acceptance in the lived community is an essential component of both recovery and desistance.

There is a considerable literature that has suggested that recovery from addiction problems is based on the transformation of personal identity (for example, Biernacki, 1986). This theme was developed by McIntosh and McKeganey (2000) who have argued that recovery is predicated on the 'restoration of a spoiled identity'. This concept has been challenged on the grounds that the notion of a spoiled identity is pejorative and that it neglects the range of alternative identities available to individuals across different social contexts (for example, as father, daughter, neighbour) and overemphasises substance misuse (Neale et al, 2011). More recently, Radcliffe (2011) extended the argument around multi-faceted identity in a paper on recovery from substance abuse among pregnant women and new mothers. Radcliffe argued that participants' motivation for recovery occurred in the context of an emerging 'maternal' identity, with pregnancy providing a turning point, or 'second chance', allowing them to construct a 'normal, unremarkable, and un-stigmatised motherhood' identity that supported their transition to recovery (Radcliffe, 2011, 984), although she did point out that this did not occur in all cases.

In the literature on desistance from offending there is also strong emphasis on identity change. Shadd Maruna's (2001) Liverpool desistance study identified that, in order to desist from crime, ex-offenders needed to develop a coherent, prosocial identity for themselves. In this study, which compared persisting and desisting offenders, the desisters were much more optimistic in their narratives and were much less likely to characterise themselves as 'doomed to deviance', than persisters who had more complex and generative life narratives. Similarly, Giordano et al (2002) proposed a four-part 'theory of cognitive transformation' describing a process involving: a general cognitive openness to change; both exposure and reaction to hooks for change or turning points; the opportunity to envision an appealing and conventional replacement self; and finally a significant transformation in the way the actor views deviant behaviour – indicating that the process is thereby complete as old behaviours are no longer seen as desirable or relevant (Giordano et al, 2002, 1002).

## Change as a process of social not personal identity: social identity theory

The focus on identity in the desistance and recovery literature has primarily been on personal identity and the transition in the self-concept. The idea here is that there is an alternative form of identity that is relevant both as a key component of the self and as a mechanism for changing aspects of personal identity. Social identity theory proposes that, in a range of social contexts, people's sense of self is derived from their membership of social groups, and that the resulting social identities structure a person's perception and behaviour — their values, norms and goals; their orientations, relationships and interactions; what they think, what they do, and what they want to achieve (Tajfel and Turner, 1979; Haslam, 2014).

The fundamental premise here is that belonging to groups is good for individuals both in terms of providing access to a range of supports and resources, and also for its impact on wellbeing. Social identities act as resources that support psychological health and adjustment (Jetten et al, 2010; 2014). Along these lines, there is evidence that internalised group memberships become personal resources that support positive adaptation to change in times of life transition (Jetten et al, 2012).

For example, Haslam and colleagues (2008) found that life satisfaction among patients recovering from stroke was greater for those who belonged to more social groups before their stroke, and who retained more of those group memberships following their stroke. In addition, the formation of new group memberships following a traumatic event has been found to predict fewer symptoms of traumatic stress over time, after controlling for individual differences in post-traumatic symptoms at baseline (Jones et al, 2012). In other words, both the maintenance of former social networks and the development of new social networks are protective and beneficial to wellbeing.

This is, however, predicated on the nature of the group. It cannot be assumed that all the groups to which individuals belong have a positive impact on physical and psychological wellbeing (Haslam et al, 2012; Jetten et al, 2014), nor that they all promote healthy behaviours and sustainable wellbeing (Oyserman et al, 2007). Because groups are strong determinants of self-definition (Turner, 1991), strong affiliation to a group that is discriminated against and socially excluded due to involvement in deviant norms and activities (for example, many using and offending social networks) may also increase group members' health vulnerability and reduce subjective wellbeing and self-esteem (Schofield and Eurich-Fulcer, 2001).

This is associated with the adverse impact of being a member of a socially excluded or stigmatised group. Stigma can threaten social identity (Major and O'Brien, 2005) as it can have an impact on self-esteem and lead to the belief that adverse life events result from being the member of a stigmatised group (Steele, 1997), such that belonging to groups of drug users and offenders can result in adverse impact on self-esteem and wellbeing. This is particularly the case as members of stigmatised groups are more at risk for mental and physical health problems such as depression, heart disease and stroke (American Health Association, 2003; Jackson et al, 1996; McEwen, 2000). While it will most commonly be the case that such adverse effects of group membership will lead to voluntary exit for the individual striving for desistance or recovery, it is possible that the whole group may change to embrace a new identity and lifestyle. Weaver and McNeill (2015), for example, describe such a transition in a friendship group whose desistance is characterised as intrinsically relational, and based on transitions in the group itself.

For this reason, it is posited that the process of desistance and recovery necessitates changes in social networks that are associated with shifts in social and personal identity. Furthermore, that successful recovery requires that these transitions are not only from using to non-using groups but also from excluded and stigmatised social networks to membership of social networks which are associated with positive perceptions of the group and the belief that being a member of the group is something valuable and beneficial.

The rationale for the current study, first reported in Best (2014), is that it describes the life narratives of those who have successfully made the transition from active substance use (and considerable offending) to working in the alcohol and drug field. This is a population who have successfully reversed a career of dependent substance use and are 'giving back' to the community through their work as treatment practitioners, generally but not exclusively working as clinicians/practitioners to help others. This group can be split into two sub-groups – those whose active addiction involved a significant level of involvement with the criminal justice system and those that did not. One of the key questions in the current study is the extent to which the recovery journeys of those with criminal justice histories involves a different experience or trajectory, and whether there is any indication that there are greater challenges in identity transition in those attempting to negotiate a new identity that involves shedding both 'addict' and offender identities.

The method employed was a mixed methods approach in which a series of standardised research measures were used to collect information on wellbeing and recovery capital, and a timeline follow-back method was used to capture key event data during and after their addiction careers. The chapter will present information on the mechanisms of transition as retrospectively reported by this population and will supplement that with qualitative information about their experience of changing social networks and its impact on their social identities.

## Method

A long-term recovery sample: this is a population who were recruited through a snowball methodology in both Australia and the UK, with initial contacts being addiction professionals who were known to be in recovery by the author and who were also known to be happy to discuss their own recovery journeys. In both countries, they were then asked to recruit other people they knew who were in a similar situation and this method led to the recruitment of the sample. Interviews were conducted primarily by telephone although some were undertaken as self-complete questionnaires or as face to face interviews depending on the preference of the interviewee. In total, 42 individuals agreed to participate in the project and completed the interview or questionnaire. All of these can be regarded as people who have been sufficiently successful in their recovery journeys that they are currently recognised as addiction professionals, although there are marked variabilities within the sample in the duration of recovery and desistance from offending.

The initial phase of data collection used primarily quantitative methods and this was supplemented with a case study approach to examine turning points in the addiction career based using the Lifetime Drug Use History (Day et al, 2008). The key conclusions from this analysis (Best, 2014) were that this was not a group of people who had strong personal and social capital during their periods of active addiction, yet were able to build recovery capital reasonably quickly and so were able to exit from their addiction lifestyles at a relatively early age. The 50 participants in the study had last used their preferred substance at a mean age of 33 (and they were on average 45 years old at the time of the research interview). For the problem alcohol users, the average age of onset was 12 years and for heroin users average age of first use was 22 years (in other words, markedly older than would be expected in typical clinical populations). However, for both substances, problem substance use typically started markedly later (particularly for the drinkers) meaning that the average age of problem substance-using career averaged at around 11 years, although there was marked variability in this within the sample.

This population had experienced multiple adversities before, during and after their substance-using careers. Around 40 per cent had experienced at least one episode of homelessness, 32 per cent had been in prison, and more than half had been arrested at least once during their active addiction careers. It is this group that is the focus of the current analysis which is restricted to participants who had both experienced a criminal justice and a substance use problem (and label) at some point in the past.

Cloud and Granfield (2009) have argued that there are a number of fundamental barriers to long-term recovery from substance use, one of which is a significant forensic history and this they refer to as 'negative recovery capital'. In the current context this is important as there is not only the challenge of escaping the behaviours and problems associated with offending and with substance misuse, but also in managing the societal responses, including the exclusion and stigmatisation as offenders and 'addicts'. Each of these represents a label that can be internalised as a form of secondary labelling leading to a negative effect on self-esteem and perceived self-efficacy.

The analysis presented in this chapter focuses on the characteristics and pathways to recovery and desistance for this group and the reported impact on personal and social identity that results.

## Substance use and criminal justice histories

Of the 42 participants in the project, 26 (61.9 per cent) had been arrested for the first time at an average age of 19 (with a range of 10–42 years). Eighteen of the study participants had lifetime experience of prison and those who had been in prison averaged 3.7 years in prison (with a range of 1 to 19 years). For those who had been to prison, their first imprisonment typically occurred when they were 23 years of age but again there was marked variability with the range extending from the age of 14 to 33 years.

In terms of their substance-using histories, the group were primarily poly-drug users with 22 individuals reporting a heroin-using history, typically starting use at the age of 20 (although again this ranged widely from first use at 13 to first use at 41). Twenty-four individuals reported lifetime problems with cocaine, typically experiencing initial problems around the age of 25, although again there was considerable variability in the age of initial problems. Thirty participants reported daily and problematic drinking at some point in their lives with the age of daily drinking starting on average at the age of 22. Additional problems were reported with cannabis, prescribed opioids, amphetamine-type stimulants and benzodiazepines (both prescribed and illicitly acquired).

Consistent with previous studies on addiction careers, the mean length of heroin-using careers was 12.2 years (range of 3 to 26 years); for alcohol, the average length of alcohol dependence was 9.5 years (although again the range was huge, extending from 1 to 46 years) and the average age of achieving abstinence was just over 30.

One of the key questions is whether those with a criminal justice history have a different or more problematic pathway to recovery and desistance as implied in the negative recovery capital model outlined by Cloud and Granfield (2009). To test this question, the 18 participants with a history of imprisonment were compared to the 21 who had no such experience (three participants did not answer this question and so have to be excluded from the analysis).

### (i) Are the desistance pathways different for those with prison histories?

There was no gender difference in the likelihood that the sample would have a history of imprisonment, and no difference in the likelihood that they would ever have been married. There was also no significant difference in their ages at the time of the interview with those with no prison history having an average age of 45.9 years and those with a prison history having an average age of 46.4 years.

Those participants without prison history, however, reported significantly more time in secondary education in school (an average of 4.6 years) than those who had been to prison (who averaged 3.6 years in secondary education; this difference was statistically significant: $t=3.04$; $p<0.01$). This would suggest that the two populations are additionally differentiated by greater social exclusion and early disadvantage among those who subsequently experienced imprisonment. This difference is also manifest in lifetime education, with the no prison group having almost twice as much tertiary education (an average of 6.0 years compared with 3.9 years for those who had been to prison at some point; again this difference is statistically significant: $t=2.20$, $p<0.05$). Thus, both in terms of secondary schooling and in terms of overall educational engagement, the population is divided by prison history, with those in recovery without a significant prison history reporting significantly greater childhood and adult engagement in education.

In terms of working lives, there is, however, no difference, with both groups reporting an average of around 16 years of full-time employment and an initial age of starting full-time work of around 20–21 years. This would suggest that the recovery experiences of each population has not been a barrier to work either during or since their addiction experiences. The group with a prison history do, however, report a much higher average rate of lifetime homelessness (averaging 1.1 occasions of homelessness each compared to 0.6 times among the 'no prison' group, although this difference is not statistically significant).

The other key historical factor is that the participants with a prison history who had been heroin users also had a significantly earlier age of first use than heroin users who had never been to prison – an average age of 18.5 years compared to an average age of 24.5 years for heroin users in the sample with no prior prison history (this difference was statistically significant: $t=2.31$, $p<0.05$). This is a very striking difference between the two groups suggesting many more risk factors in the group who had been to prison.

## (ii) Differences in current functioning and lifestyle by prison history

The first difference that is evident from an analysis of the data relates to current social networks. While the overall social network of those with a prison history is slightly larger (a mean of 33 people in the social network compared to 28 for those with no prison history), it is the number of current users who are in the network that is particularly striking. There are no meaningful differences between the groups in terms of how many people who are in recovery or who have never used are in the social networks. However, for those with no prison history, the average number of people in the social network who are current problem substance users is 0.5. In contrast, for those with a prison history, the average number of current users in the network is 2.9 (although this difference is not statistically significant). This is reflected in the average amount of time in the previous week spent with current problem substance users reported by participants – just over two hours on average for those with a prison history and 0.7 hours on average for those with no prison history.

This is important given the findings from Project MATCH reported by Longabaugh et al (2010) that one of the key predictors of effectively maintained recovery is successfully managing a transition from a network supportive of substance use to a network supportive of recovery. Thus, evidence would suggest that the group with a history of prison should have a more fragile stability to their recovery as their social networks are more occupied by those who continue to use substances in a problematic way, with clear implications for the development of a social identity of recovery. In the Social Identity Model of Recovery (SIMOR), Best et al (2015) have argued that the supplanting of an 'addict' identity with a 'recovery' identity is characterised by shifts in engagement with and commitment to groups who are active supporters of recovery and the gradual loss of identification with active using groups and the accompanying beliefs and value systems. Within this recovery model, retaining membership of social who continue to actively use (and so where substance use is normative and acceptable) is challenging to an attempt to create a strong and stable identity formed around the concept of recovery.

In spite of this difference in social network composition, there were no differences between the recovery group who had a significant prison history and those who did not in terms of their reported wellbeing at the time of the research interview. Both groups showed approximately equivalent (and high) levels of quality of life, recovery capital, physical and psychological health and participation in recovery group activities.

What this would suggest is that, to address the question of negative recovery capital, a history of imprisonment does not suggest that those who have this added barrier to overcome are destined to have a poorer or paler version of recovery. The nature of the data presented here does not, however, allow us to answer the question of whether it is less likely that those who have a history of addiction and prison are less likely to achieve recovery, given the nature of the sample and the study design.

## (iii) Recovery identity and ongoing recovery support

The majority of both groups (35 of the 38 people who answered the question) perceived themselves to be 'in recovery' and to understand this as an ongoing process of change. However, of the four people who regarded themselves as 'recovered', three had a significant history of prison. Almost all of those who participated in the project had a significant history with 12-step groups, although a slightly lower percentage of those with a prison history (42.9 per cent compared to 50.0 per cent) were actively involved with 12-step groups at the time of the follow-up interview. The evidence here would suggest that 12 steps can play a significant role in change (desistance and recovery) for those with both substance use and offending histories, and that involvement in such groups can continue well into the recovery journey.

Those with a prison history were, however, more likely to have gone through abstinence-oriented specialist treatment than those without – and this difference was statistically significant for residential detoxification (where those with a prison history averaged 1.5 in-patient detox episodes compared to 0.6 for those with no prison history). Similarly, those with a prison history were more likely to have been through residential rehabilitation, possibly suggesting more complex treatment needs in this group. Further evidence for this comes from the fact that 11 of the prison group compared to only two of the non-prison group had ever been prescribed methadone (a mu opioid agonist used to substitute for heroin in a prescribing regime designed to reduce craving and withdrawals and to minimise risk taking). The group with the prison history also report more than double the length of time in community addiction treatment during their recovery journeys and a statistically significant first date of seeking community treatment. Thus, we can conclude that the addiction problems of those with criminal justice histories were more complex and required more specialist interventions than those who did not have a criminal justice history.

### (iv) Overall conclusions on the quantitative data

There are clear indications that there is a 'double jeopardy' associated with the co-occurrence of substance addiction and criminal justice involvement, in this case defined as a history of imprisonment. Although this does not permit any inferences about cause, those who had a history of going to prison had significantly greater complexity in their backgrounds – with much less secondary schooling, much more involvement with specialist addiction treatment during the recovery journey and more ongoing contact with current problem substance users than those who did not have a previous history of imprisonment.

Nonetheless, this group also reported levels of functioning comparable with those without a prison history – both in terms of active symptoms (physically and psychologically) and in terms of strengths (employment history, quality of life and personal and social recovery capital). This suggests that, while there are additional challenges in the journey to recovery (and so it may be less likely), it would not imply that the achievements and benefits of the recovery and desistance process are in any sense 'lesser' for this group. The next section will look at personal experiences of the transition desistance and recovery using individual case studies.

## Qualitative case study 1: Jeremy's journey to recovery

Jerry is a 57-year-old male who is now well established as a senior clinician in a large national specialist treatment provider. It is now 25 years since he last used heroin and he is quite explicit in terms of his identity that he has 'completed his recovery journey', that he is now an 'ex-addict' and that he regards his criminal history as similarly something that is completely in the past. Jerry was a major importer of drugs, including heroin, and he spent two long periods in prison following convictions for possession with intent to supply heroin.

It is interesting to note that Jerry regards the onset of his life problems as not resulting from the initial experiences of withdrawals from heroin but rather that

> I didn't really view anything as a problem until I started to get arrested and put in prison.

Although he then recognised a problem, he did not find it easy to change and reported that

> I had my 'last shot' countless times, but it only lasted until I got sick or got some heroin. My lifestyle got in the way of me changing. Everyone I knew used.

When asked about what finally became the key turning point, however, he said that it was treatment that had been provoked by criminal justice system requirements:

> I got bailed to rehab, and I began to learn that it was more than simply drug use . This gave me something to work with other than just not using. Also, I started to see people I knew from the streets or prisons at meetings [Narcotics Anonymous meetings] who seemed to be doing ok.

He reports that the first year was relatively easy and that he managed this just by committing to abiding by the rules of the rehabilitation unit. However, it became much harder after he left, as a consequence of leaving the structured and supportive environment with its rules and regulations (which he likened to prison). In contrast, the transition to the community was a challenge because of the freedoms and demands that he struggled to manage. He reports that, from about two years clean

> I enjoyed life and began to experience life in a different way – no drive to use, no crime, no police, no violence. I had a job and was able to enjoy my life.

Colman and Vander Laenen (2012, 1) recently asserted that, 'desistance is subordinate to recovery' in a cohort of substance-using offenders, recruited through a snowballing method in addiction treatment and social work services. They go on to argue that 'most of our respondents (four out of five) consider their desistance from offending to be subordinate to their drug use "desistance"' (Coleman and Vander Laenen, 2012, 3). This is too simplistic an explanation for Jerry's situation where criminal justice involvement was both the trigger for problem recognition and the mechanism through which he was able to access the help and support he needed to make lasting changes.

This is evident when he was asked what currently sustains his recovery and desistance and he answered that

*Now I enjoy life. Living is something that requires maintenance, there are things to do, and responsibilities to accept. I have a status in the community, a good recreational and social life, and I have achieved some of the luxuries in life. My family — my wife and children — are important and enjoyable.*

His perception of himself as recovered and as an ex-addict means that he is selective about disclosing his recovery identity. He argued that

*Some of the people outside of work I socialise with or I am connected to through my children's schooling and sports club would not understand. I am not defined by who I used to be.*

While Jerry was happy to talk about his own addiction and recovery in the work context where he felt that his experience was able to help other people, in other contexts he is much more selective and unlikely to make this kind of confession.

For Jerry, the use of the recovery and desistance identity is tied to context and, in terms of the SIMOR (Best et al, 2015), its salience and fit is about the role and social context in which recovery and desistance are likely to arise. Consistent with the notion that membership of multiple groups is protective to health (Jetten et al, 2012), Jerry has a range of social supports and networks and so is not defined or constrained by a single identity — neither that of an addict nor that of being in recovery or desisting from offending. The social identity model that is outlined in SIMOR suggests that the stability and effectiveness of recovery change (and equally desistance) is about supplanting an addict identity with a recovery one; however, the paper goes on to assert that the longer-term stability of this identity is likely to be preserved when the 'recovery' identity loses its salience across all contexts and is replaced by a range of socially positive identities such as 'father', 'husband', 'health professional', 'golfer'. In Jerry's case, the transition is from a social identity that is constructed through a using network that was also defined by its drug-related offending (a narrow and excluded social identity) to one that is defined by a more complex and diverse set of social identities that relate to professional life, family, friends and neighbours, for example. Thus, the transition is both in the complexity and diversity of social identities and in the transition from excluded and stigmatised group memberships to prosocial identities. The mechanisms for this change are not sudden, although they can be framed within the context of turning points in the shape of events, but it is their interaction with psychological states (social identity as a frame for self-image, self-esteem and so on) that is critical.

## Qualitative case study 2: Diane's journey to desistance and recovery

At the time of the interview Diane was well established as a recovery coordinator with one of the major alcohol and drug treatment providers in the UK. She was widowed and living with her 23-year old daughter and, when asked to describe what her life was like at the time of the interview, said,

> *Life is great. I have maintained full-time employment since 2007. I have excellent relationships with most of the family, and a brilliant relationship with both of my children. I am responsible for my own destiny and I no longer consider myself an addict – I have no cravings. I can cope with anything that life throws at me.*

This, however, contrasts very strongly with her life experience of involvement in substance use, addiction and offending:

> *My husband was using without my knowledge, then after I had a nervous breakdown I started to use. I became dependent almost immediately, very quickly it became a problem. We were involved in dealing drugs and other acquisitive crime. I lost my children due to the chaotic lifestyle, and I was disowned by my family. There were regular drug busts, arrests, prisons, homelessness. My husband was murdered in 2000. Numerous suicide attempts followed this.*

Diane's heroin-using career started at the age of 24 and continued until she was 33 and there was also a transition to daily drinking towards the end of her heroin-using career that lasted for around two years. She was twice imprisoned at the age of 29 and again at 33. She first attempted to stop using heroin at 30 and had regular lapses and relapses until 34 when she started her recovery journey. She explains that

> *I tried to stop several times but never stayed abstinent for long. I completed six months in rehab but still messed up from bereavement and relapsed soon after I left.*

She goes on to say that

> *Finally, I was sent to xxxx bail hostel in 2003 and received support, friendship and rebuilt family relationships.*

When asked what finally led her to long-term recovery she reiterated the above statement by saying that it was down to

> *receiving all round support from the bail hostel, making non-using friends and starting volunteering – so I felt that I had a future.*

In describing her pathway to long-term and stable recovery she talks about the first year of

> *feeling like a kid! I had no responsibilities, I had a good friend who was a non-user and I started rebuilding lost relationships with my family.*

She then went on to describe the subsequent experience of activities as central:

> *I volunteered and then gained full-time employment. I had goals and dreams. The children came back to live with me. I discovered a new identity.*

This means that she will be selective about talking about her recovery

> *I feel no need to wear it as a badge [although] I tend to be open with work colleagues when it comes up in conversation.*

In reflecting on her recovery journey, Diane talks about two key 'turning points' – the first being sent to the bail hostel where she started to make new and positive relationships, and the second when she started volunteering – both of which started the same year and around the time that she managed to stop using heroin (she had not used for ten years at the time of the interview). She also describes starting full-time work as a key point in her recovery journey as she felt it affirmed her status and her new identity.

For Diane it is clear that a life course perspective makes sense both in terms of key trigger events that initiated addiction and then in the pathway to recovery (Sampson and Laub, 1993; Lemert, 1951). It is interesting to note that the journey to recovery is described in terms of three trigger events – a criminal justice disposal followed by the initiation of two forms of meaningful activities, volunteering and working. Again, the evidence is clear that recovery is a process that happens over time and that the transition is a dynamic process of key events and the psychological changes they trigger and sustain. This is consistent with LeBel et al's (2008) 'chicken and egg' discussion of the role that agency plays in enabling and sustaining events that come to be seen as turning points.

What the current model suggests is that the overall framing for this should be considered within a social identity model in which group memberships provide not only the access to opportunity (in the form of social and community capital (Best and Laudet, 2010; Best and Savic, 2015), but also the social supports that assist in the development of new and prosocial identities.

## Conclusion

The fundamental argument advanced in this chapter, with support provided through qualitative case studies and quantitative data, is that desistance from offending and recovery from substance use are complex processes of overcoming stigma and social exclusion. In both case studies, the individuals describe the construction of new lives and new social identities that allowed them to regain the core components of their former lives that they valued, particularly in terms of family re-engagement, and to establish new identities that were positive and prosocial through work, volunteering and hobbies.

It is argued, however, that the emergence of these identities is a fundamentally social process (for example, Jetten et al, 2012) in which it is the internalisation of positive group norms and values that binds the individual to the new group and that supports and sustains the fundamental changes in their attitudes, behaviours and values. Recently Best and Savic (2015) have advanced the Social Identity Model of Recovery (SIMOR) to explain the transition from addict identity to recovery identity but have argued that this really involves two separate processes – the transition from narrow and simple to complex and diverse social identities that is also accompanied by the transition from socially excluded to socially included identities. It is this multiple group membership that is likely to be protective and beneficial (Jetten et al, 2014) and that enables effective transition not only to desistance and recovery but to effective and full community reintegration as well.

To frame this within a recovery capital model (Granfield and Cloud, 2001), it has been suggested that a significant offending history is a barrier to long-term recovery and that it can be seen as a 'negative recovery capital' factor. What the current evidence shows is that there is no ceiling to the extent of recovery for those with a joint history of addiction and criminal justice involvement (although the study is not able to comment on whether it reduces the likelihood that such a journey will take place). Within the SIMOR model advanced above, it is the transition in social group membership that allows both access to community resources and assets, and to new social identities that enables effective desistance and recovery.

While identity has been described extensively in the desistance literature (for example, Maruna, 2001), it is the social framing of that identity change and its relationship to access to social and community resources that is central to this argument about the shared pathways of desistance and recovery.

## References

American Heart Association, 2003, Stroke risk factors, www.americanheart.org/presenter.jhtml?identifier=237

Best, D, 2014, *Strengths, support, setbacks and solutions: The developmental pathway to addiction recovery*, Brighton: Pavilion Publishing

Best, D, Laudet, A, 2010, *The potential of recovery capital*, London: RSA

Best, D, Savic, M, 2015, Substance abuse and offending: Pathways to recovery, in R Sheehan, J, Ogloff (eds) *Working within the forensic paradigm: Cross-discipline approaches for policy and practice*, Abingdon: Routledge

Best, D, Beckwith, M, Haslam, C, Haslam, A, Jetten, J, Mawson, E, Lubman, D, 2016, Overcoming alcohol and other drug addiction as a process of social identity transition: The Social Identity Model of Recovery (SIMOR), *Addiction Research and Theory*, 24, 2, 111-123.

Betty Ford Institute Consensus Panel, 2007, What is recovery? A working definition from the Betty Ford Institute, *Journal of Substance Abuse Treatment 33*, 221–8

Biernacki, P, 1986, *Pathways from heroin addiction: Recovery without treatment*, Philadelphia, PA: Temple University Press

Cloud, W, Granfield, R, 2009, Conceptualising recovery capital: Expansion of a theoretical construct, *Substance Use and Misuse 43*, 12–13, 1971–86

Colman, C, Vander Laenen, F, 2012, 'Recovery came first': Desistance versus recovery in the criminal careers of drug-using offenders, *The Scientific World Journal*, www.hindawi.com/journals/tswj/2012/657671/

Day, E, Best, D, Cantillano, V, Gaston, R, Nambamali, R, Keaney, F, 2008, Measuring the use and career histories of drug users in treatment: Reliability of the Lifetime Drug Use History (LDUH), and its data yield relative to clinical case notes, *Drug and Alcohol Review* 27, 175–81

Giordano, PC, Cernkovich, SA, Rudolph, JL, 2002, Gender, crime and desistance: Towards a theory of cognitive transformation, *American Journal of Sociology* 107, 990–1064

Granfield, R, Cloud, W, 2001, Social context and 'natural recovery': The role of social capital in the resolution of drug-associated problems, *Substance Use and Misuse* 36, 1543–70

Haslam, C, Holme, A, Haslam, SA, Iyer, A, Jetten, J, Williams, WH, 2008, Maintaining group memberships: Social identity continuity predicts well-being after stroke, *Neuropsychological Rehabilitation* 18, 5–6, 671–91

Haslam, SA, 2014, Making good theory practical: Five lessons for an Applied Social Identity Approach to challenges of organizational, health, and clinical psychology, *British Journal of Social Psychology* 53, 1, 1–20

Haslam, SA, Reicher, SD, Levine, M, 2012, When other people are heaven, when other people are hell: How social identity determines the nature and impact of social support, in J Jetten, C Haslam, SA Haslam (eds) *The social cure: Identity, health and well-being*, pp 157–74, New York: Psychology Press

Jackson, J, Brown, T, Williams, D, Torres, M, Sellers, S, Brown, K, 1996, Racism and the physical and mental health status of African Americans: A thirteen-year national panel study, *Ethnicity Discourse* 6, 132–47

Jetten, J, Haslam, SA, Iyer, A, Haslam, C, 2010, Turning to others in times of change: Social identity and coping with stress, S Sturmer, M Snyder (eds) *The psychology of prosocial behavior: Group processes, intergroup relations, and helping*, pp 139–56, Chichester: Wiley-Blackwell

Jetten, J, Haslam, SA, Haslam, C, 2012, The case for a social identity analysis of health and well-being, in J Jetten, C Haslam, SA Haslam (eds) *The social cure: Identity, health and well-being*, pp 3–19, New York: Psychology Press

Jetten, J, Haslam, C, Haslam, SA, Dingle, G, Jones, JM, 2014, How groups affect our health and well-being: The path from theory to policy, *Social Issues and Policy Review* 8, 103–30

Jones, JM, Williams, WH, Jetten, J, Haslam, SA, Harris, A, Gleibs, IH, 2012, The role of psychological symptoms and social group memberships in the development of post-traumatic stress after traumatic injury, *British Journal of Health Psychology* 17, 4, 798–811

LeBel, T, Burnett, R, Maruna, S, Bushway, S, 2008, The 'chicken and egg' of subjective and social factors in desistance from crime, *European Journal of Criminology* 5, 2, 131–59

Lemert, EM, 1951, *Social pathology*, New York: McGraw Hill

Longabaugh, R, Wirtz, PW, Zywiak, WH, O'Malley, SS, 2010, Network support as a prognostic indicator of drinking outcomes: The COMBINE study, *Journal of Studies on Alcohol and Drugs*, 71, 6, 837.

McEwen, B, 2000, The neurobiology of stress: From serendipity to clinical relevance, *Brain Research* 886, 172–89

McIntosh, J, McKeganey, N, 2000, Addicts' narratives of recovery from drug use: Constructing a non–addict identity, *Social Science and Medicine* 50, 1501–10

McNeill, F, 2014, Discovering desistance: Three aspects of desistance?, http://blogs.irss.org.uk/discoveringdesistance/2014/05/23/three-aspects-of-desistance/

McNeill, F, Farrall, S, Lightower, C, Maruna, S, 2012, How and why people stop offending: Discovering desistence, *Institute for Research and Innovation in Social Services*, http://eprints.gla.ac.uk/79860/1/79860.pdf

Major, B, O'Brien, T, 2005, The social psychology of stigma, *Annual Review of Psychology* 56, 393–421

Maruna, S, 2001, *Making good: How ex-convicts reform and rebuild their lives*, Washington, DC: American Psychological Association

Maruna, S, Farrall, S, 2004, Desistance from crime: A theoretical reformulation, *Kolner Zeitschrift fur Soziologie and Sozialpsychologie* 43, 171–94

Neale, J, Nettleton, S, Pickering, L, 2011, Recovery from problem drug use: What can we learn from the sociologist Erving Goffman?, *Drugs: Education, Prevention and Policy* 18, 1, 3–9

Oyserman, D, Fryberg, SA, Yoder, N, 2007, Identity-based motivation and health, *Journal of Personality and Social Psychology* 93, 6, 1011–27, doi: 10.1037/0022-3514.93.6.1011

Radcliffe, P, 2011, Motherhood, pregnancy, and the negotiation of identity: The moral career of drug treatment, *Social Science and Medicine* 72, 6, 984–91

Sampson, RJ, Laub, JH, 1993, *Crime in the making: Pathways and turning points through life*, Cambridge, MA: Harvard University Press

Schofield, JW, Eurich-Fulcer, R, 2001, When and how school desegregation improves intergroup relations, in R Brown, SL Gaertner (eds) *Blackwell handbook of social psychology: Intergroup processes*, pp 475–94, Oxford: Blackwell

Steele, C, 1997, A threat in the air: How stereotypes shape intellectual identity and performance, *American Psychology* 52, 613–29

Tajfel, H, Turner, JC, 1979, An integrative theory of intergroup conflict, in WG Austin, S Worchel (eds) *The social psychology of intergroup relations*, pp 33–47, Monterey, CA: Brooks/Cole

Turner, JC, 1991, *Social influence*, Milton Keynes: Open University Press

UK Drug Policy Commission, 2008, *The UK drug policy commission recovery consensus group: A vision of recovery*, London: UK Drug Policy Commission

Valentine, P, 2011, Peer-based recovery support services within a recovery community organization: The CCAR experience, in JF Kelly, WL White (eds) *Addiction recovery management*, pp 259–79, New York: Humana Press

Weaver, B, McNeill, F, 2015, Lifelines: Desistance, social relations, and reciprocity, *Criminal Justice and Behaviour* 42, 1, 95–107

# NINE

# Alcoholics Anonymous: sustaining behavioural change

*James Irving*

## Introduction

Alcoholics Anonymous (AA) is the world's largest and most recognisable recovery 'programme', and the Twelve Step Programme is central to its philosophy. AA is a global organisation of 2.2 million members (AAWS, 2001), with a reported 3,651 weekly group meetings in the United Kingdom (AAWS, 2015). AA has made many claims in its literature about the programme's effectiveness (AAWS, 2001), yet Groh (2008, 44), for example, states that: 'Overall, the AA literature is characterized by inconsistent findings, with researchers continuing to debate the role of AA in promoting abstinence (Emrick et al, 1993; Humphreys, 2004; Kownacki and Shadish, 1999; McCrady and Miller,1993; Tonigan et al, 1996).' Kelly et al (2009, 237) add to the debate, referring to almost the exact same studies, 'Rigorously conducted empirical reviews of AA-focused research indicate that AA participation is helpful for many different types of individuals in their recovery from alcohol dependence.' One author suggests that claims of AA effectiveness are ambiguous whereas the other suggests a consensus of positive opinion regarding effectiveness.

This chapter explains how AA members sustain long-term behavioural change, or in other words, how members of AA maintain their sobriety. To achieve this, I constructed a conceptual model of change from AA's core texts, *Alcoholics Anonymous* (2001) – colloquially known as the *Big book* – and *The twelve steps and twelve traditions* (1952), and a review of academic literature. The model was then empirically tested in interviews with 20 long-term abstinent members of AA who each narrated various dimensions of their recovery as it had unfolded over time.

The model has four components. First, motivation to engage (MtE) refers to the circumstances or pressures under which an individual seeks help from AA. Once a member has joined AA the transition to recovery takes time, often years, and is aided by AA's Twelve Steps, sponsorship and relationships formed among AA's wider social network. This forms the second component, structured social engagement (SSE). Third, the effects of joining and participation in AA are an increase in an individual's personal agency (PA). The concomitant effect on behavioural outcomes (BO) represents the fourth component.

## A brief history of AA

> [Q]uite simply the most successful self-help organisation ever established. (Davidson, 2002, 4)

Other recovery groups and organisations, such as the Washingtonians (1840), Fraternal Temperance Societies (1842) and Native American recovery 'circles' (1737) predated AA (Blocker et al, 2003). Yet, since its inception, AA has become a yardstick against which all other mutual-help organisations are measured (Kurtz and White, 2005). AA dates back to 10 June 1935, in Akron, Ohio (Borkman, 2006), the day that Dr Bob Smith had his last drink. His co-founder, Bill Wilson, had been abstinent for five months at that time (Kurtz, 1979).

Both men were originally part of the Oxford Group, a Christian organisation combining social activities with religion. Their teachings were religious in nature, and some of their core beliefs are reflected in AA's tone and practices (Davidson, 2002). The Oxford Group practised public and one-to-one confessions, group discussion characterised by honesty, unselfishness and repentance for past wrongdoing (Davidson, 2002). Drawing on the practice of the Oxford Group, AA also aimed for personal change, not just abstinence. However, believing that their emphasis on God would be problematic for most alcoholics, Smith and Wilson began to focus solely on helping other alcoholics achieve sobriety. Thus, AA was established in its own right rather than as a sub/splinter organisation of the Oxford Group (Valverde, 1998).

White and Kurtz (2008) note the unique and distinctive features that have helped AA surpass the achievements of every other recovery group. Among these are: AA's growth and geographical spread, with more than 2 million members across 150 countries; its influence on the treatment of drug addiction and upon the treatment 'industry' generally (White, 1998); and its lasting influence on popular culture (Room, 1989). White and Kurtz (2008) trace a core element of AA's therapeutic practices – the 'helper principle' (Riessman, 1965) – to a chain of events and relationships involving Bill Wilson and another early

AA member who had been treated by Carl Jung. Jung had suggested that, in a relatively small number of cases, recovery from alcoholism had been affected by a profound spiritual experience augmented by a commitment to supporting others in a similar predicament. This suggestion from an eminent psychiatrist helped AA to cast the medical and psychiatric professionals into a supporting role, rather than allowing their discourses to potentially co-opt and subordinate AA (Kurtz, 1979; Valverde, 1998). This 'arm's-length' approach to professional intervention has since been replicated in other studies on mutual-help groups (Humphreys, 2015).

AA believes that a person, who has experienced alcoholism and subsequently achieved stable recovery, has a greater capacity to gain the confidence of another alcoholic. Shared knowledge of a common problem has been termed 'experiential knowledge' (Borkman, 1976), being a cannon of wisdom set aside from expert and common knowledge, and so occupying a middle ground. In AA's therapeutic practices, the sharing of experience is characterised by honesty and takes the form of an uninterrupted series of monologues within a set group context – the AA meeting (Arminen, 1996; 2004). The dyadic relationship between sponsor and sponsee involves sharing deeply personal, and sometimes humiliating, information. The sponsor is familiar with the Twelve Step Programme and this reciprocal sharing process is a pre-requisite for building trust (AAWS, 1952; Smith, 2007). These practices were carried forth by the co-founders, Wilson and Smith, helping to shape AA's distinctive dynamics of communication and its therapeutic mechanisms for behaviour change.

## Models of behavioural change

Prochaska and DiClemente's (1984) transtheoretical model (TTM) of health behaviour change has 'received unprecedented research attention' (Armitage, 2009, 196). TTM has also been widely adopted in health practice in relation to weight loss, smoking cessation, alcohol and drug abuse, condom use and medical compliance (Velicer et al, 1990). The model is a theoretical, integrative description of how people modify a problem behaviour or adopt a more positive form of behaviour, based on the notion that an individual typically passes through six conceptually discrete stages: *pre-contemplation, contemplation, preparation, action, maintenance* and *termination* (Prochaska et al, 1992). However, no clear consensus exists on TTM's overall validity, Cahill et al (2010), while Kraft et al (1999) argued that there are more stages of change and Callaghan et al (2007) find no clear evidence that matching a person to treatment relative to their 'stage-of-change' status, increases behavioural improvement.

Progression through these stages is not linear. The model is usually represented in a cyclical form, suggesting that the individual progresses through the stages in a clock-wise fashion. However, an individual can regress, and so take an anti-clockwise turn. To a degree this is expected, given the high relapse rates among alcohol and drug users (Velicer et al, 1990; Mäkelä et al, 1996). Migneault et al (2005) suggest that there are other dimensions which describe where a person is in relation to each of the six stages of change, including: *processes*, *decisional balance* and *self-efficacy*.

The properties of these constructs are conceptually analogous to AA's theory of change. The psychological state of an individual prior to committing to the AA Twelve Step Programme is a clear 'fit' with these constructs. Migneault et al (2005, 438) describe *processes* as 'a set of activities in which individuals engage during behavioural change'. *Decisional balance* describes a moment in time that a person becomes open to the prospect of behavioural change and thus relates clearly to MtE. It is therefore given explanatory and theoretical primacy here as this is the first step towards behaviour change. My study presents data from long-term abstinent members of AA. Understanding motivation 'unlocks' the other concepts incorporated into the behavioural model that I propose.

## Decisional balance

> Some day he will be unable to imagine life either with alcohol or without it. Then he will know loneliness such as few do. He will be at the jumping-off place. (AAWS, 2001, 152)

Velicer (1990) and colleagues explain *processes*, *decisional balance* and *self-efficacy* as being operationalised as psychometric constructs which can be used to assess where, psychologically or behaviourally, an individual may be on each of the six stages of the TTM. For example, work on decision making attempts to address decisional balance by weighing the pros and cons an individual perceives when continuing or terminating a negative behaviour (Janis and Mann, 1977, cited in Mignealt et al, 2005).

To understand how this 'decisional balance' corresponds to behaviour change, we need to sketch the dynamics of this psycho-social variable. As a starting point, individuals who have experienced external pressures, formal and informal, can be assumed to be *contemplators* who are considering their situation in relation to changing behaviour. Ajzen's (1991) theory of planned behaviour (TPB) conceptualises attitudes according to positive or negative evaluations of future behaviour change. Armitage et al (2003) argue that this evaluation identifies underlying behavioural beliefs. The social pressure exerted upon the individual shapes a 'subjective norm' – expectations associated with positive behaviour change. Within TPB, this is understood to represent the perceived effects of entering treatment. As a corollary to subjective norms 'behavioural intention' is informed by the strength of intent to act – to what lengths would a person go to change a problematic behaviour? The tension present in conceptualising this component of behaviour change is partly overcome by assessing *attitudinal ambivalence*: '[being] unable to imagine life either with alcohol or without it' (AAWS, 2001, 152).

Armitage et al (2003) observe that a person may *simultaneously* hold supportive and non-supportive beliefs towards a particular behaviour. For example, the ephemeral calming effect of drugs or alcohol on an individual works both psychologically and emotionally, so providing 'negative reinforcement via amelioration of an unpleasant negative affect' (Witkiewitz et al, 2005, 16). Removing the unpleasant feelings associated with withdrawal from excessive alcohol use, by drinking more alcohol, despite the known consequences, evidences an inability to cope without drinking.

Thus, as these 'attitudes of ambivalence' are equalised, a cross-over effect characterises the individual's thinking that locates him or her at the contemplation, preparation or action stage. Cross-over is achieved when the perceived pros and cons associated with a behaviour become more closely aligned, a balancing of the scales. As the 'decisional balance' becomes ripe for tipping, the individual becomes more receptive to the notion of positive change and more capable of processing salient information, as he or she prepares to take action (Armitage and Connor, 2000).

## Alcoholics Anonymous' active theory of change

First, I consider the *mechanisms* underlying an 'active theory of change'. Identification with other self-identified alcoholics is achieved at AA meetings and supported by peer interaction. The Twelve Step Programme directly addresses alcohol dependency. Each individual is supported through the programme by a sponsor who has achieved a substantial length of continuous sobriety having been through the Twelve Steps him or herself. AA's active theory of change also rests on the development of a spiritual dimension to be nurtured and incorporated into an individual's life. Members of AA describe experiencing a change in behaviour towards alcohol that goes beyond the usual clinical outcome measures such as reduced alcohol intake and medical co-morbidities (Humphreys, 2004).

Because AA is a complex entity, no single mechanism can account for change (Kurtz, 1979; Smith, 2007). As Kelly and McCrady (2008) argue, it is likely that there are simultaneous mechanisms occurring in an individual that are both psychologically and socially activated. An individual may feel 'pulled' deeper into the AA Fellowship as he or she attends AA meetings, acquires a sponsor, applies the Twelve Step Programme, and participates in the supportive network of recovering alcoholics (Smith, 2007).

## AA meetings

The formal arena and first point of contact for those seeking help from AA is the meeting. The basic purpose is that AA members may 'share our experience, strength and hope with one another' (AAWS, 1952, preamble). There are two basic types of AA meetings. Closed meetings are for members and potential members only, those with a 'desire to stop drinking', (AAWS, 1952, 143). The 'open' meetings are accessible to all, although members of the public would not be allowed to participate in any of the rituals and practices of the meetings (Donovan, 1984; Borkman, 2008).

In 'speaker/discussion' (open or closed) meetings (Smith, 2007; Arminen, 1996; 2001; Kelly and McCrady, 2008) AA members are invited to open the meeting by speaking on a chosen topic derived from either the basic text, *Alcoholics Anonymous* (2001), *As Bill sees it* (1967), or *Twelve steps and twelve traditions* (1952). The speaker narrates or 'shares' experience on the chosen topic, reflecting and quoting the tenor of AA literature. This will be his or her own experiential monologue and interpretation of a particular Step(s) or principles of AA.

Individual and group cohesion is predicated on AA's belief that, where healthcare professionals, family and friends have failed, '*the ex-problem drinker…can generally win the entire confidence of another alcoholic in a few hours*' (AAWS, 2001, 18, my emphasis). This dialogue of open vulnerability is deemed crucial in establishing trust and a common identity among new members. At AA meetings the new member is exposed to Borkman's (1976) 'experiential knowledge'; hearing the language of AA and how other members stay sober (Sommer,

1997; Roberts, 1988; Smith, 2007). New members are encouraged to listen for the 'similarities, not the differences', it is hoped that the new member begins to connect their own experience to that of other members. Kurtz (1979, 61) notes that the narrator offers a 'profound honesty of personal weaknesses', one that demands no reciprocity, but demonstrates the necessity of honesty as a pre-requisite for 'getting the Programme' and maintaining recovery. Attendance at an AA meeting helps bring an end to the loneliness that most alcoholics feel (Allen et al, 1981). In other words, attendance conceptually transforms the 'I' of the singular, isolated individual into a 'We' – a group of like-minded alcoholics. This establishes a common identity, a common set of reasons for drinking, and a common set of strategies for recovery (Donovan, 1984, 411).

Vaillant (2003; 2005) and Gossop et al (2003) found that men who had attended AA on a weekly basis (or more frequently) spent fewer days intoxicated and were likely to achieve stable abstinence. Ogborne and Bornet (1982; Jin et al, 1998) maintain that relapses are an inevitable part of recovery in AA, particularly among newcomers. AA conceptualises relapses – or 'slips' – as a failure to maintain participation in the AA programme (AAWS, 2001). Smith (2007; see also Kurtz, 1979; Rudy, 1980; Sheeren, 1998) argues that the abstinent AA member becomes vulnerable to existing psychological vulnerabilities, which are held in abeyance by participation in the AA programme. Smith indicates the potential for relapse in AA is pre-figured by the gradual withdrawal from AA meetings: 'I got so complacent about meetings. I didn't need them anymore. But as it says in the Book, the disease is powerful. And all we have to fight it with is this programme' (Smith, 2007, 47).

## Sponsorship in AA

Sponsorship is not a mandatory practice, but is strongly encouraged. AA sponsors sometimes sponsor more than one person (Whelan et al, 2009), and it is also considered 'good' AA practice for sponsors to be sponsored themselves (Strobbe, 2009). Salient points from the pamphlet *Questions and answers on sponsorship* (AAWS, 2005) are summarised as:

- A sponsor does everything possible, within the limits of personal experience and knowledge, to help the newcomer get sober and stay sober through the AA programme.
- They field any questions the new member may have about AA.

- Sponsorship gives the newcomer an understanding, sympathetic friend when one is needed most — it assures them that at least one person cares.

Witbrodt and Kaskutas (2005) report that having an available sponsor in early recovery is more important than any other activity for alcohol-dependent individuals. Whelan et al (2009, 419) suggest that successful sponsor/sponsee relationships perhaps 'flatten out' rather than 'age out' over a number of years as the need for intense support lessens after early recovery. Smith (2007; compare Whelan, 2009; Zemore et al, 2004) points out that AA recommends that sponsors and sponsees should be of the same sex, as AA 'wisdom' teaches that the vulnerable newcomer in early sobriety may confuse help with romantic notions. Although there are exceptions to this same sex 'rule' in that homosexual members of AA often acquire a sponsor of the opposite sex, this reinforces the same logic.

Sponsorship is the only formalised relationship in AA, and is normatively prescribed for working through the Twelve Steps (AAWS, 1952, 59; Chappel, 1994). It is understood to strengthen the sponsor's own recovery while simultaneously helping the newcomer (Project MATCH Research Group, 1993; 1998; Zemore et al, 2004; Zemore, 2007). Pagano et al (2004; 2010) found that, in terms of relapse prevention, sponsorship was itself a protective factor among those who sponsor AA members, and demonstrates fidelity to AA through encouragement to complete the Twelve Steps and attending meetings regularly (Whelan et al, 2009). There is a clear comparison to be made here with Maruna's (2001) analysis of offender/ex-offender generativity, as the author indicates generative pursuits have therapeutic effects. Exoneration, restitution and therapy, according to Maruna, occur when helping others alleviates guilt and shame, while helping the ex-offender (ex-alcoholic), maintain desistance/abstinence efforts, by coming to terms with past mistakes and moving on. Maruna goes on to cite AA's Twelve Steps as a source of empowerment derived from continually engaging with new members seeking abstinence (Maruna, 2001, 125).

AA's behavioural model of an alcoholic is that he or she loses control once drinking has commenced. AA holds that the merely abstinent person, the 'dry drunk', still carries the artefacts of character displayed by the drinking alcoholic: grandiosity, infantile defiance and so forth (Denzin, 1987). Having worked the Twelve Step Programme, the 'sober' AA individual lives free from these psychological and behavioural defects of character (Kurtz, 1979). Morgernstern et al (1997) notes that

AA's method of targeting the psychologically maladapted characteristics of the alcoholic, such as grandiosity, is unique. AA makes explicit the link between this dysfunction and continuing alcohol abuse. Without the Twelve Step Programme, and the 'tools' to manage these problems, AA doctrine teaches that the 'the person I was drank' if sufficient change does not occur: 'the person I am will drink again' (Borkman, 2008).

Although this assessment may appear condemnatory, AA's Twelve Steps offer a chance of reform and redemption. AA frames individual frailties as 'character defects' (see Steps Six and Seven below), these are reconfigured in AA's philosophy and Programme, providing, simultaneously the motive and method that drives effort and success.

## Surrender and reconceptualising reliance: Steps One, Two and Three

The book, *Alcoholics Anonymous* (AAWS, 2001), and the *Twelve steps and twelve traditions* (AAWS, 1952) explain exactly how to carry out each of the Twelve Steps. The objective regarding Step One is that the individual should 'surrender', focusing particularly on the inability to control his or her alcoholism. Step One achieves this by moving past experiences from the unconscious to the conscious mind, 'going back in our drinking histories, we could show that years before we realized it, our drinking was out of control' (AAWS, 1952, 23). Tiebout (1945, 5) suggests that, in the process of surrender, 'the unconscious forces of defiance and grandiosity actually ceases to function effectively', enabling the individual to accept his or her alcoholism.

Step Two encourages belief that a 'Power greater than ourselves could restore us to sanity'. This process requires substitution: 'you can if you wish make AA itself your 'higher power' (AAWS, 1952, 27). The underpinning logic here is that there is a group of people who have found a 'solution', while your own efforts have amounted to failure; in this sense the group is a power greater than yourself. Step Three advocates that the individual should 'turn our will and our lives over to the care of God as we understood Him'. The key to understanding this Step is a willingness to believe that efforts to control alcohol consumption should be left to the AA programme.

## AA's 'Practical' Steps: Four, Five, Eight and Nine

For these Steps, the objective is the amelioration of other dysfunctional areas of an individual's life, such as sex, debt, anger and criminality, in part by making lists and apologising to people (AAWS, 2001, 69, 78). AA locates these behavioural and emotional problems within the individual, on the basis that contorted emotions, desires and unrealistic expectations are a result of 'false' pride exacerbated by an inflated ego (Tiebout, 1945; Kurtz, 1979).

Step Four requires the individual to 'Make a fearless moral inventory of ourselves'; and Step Five to 'Admit…the exact nature of our wrongs' (AAWS, 1952, 43, 56). In practice, Step Four advises the individual to draw up a table, listing the nature of his or her resentment, to whom the resentment is directed and what area of life he or she perceives to be affected (AAWS, 2001, 65; Swora, 2004). AA doctrine asserts that the alcoholic 'leads a double life', and that negative experiences occur during excessive drinking, resulting in acute moral failing and an increasing sense of self-loathing. These events cause great distress, keeping the alcoholic in a state of 'constant fear and tension – that leads to more drinking' (AAWS, 2001, 73).

Step Four teaches that an individual must relinquish the 'tormenting ghosts of yesterday', and to do this in a practical sense. Step Five states that the individual must 'talk to somebody about them' (AAWS, 1952, 56). After the 'survey of the human wreckage left in his wake', these actions have the claimed therapeutic effect of forgiveness for him or her and forgiving those that had actually harmed the individual: 'As the pain subsides, a healing tranquillity takes its place' (AAWS, 1952, 63).

According to Donovan (1984), the act of disclosing innermost fears and negative behaviours in Step Four gives the pre-appointed sponsor access to the sponsee's internal state. The private sphere of the inner world thus becomes public, as members may choose to 'share' elements of their Steps Four and Five experience in meetings, fulfilling AA's tenet to 'Share experience strength and hope'. Experiences are re-framed into a positive allegorical narrative, confirming the absence of guilt and shame. Anderson and Gilbert (1989) reported that individuals felt Steps Four and Five were the most difficult parts of the AA Programme, but that the self-disclosure skills learned while practicing these steps aided the recovery process. Swora (2004) assessed the nature of the 'healing effects' of AA, finding that the re-living of past and painful memories serves to function as a protective factor by reminding members of the negative consequences of drinking.

Step Eight is 'Make a list of all persons we had harmed' (AAWS, 1952, 43, 79, 85) and, following on from this, Step Nine can be understood as therapy in action as the given objective is making direct amends to those persons harmed. There are caveats, for instance, divulging the details of extra marital affairs 'upon the shoulders of an unsuspecting wife or husband' (AAWS, 1952, 88). Nevertheless, AA encourages the individual to establish the 'willingness' to make amends where possible (Borkman, 2008).

## The 'Middle Steps', Six and Seven: Towards reflexive growth

Steps Six and Seven are perhaps the most abstract in nature. Steps Four and Five give the individual a retrospective 'map' of harms done, potential 'triggers', and 'defects' which, if not managed, will again result in negative behaviour or drinking. Thus, satiating such 'warped' desires, 'enjoying' various forms of malign behaviour, 'lust', 'self-righteous anger', 'gluttony' and 'slothfulness' has led to imperfections of character. Step Six asks that the individual is 'entirely ready to have God remove all these defects of character' (AAWS, 1952, 64). The alcoholic's behaviour, according to AA theory, is made up of incompatible and unsustainable demands for satisfactions of basic desires. Step Six requires a measure of 'character building'; that is a call to practice a greater degree of moral action, framed as an internal narrative. This narrative informs and develops the individual's sense and capacity for reflexivity, further suggesting that the individual should strive to avoid indulgent behaviours.

Step Seven directs a person to 'Humbly ask Him to remove our shortcomings' (AAWS, 1952, 76). This level of abstract spiritual practice is guided by the theory that, as drinking alcoholics, spiritual values were placed second to material and emotional satisfactions, thus blocking spiritual growth (Swora, 2001). Step Seven is characterised by individuals either praying or being mindful of certain traits or behaviours that need changing, with the help of the Higher Power.

## Maintaining spiritual growth and sobriety: Steps Ten, Eleven and Twelve

Steps Ten, Eleven and Twelve are sometimes referred to as the 'maintenance steps' (Borkman, 2008, 21), which should negate the possibility of having to repeat the 'moral inventory' and making 'direct amends' by maintaining a 'fit spiritual condition' (AAWS, 2001, 85). Step Ten is the capacity to act in a reflexive manner, correcting mistakes by taking a 'personal inventory'. AA doctrine reminds members that they are not 'cured of alcoholism', rather that 'We are not fighting it, neither are we avoiding temptation. We feel as though we have been placed in a position of neutrality, safe and protected' (AAWS, 2001). Step Eleven is the practice of further self-reflection: 'we constructively review our day. Were we resentful, selfish, dishonest...we ask God's forgiveness and inquire what corrective measures should be taken' (AAWS, 2001, 86).

In AA's literature, recovery culminates in Step Twelve: 'Having had a *spiritual awakening* as the result of these steps, we tried to carry this message to alcoholics, and to practice these principles in all our affairs' (AAWS, 1952, 109; my emphasis). AA regards spirituality as its 'core' principle, generating feelings of kinship with self, a Higher Power and other members of AA. Tonigan (2007) suggests that AA attendance, length of sobriety and practicing Steps Eleven and Twelve result in an increase in spirituality. Conversely, Winzelberg and Humphreys (1999) found that, regardless of 'God belief', AA attendance could not be predicted 12 months after treatment. In spite of AA's doctrine that the 'disease' of alcoholism necessitates a spiritual approach, studies have drawn no conclusive evidence that a spiritual dimension is, per se, a clearly definable mechanism of change. Murray et al (2003) assert that those members of AA with higher levels of reported beliefs in a God/ Higher Power did *not*, contrary to AA's doctrine on recovery, have better life satisfaction or greater lengths of sobriety.

To summarise, AA teaches that the drinker must hit 'rock bottom' to be motivated to engage with AA and achieve abstinence. Abstinence and a sober way of life are taught to newcomers via participation at AA meetings, whereupon a sponsor guides the individual through the Twelve Step Programme. Once immersed in AA's therapeutic practices, pre-existing behavioural, emotional and psychological problems are ameliorated as the individual progresses in AA. Overall, success for AA participants is summed up as the experience of a 'new freedom and happiness' and, in particular, relating to self-efficacy measures: 'We will intuitively know how to handle situations which used to baffle us' (AAWS, 2001, 83, 84).

## Building the acute ideal type model

> Under the lash of alcoholism, we are driven to AA...and there we discover the fatal nature of our situation. (AAWS, 1952, 24)

This chapter aims to connect AA's therapeutic mechanisms to a model of change. My study illuminates how engagement with AA has shaped abstinence. To do this, I developed a theoretical model from academic and AA literature which was tested and revised using data from interviews conducted with 20 long-term abstinent members of AA. The overall goal, here was to develop a model of behaviour change to inform a clearer understanding of AA and draw out the effects of membership of AA.

The model of behavioural change that is developed and described, guides my analysis, helping to articulate the main arguments and informing the discussion. Figure 9.1 distils the main concepts associated with AA's philosophy and therapeutic practices of change, situating these within other academic perspectives on behaviour change.

**Figure 9.1:** Ideal model of change.

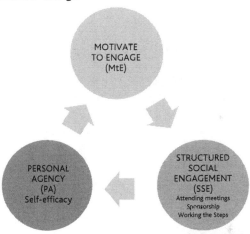

Each basic component of the model has a theoretical underpinning and here the provision of empirical evidence demonstrates how engagement with AA supports this basic model.

## Motivation to engage (MtE)

Polcin and Weisner (1999) argue that pressure from family and friends to enter treatment did not feature highly as a motivating factor in their study. The narratives of the recovering alcoholics interviewed for my research did, however, suggest that pressure from family and friends had a strong influence in the decision to seek help. For example, Mary's drinking and the subsequent breakdown of her marriage and problematic relationship with her children resulted in her husband threatening to involve social services.

> [Ex-husband] *was going to phone social services and going to have the kids taken off me.* [Mary, early 40s, 14 years of continuous sobriety]

Motivation and agency lie at the heart of all discourse of purposive action. High motivation to change predicts better outcomes among AA members: coerced samples tend to fare worse, and studies using quantitative methods which approximate randomised control trials demonstrate poor outcomes. Tonigan (2008) reflects Ditman et al's (1967) frequently cited study that 'proves' AA is ineffectual among individuals forced to attend AA under threat of legal sanction. We still need to 'unpack' and illuminate how an individual moves from a coerced state to become motivated to stay sober and continue involvement in AA's structured social engagement.

## Structured social engagement (SSE)

During the first 90 days of recovery 75 per cent of AA members acquire a sponsor (AAWS, 2015). One of the key predictors of maintaining abstinence has been the role of sponsorship in AA (Tonigan and Rice, 2010). Sponsorship allows a new member to anchor their unstable and negative experience in a person who has knowledge and experience in staying sober and, moreover, is familiar with recovery and the Twelve Steps (Denzin, 1987). Being a sponsor marks a person out in AA as one who can be trusted to give good advice and to guide a sponsee through the principles set out in the Twelve Steps.

> I think...if you asked me what, what's the biggest influence in your recovery that's helped you to stay sober it's sponsoring. It's sponsorship because every time, every time I sit down with someone to do some Step work, um, I, I'm, I'm, I'm going through it myself, I'm reaffirming it myself...It's a recommitment, it's a reaffirmation for myself to what it means to be able to work this Step...and, and that's been the key for me and that's not been easy and I didn't actually start seriously sponsoring people 'til I was six or seven years sober. [Elaine, mid-50s, 20 years of continuous sobriety]

Elaine's experience reflects the positive benefits of sponsoring people in AA, and how that continues to have an impact on her own recovery.

Following Coleman (1988), social capital exists in the relations among members of a group. A sub-category of social capital in Coleman's formulation is human capital. This is a non-tangible 'good' that can be passed from person to person as a skill that, once acquired, may help that person achieve a goal or objective, one that is not possible individually. Through participation in AA's various forms of SSE, social capital is accessed at AA meetings. There, an individual finds a sponsor, a trust-dependent relationship in which human capital facilitates productive and positive activity: time spent with a sponsor supports the mutual goal of abstinence. Membership of AA may also perform other functions which, although not explicitly therapeutic, may also help an individual's circumstances.

## Personal agency (PA)

Bandura's (1977; 2003) concept of self-efficacy explains how individuals develop strategies to avoid relapse and pursue hitherto unobtainable socially approved goals. The goals and strategies employed to manage alcohol are different to the long-term changes in attitudes towards alcohol. In early recovery AA members are taught strategies of avoidance, whereas many members of AA with long-term sobriety keep alcohol in their homes for social occasions.

Loz summarises a range of strategies used to manage social contexts in early recovery where alcohol is present.

> *When I was first around* [AA slang for being a newcomer], *I just used to avoid most parties and stuff like that. When I couldn't avoid 'em, I'd arrange to, say, phone my sponsor an hour into the party or whatever it was. One time, at my cousin's wedding, about three months in* [three months sober in AA] *I phoned him* [sponsor] *and just talked through how I was feeling. I was just fucking bored really, speeches went on for ages and I was starving. Guess it was the old hungry, angry, lonely, tired thing kicking in. Or have the excuse that I was driving, on antibiotics, owt like that really. When I did have to carry a drink, I'd try and remember to carry it in my left hand, just so I wouldn't accidently, you know, without thinking, take a drink of it, always drank from me right hand see.* [Loz, mid-30s, eight years of continuous sobriety]

Loz refers to another of the AA's slogans that teach a person to become a more reflexive agent. New members are taught to be mindful of feeling hungry, angry, lonely and tired. Loz realised he was getting annoyed/angry at the length of speeches, hungry and lonely, that is, he felt the need to speak to another recovering alcoholic [his sponsor] with more experience at dealing with situations such as weddings. It is understood that any of these physiological and psychological states puts an individual at higher risk of relapse (Marlatt and Donovan, 2005).

The model illustrated in Figure 9.1 represents an 'ideal type' – an acute and simplistic conceptualisation of behaviour change experienced by members of AA. To develop this model further, a temporal dimension must be added that illustrates how sustaining abstinence is achieved (see Figure 9.2). What is important for testing the mediating effects of AA is that the model includes moderators which represents how the individual experiences and copes with stressful life events that threaten disengagement from AA.

**Figure 9.2:** Hypothetical temporal model of change.

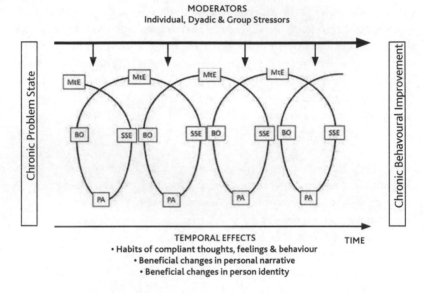

## Hypothetical model of AA-mediated behavioural change: temporal components

This model (Figure 9.2) provided a 'tool' to test, deductively, my findings. The model here functions to illustrate the moderators – individual, dyadic and groups stressors. These can be described as situations and contexts which may threaten disengagement from AA. Maintaining abstinence is dependent on the strength of AA's mediating effects and activities. So, the level or magnitude of the moderators (threats) is mediated by the relative strength of understanding and commitment to AA's therapeutic practices evidenced in the narrative accounts, with examples used to show commitment to MtE, SSE and PA. The mediators explain the relationship, how engagement with

MtE, for example, mediates the negative or moderating effects of the stressors; thus the individual either maintains sobriety or 'spins off' the helix and risks relapse.

As time in AA and maintaining abstinence accumulates, the individual 'travels' towards 'chronic behavioural improvement'. Positive behaviour change is 'captured' and evidenced in the component 'behavioural outcomes' (BO): as a result of engagement with AA, the individual 'stays on' rather than being 'pushed off', the helix. Conceptually, recovery is understood as an elongated process, as participants in my research had between five and thirty years of continuous abstinence, which is why the ideal model in its second iteration resembles a helix. The helix helps to explain how threats to disengage from AA's therapeutic practices are experienced and managed over time.

The 'temporal effects' of long-term engagement with AA have been derived from a careful study of AA theraputic mechanisms of change – participation in AA targets thoughts, feelings and behaviour. Specifically, commitment to attending AA meetings, working with a sponsor and 'practising' AA's Twelve Steps result in a change in personal narrative and identity exchange – the substitution of an identity as a 'drinking alcoholic' for one of a sober alcoholic.

There are, however, threats to an individual which emanate from within AA. These are salient findings which shed further light on the functioning of the organisation. This section illustrates one of the negative consequences – or perceived negative consequences – the limitations of sponsorship.

Suicide attempts featured in the narratives of three participants. In this example, Elaine provides a moving account of a sponsee who committed suicide, having been sober for ten years and a frequent attender at AA meetings. This demonstrates how Elaine copes with the moderating effects of the sense of loss and how engagement with AA mediates the worst effects – put simply, the strategies used to stay sober.

> *Well, I failed ultimately this year. [XXXX], she, she took her own life...Sponsored her for ten years. I didn't know her level of suffering. How could I? Um, [pause] did I fail as a sponsor? Not for me to judge. Ultimately, yeah, but how responsible am I for that? That's, that's a terrible question that I've been tormenting myself with. But, she believed, Jamie, and I know this very well, she believed in the Twelve Steps. She knew it could change her life and she didn't pick a drink up, even to commit suicide, not with drink...She knew what was possible but she knew what the programme could do for, to people's lives and, my god, did she*

*try. But, her mental health destroyed her...I don't know, I mean, I regret some things and I don't regret some others that perhaps I should but, [pause] the only way I can sponsor is taking no, taking no credit for someone who doesn't drink and taking no responsibility when someone picks up* [AA slang for drinking]...*I'll take no credit for you staying sober, however long it is, and I'll take no responsibility for if you pick up. Um, you know, there's no credit to anyone's life really other than that she didn't drink for ten years and I can't be responsible for her getting to the stage mentally where she couldn't, she couldn't hack it.* [Elaine, mid-50s, 20 years of continuous sobriety].

Elaine takes psychological 'refuge' in the principles of AA, learned as a result of long-term engagement. Elaine, thus manages a proportion of guilt and emotional pain she feels at the tragic loss of a sponsee. Elaine frames the account using the three following devices learned in AA:

1. AA works – the suicide knew of the transformative effects of AA, and, 'importantly', she died sober;
2. AA or sponsors cannot 'solve' all problems – some severe and enduring mental health difficulties are beyond AA's curative effects. This is a reference to the book *Alcoholics Anonymous* (AAWS, 2001, 58), which regards the chances of those 'who suffer grave emotional and mental disorder' as having slim chances of recovery; Elaine takes little responsibility for any success or failure she may have had in the recovery of a sponsee.

This last point is a reference to Kurtz's (1979) *Not-God* thesis, which revolves around the alcoholic's struggle for control, initially over alcohol intake and then, in recovery, learning personal limitations, essentially not believing in God-like powers of control.

AA members access key resources which support an individual in a time of crisis. The overall aim here has been to shift the focus from short-term gains suggested in my original model – the 'ideal type' – to incorporate an analysis of threats to disengagement from AA, demonstrating the cognitive-behavioural coping mechanisms used. In my participants' accounts, threats were dealt with 'linguistically', in terms of internal dialogue and 'self-talk'. Reference to the AA discourse such as common recovery couplets: AA 'slogans' (Live and Let Live), and reference to AA's core texts, pepper the narratives of individuals as they make sense of, and formulate, strategic responses to threats. I coined the term 'linguistic echoes' to encapsulate the use of therapeutic phrases and references found in AA's core texts, which are used by participants as a structuring device that in essence scaffolds each person's recovery. As the accounts given are retrospective in nature, we can observe how these are 'crafted' and framed by individuals, using, in this example AA's literature and key phrases.

Further, as argued, my model changed, becoming elongated over time to resemble a helix. The purpose of this approach is both analytical and conceptual. At a conceptual level, the purpose was to 'test' the model proposed earlier – the 'ideal type' – to tease out its strengths and weaknesses. As a corollary of this analysis and approach, we can begin to observe some of the, under-researched, unintended and negative effects of long-term engagement with AA.

## Changes to the model: AA's mediating effects

Figure 9.3 shows changes made to the second version of the hypothetical model of AA-mediated behavioural change in the light of the field data. The 'book-ends' of the model reflect the trajectory of recovery for this cohort from a 'state of denial' to a 'state of recovery'. This shift reflects a significant and increased awarness of the internal as well as behavioural changes experienced, by this cohort. This analysis was an iterative process. As participants gave surprisingly frank and reflexive accounts of their inner worlds and experiences, the model incorporated these findings to better represent the complexitiy of behavioural change.

The temporal effects are now: acceptance of AA's recovery script; use of linguistic echoes; and more highly developed capacity for self-reflection and self-control. Participation in AA's therapeutic practices mediates or explains how the individual starts from a state of denial, moving towards behavioural improvement. The helix is labelled so as to demonstrate each conceptual component. The analysis accompanying these concepts, MtE, SSE and PA, has been demonstrated in the data collected from participants.

The empirical evidence and a close reading of AA's literature shows and explains how and why these effects occur. AA's therapeutic practices predict behavioural change  The temporal dimension of this model was investigated by interviewing individuals whose abstinence and membership of AA had been constant over a number of years.

Almost all interviewees described attitudes to alcohol similar to those expressed in AA's literature. The language the participants used was also strikingly similar. Jill's account of her changed attitude towards

**Figure 9.3:** AA's mediating effects

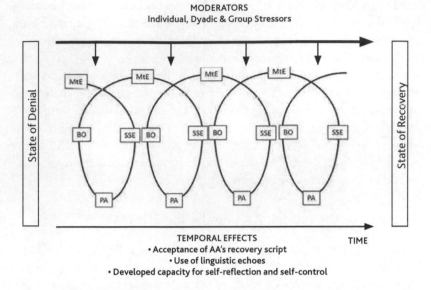

alcohol demonstrates the embeddedness of AA's discourse in terms of her relationship with alcohol,

> *I do keep alcohol in the house because I have friends who come for supper and who like to have a drink, and there's a bottle of wine in the fridge – I'm not even interested – it doesn't – I'm not afraid of alcohol. I don't think this is probably going to make sense; I'm not afraid of having alcohol in the house because, just because I don't drink it, doesn't mean that other people can't drink it. The fact that it's here doesn't pose a problem to me; my obsession and my compulsion to drink alcohol has totally gone. Whether that's a result of my having worked the steps, I don't know; whether it's the result of a spiritual awakening, I don't know, I don't need to know…the bottle of wine in the fridge that's been sitting there, that will sit there for months and will continue to sit there for months.*
> [Jill, mid-50s, 14 years of continuous sobriety]

Jill talks of the 'obsession' and 'compulsion' to drink alcohol being removed. Steps One to Four, Six, Seven and Twelve explicitly describe one of the chief characteristics of alcoholism as an 'obsession'. For example, Step One (AAWS, 1952, 24, 22) speaks of a 'mental' and 'merciless obsession for destructive drinking', and that there is, 'no such thing as the personal conquest of this compulsion'. Step Two (AAWS, 1952, 32) teaches that, 'God could enter us and expel the obsession' and Step Twelve (AAWS, 1952, 107), 'we were unable to be rid of the alcohol obsession'. There are 19 instances in AA's core texts – the *Big book* (2001) and the *Twelve steps and twelve traditions* (AAWS, 1952) – of alcohol and the solution to the problem of alcoholism being described as an 'obsession'.

Further, Jane explains how, cognitively, self-regulation is bound closely with AA's therapeutic discourse.

> *There are normal drinkers out there who can drink alcohol and there's me who can't and I'm quite happy to sit with a mineral water or an orange juice and watch other people drink. It doesn't bother me. It, it's really a non-event because what other people drink is none of my business and I don't have an envious relationship with that. I'm not even particularly conscious of what people are drinking most of the time. What matters is what I'm drinking and the reason for being in the pub in the first place, which for me, it's a social thing...Um, if I was going because I thought that I might get a vicarious thrill by being around people who were drinking a lot of booze then I'd start worrying there'd be something going on with me.* [Jane, 21 years of continuous sobriety]

First, Jane demonstrates the necessity to separate herself from the 'normal drinker', establishing herself as someone who simply 'can't' drink alcohol. Second, Jane offers an almost exact replication of the behavioural outcomes, in terms of socialising with friends in places where alcohol is served, as found in the book *Alcoholics Anonymous*:

> So our rule is not to avoid a place where there is drinking, *if we have a legitimate reason for being there*...Therefore, ask yourself on each occasion, 'Have I any good social, business, or personal reason for going to this place? Or am I expecting to steal a little *vicarious* pleasure from the atmosphere.' (AAWS, 2001, 101, emphasis in original)

The chief aim of this section has been to 'weave' together, and illustrate how the temporal effects of long-term participation in AA, the use of 'linguistic echoes' and self-regulation, affect behavioural outcomes (BO). From the analysis of the data, it became apparent that each of the participants narrated a more nuanced and sophisticated understanding of themselves and their identity as a sober alcoholic in AA, and that they demonstrated a marked shift towards positive behaviour.

## Discussion

The overall trajectory of behavioural change points towards positive outcomes, specifically abstinence. This chapter offers a model of how an individual is motivated to maintain sobriety while employing AA and its therapeutic practices as a structure of support. Alcoholism is readily understood to be a chronic and re-occurring problem state, often spanning many years (Dennis et al, 2008). Likewise, recovery is seldom achieved via acute, short-term interventions. Rather, achieving recovery is a process that similarly lends itself to chronicity – stable recovery is estimated to take five years (Betty Ford, 2007; Best et al, 2010).

Thematically, mastering techniques of self-control have been at the heart of the analysis. Individuals interviewed for this study used key expressions or linguistic devices found in the AA literature when narrating their life stories and experiences. AA has a mediating effect by exposing the individual to a recovery script. The vehicle for embedding the recovery script is the 'linguistic echoes', the therapeutic expressions learned via participation in AA.

These 'linguistic echoes' recurred in the respondents' transcripts with extraordinary ubiquity. Where possible, these examples were made by italicising key words and phrases. This represents another new finding, and an interesting addition to Borkman's (1976) analysis of shared experience, conveyed in mutual-help groups as 'experiential knowledge'. The argument made supports Borkman's (1976, 446) notion that this form of knowledge is acquired following direct experience with alcoholism. This knowledge represents a therapeutic 'source of truth' for recovering alcoholics to be shared. This source of information is validated by a collective experience representing broad, shared themes that characterise the shared problem. Marked similarities between my participants' narratives and phrases identified in AA's texts demonstrated how they structured their understanding of themselves in relation to alcoholism. These were the 'linguistic echoes' used as a support resource.

These findings add to the emerging work being carried out on recovery practices for those persons suffering from drug and alcohol addiction. Best et al (2015) argue that identity change is realised in AA through a process that is socially negotiated for example, participation with AA's opportunities for SSE. Further, AA mediates the recovery 'journey' through social learning – attending AA meetings, sponsorship and reading AA's literatures which expose the individual to a therapeutic language, thus helping the AA member's recovery within AA's framework and overall philosophy.

Assessing the literature on social identity and recovery, Buckingham et al (2013) find that participation in AA usurps a previous 'addict' identity, replacing this with a strong sober identity that supports recovery. Moos (2007) identified key factors associated with maintaining recovery, including the ability to learn techniques of recovery from peers (sponsors), via meaningful shared activities. Group membership furnishes AA members with a robust social identity, further consolidated by the use of 'linguistic echoes'. This phenomena or behavioural outcome can be further understood as a 'warrant' of knowledge, which demonstrates a deep level involvement as the individual makes the transition to regular participation in a group that is pro-abstinent. Frequent contact with recovery or pro-abstinent goal orientated groups exposes the individual to recovery values and norms of 'sober' social practice. These shape values and expectations that strongly predict abstinence (Best et al, 2008a; 2013). Thus, membership of AA provides a common shared sense of identity that connects the overall aims of the group to individual expectations and hopes, becoming 'one of us' (Haslam et al, 2005; Jetten et al, 2014).

Lastly, and tentatively, recent work by Rowe and Soppitt (2014) assesses the malleability and variability of client motivation in offender oriented desistance programmes. Focusing on the effects of two interventions, Rowe outlines two pertinent points. First, motivation to desist was directly related to problematic alcohol consumption, in two cases 'it's mostly drink, I need to get off the drink' (Rowe, 2014, 403). Second, clients reported that trust was a prerequisite to building relationships necessary to support desistance, 'meaningful and sustained relationships of trust' and 'assisting and befriending' (Rowe, 2014, 408). AA's primary purpose is to promote abstinence and help other alcoholics in their efforts to gain sobriety. AA's mechanisms and goals are analogous with those outlined in Rowe's findings.

Increasingly, the literature on desistance is exploring and comparing desistance and recovery models. LeBel et al (2015) assess the role of the 'wounded healer' or 'professional-ex' that formerly incarcerated persons play in the desistance process – more specifically helping others to desist. The wounded healer role in AA supports the goal of abstinence by, 'sharing experience, strength and hope' (LeBel, 2015, 110) and helping new members work through the Twelve Steps (AAWS, 1952). The added value a wounded healer brings to the therapeutic alliance forged in AA between the sponsor and sponsee in AA, as Humphreys (2014, 15, cited in Lebel et al, 2015, 110), argues is through 'having been there too'. From a 'generativity' perspective (McAdams and St Aubin, 1992, 1003), sponsors are helping 'the next generation' through supporting others to achieve and maintain abstinence, ensuring that, 'When anyone, anywhere, reaches out for help, I want the hand of AA always to be there' (AAWS, 1965).

Zemore and colleagues (2004, 1023), found that sustained engagement with the sponsor/sponsee relationship, while being a protective factor for both the sponsor and sponsee against a return to drinking, may also 'strengthen group bonding' – producing a clear generative effect. What is clear is that desistance research has looked – and continues to look – to the field of recovery literature and the longer more established empirical work on Alcoholics Anonymous, drawing from this rich source, for concepts and theories that shed further light on mechanisms that support desistance. Interestingly, the account given by Elaine draws our attention to the fact that, while in general, generative actions and the outcomes thereof are positive – the tacit assumption in the work of Maruna (2001; Maruna et al, 2009; LeBel et al, 2015) – undertaking generative-sponsorship work may have negative consequences.

Recently, research(ers), are beginning to sketch the conceptual fit between recovery from addiction and desistance from offending, but have refrained from concluding any casual direction that one shift in behaviour may have on another. Coleman and Vander Laenen (2012, 3), in their study of desisting drug users, explicitly state that 'respondents consider their desistance from offending to be subordinate to their drug use desistance'. Desistance occurs as an unconscious effect of a drug-free lifestyle. Coleman and Vander Laenen's (2012, 6) work suggests that a key difference between recovery and desistance may be, 'the final goal of change', a subjective change, whereby one 'experiences' recovery. Marsh's (2011) study suggests that subjectively experienced change precedes structural opportunities (employment, for example), supporting the construction of a new prosocial identity (see also, LeBel et al, 2008). Marsh (2011) interrogates the core elements of AA's 'Twelve Step script' (which I call AA's 'recovery script'), in an effort to draw out the overlaps and commonalities with Maruna (2001) and Vaughan's (2007; 2011) desistance narrative approach. Marsh found that offenders' perspectives on past harms are augmented by moral reflection, likewise Vaughan (2007) specified that a moral assessment allows would-be desisters to shape their present and future identities, thus supporting efforts to cease offending. The process described earlier in Step Four (AAWS, 1952), often termed a 'moral inventory', gives clear guidance on just how one may reflect on, and make restitution for past wrongdoing, but with the aid of a sponsor, rather than undertaking a potentially, emotionally treacherous activity alone.

In addition, Maruna et al (2004, 273) examines the effects of labelling and de-labelling on identity, noting that rehabilitation is highly related to the notion of recovery in the field of addiction treatment. Laudet and Best (2010) assess the predictors of long-term desistance that Laub and Sampson (2003) identify, finding common change factors associated with the recovery process, such as transformation of personal identity, inter-personal, life and coping skills. In sum, both desistance and recovery models of change emphasise a commitment to developing prosocial values and beliefs.

## Conclusion

A review of literature on AA identified three concepts key to understanding participation in AA: motivation to engage (MtE), structured social engagement (SSE) and personal agency (PA), resulting in desired behavioural outcomes (BO). From these I constructed a hypothetical model of AA-mediated behavioural change, constituted by these elements. Findings from 20 in-depth qualitative interviews, conducted with long-term abstinent members of AA supported this model. As all the respondents were sober for many years, it became necessary to draw this model out over time, to demonstrate the temporal effects. Visually, this became an elongated 'helix' representing their recovery journey in AA.

Analysis of interview data revealed the coping strategies that these members employed to ensure engagement with AA during stressful life events that threatened abstinence, or spinning off the 'helix'. Changes to the hypothetical model following data analysis, represent an original development in the study of AA and its therapeutic mechanisms. The model identifies the mechanisms of change, locates these within the context of AA and demonstrates how change is subjectively experienced. In addition, this model underscores the need to re-conceptualise the notion that recovery from alcohol and drug use is chronic in nature – recovery takes time. Learning how one lives a sober lifestyle is predicated, in AA, upon the support of peers. AA members use key expression learned from participation at AA meetings and from reading AA's core texts – I have called these expressions 'linguistic echoes'.

Of import, here is a working model that identifies how external factors, pressures to change and therapeutic activities are subjectively understood and experienced. In addition, examination of AA's Twelve Step recovery technology and the interpretation of this technology by my participants give clear insights into the cognitive understanding and changes that each individual undergoes to maintain sobriety and sustain long-term behavioural change. The accounts provided here illustrate the experience of membership of AA; but this is not an all-encompassing explanation or model that stretches to revealing behaviour change in other Twelve Step organisations. Furthermore, while members of this study may well have engineered and incorporated the identity of a recovering alcoholic, and limited the stigmatising effects of their drinking through long-term abstinence and membership of AA, more work needs to be carried out to assess AA's capacity to support the desistance process – as a group, AA members have made merry, made bad, made sense, and finally made good, for over eight decades – AA still has much to teach us.

## References

AAWS (Alcoholics Anonymous World Services), 1952, *Twelve steps and twelve traditions*, New York: AAWS

AAWS (Alcoholics Anonymous World Services), 1965, *Responsibility statement*, AA International Convention in Toronto

AAWS (Alcoholics Anonymous World Services), 1967, *As Bill sees it: The A.A. way of life...selected writings of A.A.'s co-founder*, New York, NY: AAWS

AAWS (Alcoholics Anonymous World Services), 2001, *Alcoholics Anonymous: The story of how many thousands of men and women have recovered from alcoholism* (4th edn), New York: AAWS

AAWS (Alcoholics Anonymous World Services), 2005, *Questions and answers on sponsorship*, New York: AAWS, www.aa.org/assets/en_US/p-15_Q&AonSpon.pdf

AAWS (Alcoholics Anonymous World Services), 2015, Alcoholics Anonymous 2015 Membership Survey, http://www.alcoholics-anonymous.org.uk/download/1/Library/Documents/2015%20Survey/2015%20Survey%20Pamphlet.pdf

Ajzen, I, 1991, The theory of planned behavior, *Organizational Behavior and Human Decision Processes*, 50, 179–211

Allen, HA, Peterson, JS, Whipple, S, 1981, Loneliness and alcoholism: A study of three groups of male alcoholics, *The International Journal of the Addictions* 16, 7, 1255–8

Anderson, JG, Gilbert, FS, 1989, Communication skills training with alcoholics for improving performance of two of the Alcoholics Anonymous recovery steps, *Journal of Studies on Alcohol* 50, 4, 361–7

Arminen, I, 1996, The construction of topic in the turns of talk at the meetings of Alcoholics Anonymous, *International Journal of Sociology and Social Policy* 16, 5/6, 88–130

Arminen, I, 1998, Sharing experiences, *The Sociological Quarterly* 39, 3, 491–515

Arminen, I, 2001, Closing of turns in the meetings of Alcoholics Anonymous: Members' methods for closing 'sharing experiences', *Research on Language and Social Interaction* 34, 2, 211–51

Arminen, I, 2004, Second stories: The salience of interpersonal communication for mutual help in Alcoholics Anonymous, *Journal of Pragmatics* 36, 2, 319-347

Armitage, CJ, 2009, Is there utility in the transtheoretical model?, *British Journal of Health Psychology* 14, 2, 195–210

Armitage, CJ, Conner, M, 2000, Social cognition models and health behaviour: A structured review, *Psychology and health* 15, 2 , 173-189

Armitage, CJ, Povey, R, Arden, MA, 2003, Evidence for discontinuity patterns across the stages of change: A role for attitudinal ambivalence, *Psychology and Health* 18, 3, 373–86

Bandura, A, 1977, Self-efficacy: Toward a unifying theory of behavioral change, *Psychological Review* 84, 2, 191

Bandura, A, Locke, EA, 2003, Negative self-efficacy and goal effects revisited, *Journal Of Applied Psychology* 88, 1, 87–99

Best, D, Laudet, A, 2010, *The potential of recovery capital*, London: RSA

Best, D, Lubman, D, 2012, The recovery paradigm: A model of hope and change for alcohol and drug addiction, *Australian Family Physician* 41, 593–7

Best, D, Day, E, Homayoun, S, Lenton, H, Moverley, R, Openshaw, M, 2008a, Treatment retention in the Drug Intervention Programme: Do primary drug users fare better than primary offenders?, *Drugs: education, prevention and policy* 15, 2, 201-209

Best, D, Ghufran, S, Day, E, Ray, R, Loaring, J, 2008b, Breaking the habit: A retrospective analysis of desistance factors among formerly problematic heroin users, *Drug and Alcohol Review* 27, 6, 619–24

Best, D, Bamber, S, Battersby, A, Gilman, M, Groshkova, T, Honor, S, McCartney, D, Yates, R, White, W, 2010, Recovery and straw men: An analysis of the objections raised to the transition to a recovery model in UK addiction services, *Journal of Groups in Addiction & Recovery* 5, 3-4, 264-288

Best, D, Loudon, L, Powell, D, Groshkova, T, White, W, 2013, Identifying and recruiting recovery champions: Exploratory action research in Barnsley, South Yorkshire, *Journal of Groups in Addiction & Recovery* 8, 3, 169-184

Best, D, Beckwith, M, Haslam, C, Haslam, A, Jetten, J, Mawson, E, Lubman, D, 2015, Overcoming alcohol and other drug addiction as a process of social identity transition: The social identity model of recovery (SIMOR), *Addiction Research and Theory*, early online, doi: org/10.3109/16066359.2015.1075980

Betty Ford Institute Consensus Panel, 2007, What is recovery? A working definition from the Betty Ford Institute, *Journal of Substance Abuse Treatment* 33, 221–8

Blocker, JS, Fahey, DM, Tyrrell, IR, 2003, *Alcohol and temperance in modern history: An international perspective*, Volume 1, Santa Barbara, CA: ABC-Clio

Borkman, T, 1976, Experiential knowledge: A new concept for the analysis of self-help groups, *Social Service Review* 50, 3, 445–56

Borkman, T, 2006, Sharing experience, conveying hope: Egalitarian relations as the essential method of Alcoholics Anonymous, *Nonprofit Management and Leadership* 17, 2, 145–61

Borkman, T, 2008, The twelve-step recovery model of AA: A voluntary mutual help association, *Recent Developments in Alcoholism* 18, 9–35

Buckingham, S, Frings, D, Albery, I, 2013, Group membership and social identity in addiction recovery, *Psychology of Addictive Behaviors* 27, 4, 1132–40, doi: 10.1037/a0032480

Cahill, K, Lancaster, T, Green, N, 2010, Stage-based interventions for smoking cessation, Cochrane Tobacco Addiction Group, *Cochrane Database of Systematic Reviews*, 11, doi: 10.1002/14651858. CD004492.pub4

Cain, C, 1991, Personal stories: Acquisition and self-understanding in Alcoholics Anonymous, *Ethos* 19, 2, 210–53

Callaghan, RC, Taylor, L, Cunningham, JA, 2007, Does progressive stage transition mean getting better? A test of the transtheoretical model in alcoholism recovery, *Addiction* 102, 10, 1588–96

Chappel, JN, 1994, Working a program of recovery in Alcoholics Anonymous, *Journal of Substance Abuse Treatment* 11, 2, 99–104

Cloud, W, Granfield, R, 2008, Conceptualizing recovery capital: Expansion of a theoretical construct, *Substance Use and Misuse* 43, 12–13, 1971–86

Coleman, JS, 1988, Social capital in the creation of human capital, *American Journal of Sociology* 94, S95–S120

Colman, C, Vander Laenen, F, 2012, 'Recovery came first': Desistance versus recovery in the criminal careers of drug-using offenders, *The Scientific World Journal*, www.hindawi.com/journals/tswj/2012/657671/

Davidson, R, 2002, The Oxford Group and Alcoholics Anonymous, *Journal of Substance Use* 7, 3–5

Dennis, M, Foss, M, Scott, C, 2008, An 8-year perspective on the relationship between the duration of abstinence and other aspects of recovery, *Evaluation Research* 31, 585–612

Denzin, NK, 1987, *Treating alcoholism: An Alcoholics Anonymous approach*, Newbury Park, CA: Sage

Ditman, KS, Crawford, GG, Forgy, EW, Moskowitz, H, MacAndrew, C, 1967, A controlled experiment on the use of court probation for drunk arrests, *American Journal of Psychiatry* 124, 160–3

Donovan, ME, 1984, A sociological analysis of commitment generation in Alcoholics Anonymous, *British Journal of Addiction* 79, 4, 411–8

Emrick, CD, Tonigan, JS, Montgomery, H, Little, L, 1993, Alcoholics Anonymous: What is currently known?, in F Barbara, S McCrady, E William, R Miller (eds) *Research on Alcoholics Anonymous: Opportunities and alternatives*, pp 41–76, New Brunswick, NJ: Publications Division, Rutgers Center of Alcohol Studies

Farrall, S, Calverly, A, 2006, *Understanding desistance from crime*, Buckingham: Open University Press

Gossop, M, Harris, J, Best, D, Man, L-H, Manning, V, Marshall, J, Strang, J, 2003, Is attendance at Alcoholics Anonymous meetings after inpatient treatment related to improved outcomes? A 6-month follow-up study, *Alcohol and Alcoholism* 38, 5, 421–6

Groh, DR, Jason, LA, Keys, CB, 2008, Social network variables in Alcoholics Anonymous: A literature review, *Clinical Psychology Review* 28, 3, 430–50

Haslam, SA, O'Brien, A, Jetten, J, Vormedal, K, Penna, S, 2005, Taking the strain: Social identity, social support and the experience of stress, *British Journal of Social Psychology* 44, 355–70

Humphreys, K, 2004, *Circles of recovery: Self-help organisations for addictions*, Cambridge, UK: Cambridge University Press

Humphreys, K, 2015, Addiction professionals are not the gatekeepers of recovery, *Substance Use and Misuse* 50, 8–9, 1024–7, doi: 10.3109/10826084.2015.1007678

Janis IL, Mann L, 1977, *Decision making: A psychological analysis of conflict, choice, and commitment*, New York: Free Press

Jetten, J, Haslam, C, Haslam, SA, Dingle, G, Jones, JM, 2014, How groups affect our health and well-being: The path from theory to policy, *Social Issues and Policy Review* 8, 103–30

Jin, H, Rourke, SB, Patterson, TL, Taylor, MJ, Grant, I, 1998, Predictors of relapse in long-term abstinent alcoholics, *Journal of Studies on Alcohol and Drugs* 59, 6, 640–6

Kelly, JF, McCrady, BS, 2008, Twelve-step facilitation in non-specialty settings, *Recent Developments in Alcoholism* 18, 321–46

Kelly, JF, Magill, M, Stout, RL, 2009, How do people recover from alcohol dependence? A systematic review of the research on mechanisms of behaviour change, *Alcoholics Anonymous. Addiction Research & Theory* 17, 3, 236–259

Kownacki, R, Shadish, W, 1999, Does Alcoholics Anonymous work? The results from a meta-analysis of controlled experiments, *Substance Use and Misuse* 34, 13, 1897–916

Kraft, P, Sutton, SR, Reynolds, HM, 1999, The transtheoretical model of behaviour change: Are the stages qualitatively different?, *Psychology and Health* 14, 3, 433–50

Kurtz, E, 1979, *Not-God: A history of Alcoholics Anonymous*, San Francisco, CA: Hazledon Foundation

Laub, JH, Sampson, RJ, 2003, *Shared beginnings, divergent lives: Delinquent Boys to age 70*, Cambridge, MA: Harvard University Press

LeBel, TP, Burnett, R, Maruna, S, Bushway, S, 2008, The 'chicken and egg' of subjective and social factors in desistance from crime, *European Journal of Criminology* 5, 2, 130–58

LeBel, TP, Richie, M, Maruna, S, 2015, *Criminal Justice and Behaviour* 42, 1, 108–20

McAdams, DP, De St Aubin, E, 1992, A theory of generativity and its assessment through self-report, behavioral acts, and narrative themes in autobiography, *Journal of Personality and Social Psychology* 62, 6, 1003

McCrady, BS, Miller, WR, 1993, *Research on Alcoholics Anonymous: Opportunities and alternatives*, Piscataway, NJ: Rutgers Center of Alcohol Studies

Mäkelä, K (ed), 1996, *Alcoholics Anonymous as a mutual-help movement: A study in eight societies*, Madison, WI: University of Wisconsin Press

Marlatt, AG, Donovan, DM, 2005, *Relapse prevention: Maintenance strategies in the treatment of addictive behaviour*, New York: Guilford Publications

Marsh, B, 2011, Narrating desistance: Identity change and the 12-step script, *Irish Probation Journal* 8, 49–68

Maruna, S, 2001, *Making good: How ex-convicts reform and rebuild their lives*, Washington, DC: American Psychological Association

Maruna, S, LeBel, TP, Mitchell, N, Naples, M, 2004, Pygmalion in the reintegration process: Desistance from crime through the looking glass, *Psychology, Crime and Law* 10, 3, 271–81

Migneault, JP, Adams, TB, Read, JP, 2005, Application of the transtheoretical model to substance abuse: Historical development and future directions, *Drug and Alcohol Review* 24, 5, 437–48

Moos, RH, 2007, Theory-based active ingredients of effective treatments for substance use disorders, *Drug and Alcohol Dependence* 88, 2–3, 109–21

Morgenstern, J, McKay, JR, 2007, Rethinking the paradigms that inform behavioral treatment research for substance use disorders *Addiction* 102, 9, 1377–89

Murray, TS, Malcarne, VL, Goggin, K, 2003, Alcohol-related god/higher power control beliefs, locus of control, and recovery within the Alcoholics Anonymous paradigm, *Alcoholism Treatment Quarterly* 21, 3, 23–39

Ogborne, AC, Bornet, A, 1982, Brief report: Abstinence and abusive drinking among affiliates of Alcoholics Anonymous: Are these the only alternatives?, *Addictive Behaviors* 7, 2, 199–202

Pagano, ME, Friend, KB, Tonigan, JS, Stout, RL, 2004, Helping other alcoholics in Alcoholics Anonymous and drinking outcomes: Findings from Project MATCH, *Journal of Studies on Alcohol* 65, 6, 766–73

Pagano, ME, Post, SG, Johnson, SM, 2010, Alcoholics Anonymous-related helping and the helper therapy principle, *Alcoholism Treatment Quarterly* 29, 1, 23–34

Polcin, DL, Weisner, C, 1999, Factors associated with coercion in entering treatment for alcohol problems, *Drug and Alcohol Dependence* 54,1, 63–8

Prochaska, JO, Di Clemente, CC, 1984, *The transtheoretical approach: Crossing the traditional boundaries of change*, Homewood, IL: J Irwin

Prochaska, JO, DiClemente, CC, Norcross, JC, 1992, In search of how people change: Applications to addictive behaviors, *The American Psychologist* 47, 9, 1102–14

Project MATCH Research Group, 1993, Matching Alcoholism Treatment to Client Heterogeneity: Rationale and methods for a multisite clinical trial matching patients to alcoholism treatment, *Alcoholism: Clinical and Experimental Research* 17, 6, 1130–45

Project MATCH Research Group, 1998, Matching alcoholism treatments to client heterogeneity: Treatment main effects and matching effects on drinking during treatment, *Journal of Studies on Alcohol and Drugs* 59, 6, 631–39

Riessman, F, 1965, The 'helper-therapy' principle, *Social Work* 10, 24–32

Roberts, N, 1988, *Getting better: Inside Alcoholics Anonymous*, New York: William Morrow

Room, R, 1989, Alcoholism and Alcoholics Anonymous in US films, 1945–1962: The party ends for the 'wet generations', *Journal of Studies on Alcohol and Drugs* 50, 4, 368

Rowe, M, Soppitt, S, 2014, 'Who you gonna call?' The role of trust and relationships in desistance from crime, *Probation Journal* 61, 4, 397–412

Roy, A, Linnoila, M, 1986, Alcoholism and suicide, *Suicide and Life-threatening Behavior* 16, 2, 244–73

Rudy, DR, 1980, Slipping and sobriety: The functions of drinking in Alcoholics Anonymous, *Journal of Studies on Alcohol and Drugs* 41, 7, 727

Seddon, T, 2007, Coerced drug treatment in the criminal justice system: Conceptual, ethical and criminological issues, *Criminology and Criminal Justice* 7, 3, 269–86

Sheeren, M, 1988, The relationship between relapse and involvement in Alcoholics Anonymous, *Journal of Studies on Alcohol* 49, 1, 104–6

Smith, AR, 2007, *The social world of Alcoholics Anonymous: How it works*, Lincoln, NE: iUniverse

Sommer, SM, 1997, The experience of long-term recovering alcoholics in Alcoholics Anonymous: Perspectives on therapy, *Alcoholism Treatment Quarterly* 15, 1, 75–80

Strobbe, S, 2009, *Alcoholics Anonymous: Personal stories, relatedness, attendance and affiliation*, Doctoral dissertation, Ann Arbor, MI : University of Michigan

Swora, MG, 2001, Personhood and disease in Alcoholics Anonymous: A perspective from the anthropology of religious healing, *Mental Health, Religion and Culture* 4, 1, 1–21

Swora, MG, 2004, The rhetoric of transformation in the healing of alcoholism: The twelve steps of Alcoholics Anonymous, *Mental Health, Religion and Culture* 7, 3, 187–209

Tiebout, HM, 1945, *The act of surrender in the therapeutic process*, New York: National Council on Alcoholism

Tonigan, JS, 2008, Alcoholics Anonymous outcomes and benefits, *Recent Developments in Alcoholism* 18, 357–72

Tonigan, JS, Rice, SL, 2010, Is it beneficial to have an Alcoholics Anonymous sponsor?, *Psychology of Addictive Behaviors* 24, 3, 397

Tonigan, JS, Toscova, R, Miller, WR, 1996, Meta-analysis of the literature on Alcoholics Anonymous: Sample and study characteristics moderate findings, *Journal of Studies on Alcohol* 57, 1, 65–72

UK Drug Policy Commission, 2008, *The UK Drug Policy Commission recovery consensus group: A vision of recovery*, London: UK Drug Policy Commission

Valverde, M, 1998, *Diseases of the will*, New York: Cambridge University Press

Valverde, M, White-Mair, K, 1999, 'One day at a time' and other slogans for everyday life: The ethical practices of Alcoholics Anonymous, *Sociology* 33, 2, 393–410

Vaillant, GE, 2003, A 60-year follow-up of alcoholic men, *Addiction* 98, 8, 1043–51

Vaillant, GE, 2005, Alcoholics Anonymous: Cult or cure?, *The Australian and New Zealand Journal of Psychiatry* 39, 6, 431–6

Vaughan, B, 2007, The internal narrative of desistance, *British Journal of Criminology* 47, 390–404

Vaughan, B, 2011, Subjectivity, narration and desistance [Subjectivité, récit et abandon de la délinquance], in M Mohammed (ed) *Sortir de la délinquance: Théories, enquêtes, perspectives internationals*, Paris: La Decouverte

Velicer, WF, DiClemente, CC, Rossi, JS, Prochaska, JO, 1990, Relapse situations and self-efficacy: An integrative model, *Addictive Behaviors* 15, 3, 271–83

Whelan, PJP, Marshall, EJ, Ball, DM, Humphreys, K, 2009, The role of AA sponsors: A pilot study, *Alcohol and Alcoholism* 44, 4, 416–22

White, W, 1998, *Slaying the dragon: The history of addiction treatment and recovery in America*, Bloomington, IL: Chestnut Health Systems

White, W, Kurtz, E, 2005, The varieties of recovery experience: A primer for addiction treatment professionals and recovery advocates, *International Journal of Self Help and Self Care* 3, 1/2, 21

White, WL, 2008, Recovery: Old wine, flavor of the month or new organizing paradigm?, *Substance Use and Misuse* 43,12–13, 1987–2000

White, WL, Kurtz, E, 2008, Twelve defining moments in the history of Alcoholics Anonymous, in *Recent developments in alcoholism*, pp 37-57. Springer New York.

Winzelberg, A, Humphreys, K, 1999, Should patients' religious beliefs and practices influence clinicians' refereal to 12-step groups? Evidence from a study of 3,018 male substance abuse patients, *Journal of Consulting and Clinical Psychology* 67, 790-794

Witbrodt, J, Kaskutas, L, 2005, Does diagnosis matter? Differential effects of 12-step participation and social networks on abstinence, *The American Journal of Drug and Alcohol Abuse* 31, 4, 685–707

Witkiewitz, K, Marlatt, AG, Walker, D, 2005, Mindfulness-based relapse prevention for alcohol and substance use disorders, *Journal of Cognitive Psychotherapy: An International Quarterly* 19, 3, 211–28, http://hypnotherapy.braham.net/wp-content/uploads/2015/08/Mindfulness-Based-Relapse-Prevention-from-Alcohol-and-Substance-Use-Disorders.pdf

Zemore, SE, Kaskutas, LA, Ammon, LN, 2004, In 12-step groups, helping helps the helper, *Addiction* 99, 8, 1015–23

Zemore, SE, 2007, Helping as healing among recovering alcoholics, *Southern Medical Journal* 100, 4, 447–50

# TEN

# Endnotes and further routes for enquiry

*Anne Robinson*

The concerns and the focus of chapters in this volume have varied, although all in their different ways have explored identity in the context of personal change. However, it is hardly a new observation that, within wider interests around desistance, the question of identity – and reshaping, rediscovering or finding a new sense of self – has proved tricky for researchers. Maruna et al, for example, note that

> In general, criminologists have been eager to study desistance, but wary of the idea of personal transformation. The difference is that, whereas desistance is tangible and measurable (at least in theory), identity change is anything but. One can 'prove' that someone has not offended – or at least that they have not gotten caught – but this is not proof that a person has 'changed'. (2009, 30)

As our chapters have shown, identity itself, and identity change (or, in our terms, transformation) can be conceptualised in different ways. This reflects the breadth and diversity of thinking across the desistance and recovery literatures. The emphases fall on internal cognitive processes or emotions in some quarters (see Giordano et al, 2002; 2007; Vaughan, 2007; Paternoster and Bushway, 2009), external relations and validations in others (Maruna et al, 2004 or, in a different vein, Best et al, 2015) and narratives of self in yet others (Maruna's (2001) *Making good* being the most prominent example). These present different perspectives on, and understandings of, agency, motivations and mechanisms enabling the process of change. In this final chapter I begin with some closing thoughts on the nature of identity, what spurs individuals on towards change, and the relationships and generative activities that enable them to sustain it over time. I then review promising research approaches that might provide valuable insights into personal change, as a complement to large-scale studies. I draw on empirical studies elsewhere, but focus significantly on the exemplars within this book to illustrate the benefits (and also the limitations) of these methods and what their findings may tell us.

## So what do we mean by self and identity? And what about personal change?

Across the varying perspectives on identity, there is a general consensus that identities are not fixed and are subject to change and (re)negotiation over time. The social identity model of recovery (SIMOR) proposed by Best and colleagues (2015) particularly stresses the effects of exposure to the norms, values and expectations of non-substance-using or prosocial groups on the individual moving towards recovery. Continued contact with positive groups and social networks encourages the individual to internalise new values, beliefs and perspectives, and to develop a different 'socially-derived sense of self' (2015, 3). The suggestion is that a former problematic identity – for example, the 'addict identity' – is supplanted by a prosocial 'recovery identity' that is supported and validated by social networks unconnected with substance-use (or offending).

As highlighted by James Irving (Chapter Nine, this volume) in his account of AA, group identification aids receptiveness to change and the adoption of new norms and behaviours. Group membership and affiliation is particularly powerful in the kinds of peer support and mutual aid initiatives in the addictions field (sadly, much less so in the organisational context of criminal justice). However, these ideas about identity construction – and, particularly, shifts in identity – are premised on the notion that influences work, as it were, from the outside in, providing opportunities for learning, social support and ways of framing problems and solutions. To illustrate this last point in relation to AA, Irving coins the term 'linguistic echoes' and Best et al (2015) refer to the 'lexicon' deriving from the Twelve Step script. Models such as SIMOR based on social identity theory thus helpfully point to social practices that may enhance desistance and recovery, but may not in themselves suggest deep insights into the dynamics of change within the individual (as opposed to the observable aspects of inter-relations and active networks).

In contrast, theorising about the narrative construction of identity focuses on the idea of the 'storied self' and internal processes of change (see Hamilton, Chapter Two, this volume). McAdams (1993) has suggested that each individual develops a personal myth that helps make sense of experiences at different life stages and integrates their past, present lives and anticipated futures. Drawing on McAdams' (1985) earlier work, Maruna explains that

> The narrative identity can be understood as an active identity-processing structure, a cognitive schema, or a construct system that is both shaped by and later mediates social interaction. Essentially, people construct stories to account for what they do and why they did it. These narratives impose an order on people's actions and explain people's behaviour with a sequence of events that connect up to explanatory goals, motivations and feelings. (2001, 40)

In this 'pure' form, this seems to highlight the cognitive aspects of identity formation, certainly in terms of deriving meanings from experiences and life events, and establishing a coherent, though evolving, self-concept over time. However, according to Vaughan (2007), the internal conversations that take place involving interpretations and reappraisals of these experiences and events, are affected by emotions, implying subjectivity rather than rationality. Furthermore, narrative theory emphasises and seeks to understand the ways in which individuals respond to situations based on their highly personalised views of 'reality' and what they see as the options realistically open to them (Maruna, 1999). Narrative methodologies invite understanding of narratives as temporally and contextually specific. That is, they are created at particular times and in particular social contexts. Narratives may also be created for specific social purposes – to explain behaviour to others and elicit desired responses, as conscious efforts at self-presentation, to frame future aspirations as consistent with past preferences, and so on. This means that the findings of narrative studies – especially those with small numbers of participants – may be limited in the extent to which they can be generalised to wider populations. That said, studies such as Hamilton's (Chapter Two, this volume) still present considerable potential for exploring subjective experiences of change, with aspects unique to the individual and aspects shared to greater or lesser degrees with others. Calverley (2013; and Chapter Six, this volume), for example, has suggested some commonalities of experience and supports for change among the populations of Indian, Bangladeshi and black participants in his study.

The most sustained forms of narratives are (auto)biographical. Whereas life history approaches have a long tradition in sociology, albeit relatively neglected in recent times (see Roberts, 2002, for an overview), biographical studies have really come into their own within desistance research. Prospective studies tracking participants over a number of years (for example, Halsey and Deegan, 2015, and see comments in Robinson, Chapter Five, this volume) are able to illustrate how a sense of biography is shaped over time and through the interaction of individual agency and social circumstances. The Liverpool Desistance Study, undoubtedly the most influential research involving biographical 'self-stories', is not prospective in this way. Nevertheless in *Making good*, Maruna (2001) offers a powerful analysis of the unfolding life stories shared by participants. Interestingly, he does not suggest that individuals fashion a 'replacement self' as proposed by Giordano et al (2002). Rather, he finds that those individuals who are successful in their desistance, employ similar plot devices in constructing their stories of recovery, which he has famously termed a 'redemption script'. Significantly, this involves, not a 'knifing off' of a past self (Laub and Sampson, 2003) but a reworking of existing identity and reconnection with the 'real me' that was lost during periods of offending and drug use:

> Narrators in this sample carefully established their essential nature through personally significant foreshadowing episodes. Even when they were 'at their worst', the desisting narrators emphasised that 'deep down' they were good people…the ex-offenders look in their past to find some redeeming value and emphasise their 'essential core of normalcy' (Lofland, 1969, 214)…Instead of discovering a 'new me', the desisting ex-offender reaches back into early experience to find and re-establish an 'old me' in order to desist. (Maruna, 2001, 89)

The value of this for the desister is that his or her story establishes an essential continuity of self-hood, as well as imbuing what would otherwise be extremely detrimental experiences with a degree of worth and, potentially, moral purpose in terms of guiding future actions and generative activities.

This rediscovery of a previous self is partially reflected in the findings of Sarah Goodwin's study of female offenders (Chapter Four, this volume). However, in her account this is dependent on her participants having a sufficiently strong 'good' past and prosocial roles to refer back to. That then allows a reconnection to the self that existed before the domestic violence, drug use or whatever else threatened self-hood and sense of self-efficacy. Yet, this is dubious in desistance and recovery processes for young people for whom offending, drug use, prostitution, experiences of abuse or intimate partner violence (IPV), for example, has coincided with an early stage of identity development. These young people may have little by way of narrative resources to draw upon in building alternative versions of their personal histories and essential selves (see Robinson, Chapter Five, this volume). Tellingly, in presenting the life stories of 12 young men who were each first incarcerated at an early age, Halsey and Deegan (2015) note the experiences, relationships and internal scripts – many of which are negative – that contribute to the fragility of their subjective selves (and thus their accounts of themselves).

As this illustrates, narrative identities are not constructed entirely separate from social experiences and relationships. Here, drawing on interactionist perspectives may offer interesting insights. Reflecting Herbert Mead's (1934) description of the relationship between 'I' (the ego or acting self) and 'me' (essentially, the socialised self), Jenkins (2006) suggests that *selfhood* is the individual's self-perception based on the qualities and character traits that he or she possesses, whereas *personhood* is observed in interactions in the external world and membership of social groups. In his view, the two are intimately connected in the sense that

> 'Your external definition of me is an inexorable part of my internal definition of myself – even if only in the process of rejection or resistance – and vice versa. Both processes are among the routine everyday practices of actors. Nor is one more significant than the other'.(Jenkins, 2006, 27)

Jenkins' model therefore refers to a constant dialectic between internal and external definitions. Effectively, this connotes an on-going internal conversation about their interpretation, significance and meaning. So it follows that each individual, to a greater or lesser degree, has a reflexive sense of his or her particular identities and so where he or she 'fits' in the social world. Needless to say, in the case of offenders, drug users and so on, the issue is so often the lack of 'fit' with mainstream society and the conventional 'respectability package'. Indeed, this is why the recovery movement explicitly homes in on stigma and exclusion.

Symbolic interactionist perspectives also underpin Giordano et al's (2002) theory of cognitive transformations and their subsequent focus on the dual roles of cognitions and emotions in change (2007). In this later work, emphasis is placed on role-taking and the various emotional satisfactions arising from new roles, including what the authors term 'positive reflected appraisals' that might be found in love relationships, in particular. This has not been explicitly argued before. Yet it seems intuitive that emotional attachments to partners and to social roles can promote receptivity, as well as access, to the 'cognitive blueprints' that enable the individual to act differently, and ultimately to achieve recognition as a changed individual. Of course, emotional and cognitive developments do not take place in isolation from social context and experiences. The emotional self is in part shaped by, for example, being a woman, being poor, being socially marginalised, being a member of a minority ethnic group, and also by feelings connected to experiences such as victimisation, discrimination or disrespect (Halsey and Deegan, 2015). Significantly, Giordano et al (2007) describe developmental processes which typically feature decreases in both the negative emotions attached to childhood experience and the positive emotions associated with offending, at the same time as an increase in capacities and skills in emotional management. However, for some individuals, their history of damage and destructive emotions makes this developmental journey extremely challenging, with the prospect of lapses or 'derailments' constantly present. The criminological literature can certainly furnish plenty of examples! And difficult progress towards adulthood and the 'replacement self' associated with desistance may be further compounded by the emotional impacts of on-going structural disadvantage and poverty.

So desistance and recovery take place in social contexts. New and exciting work (Weaver, 2016; 2012; 2013a) is also starting to explore the hitherto neglected relational context. This adds a welcome dimension to the analysis of the dynamics of change, especially in terms of motivations for making commitment to what may look like a highly uncertain future self. In Giordano at al's (2002) work, for example, it is not clear what might initiate the 'cognitive shifts' they identify. Similarly, Paternoster and Bushway (2009) refer to decisions to change arising from the individual experiencing a 'crystallisation of discontent' with his or her lifestyle. But how and why does this arise? Furthermore, what prompts the processes of change – discernment (or review), deliberation and dedication – outlined by Vaughan (2007)? Beth Weaver (2016) suggests that relational concerns may play a significant part, theorising from a highly innovative study of the collective histories of six men who were all members of a gang in their teenage years. Many academics have charted individual life histories, but this is the first serious attempt to trace the evolution of the network of relationships within a peer group that supports, first, their delinquency and, then, their efforts to desist from crime and substance use.

The crux of Weaver's argument is that successful desistance from crime is dependent on the pursuit of relational as well as individual concerns. This challenges the view of desistance in other models as an essentially individual project, assisted by others and by new social roles, but lacking the sense of joint goals, of negotiation and reciprocity that Weaver is able to bring to her analysis. Thus she suggests that, in desistance, 'both the individual and the social relation undergo reflexive change in tandem with each other' (2016, 55). This means, for example, that an individual may accept the need for behavioural change in order to maintain a relationship that he and his partner value, and so retain the 'relational goods' that the relationship provides for both. Here, interestingly, helpful social relations are characterised by both subsidiarity (putting another person's interests and goals above your own) and solidarity. These are evidenced in the group relationships that Weaver depicts, as group members, over time, offer practical, emotional and other supports to each other (and in many instances are also apparent within their long-standing marital relations). She explores a further aspect of identity, which she terms identity-in-relation, seen here as the group members in her study establish different ways of being, for example, a partner, friend, work-mate, which inevitably involves more than just their own efforts, because some sort of change or shift is also implied for the other party or parties in that social relation.

This brief overview has outlined approaches to identity and self-hood that suggest varied understandings of change processes. Although they are presented here for analytical purposes as taking distinct starting points, in reality the distinctions are often less sharp, as each attempts to account for the complex interplay of individual agency with social opportunities, roles and wider structures. The authors also share interest – albeit from their different perspectives – in the impacts of relationships, availability of social roles and the potential of generative activities. The latter is explored in more detail in the following section.

## Exploring generativity

'Wounded healer' roles have historically been embedded in the field of addictions, particularly sponsorship in twelve step programmes (see Irving, Chapter Nine, this volume), and these have inevitably been the focus of research. Meanwhile the notion of generativity has also gained ground in the desistance literature, largely because of its prominence within *Making good* (Maruna, 2001). Sadly, though, criminal justice practice does not offer generative opportunities itself and in many instances discourages individuals from seeking them elsewhere (see comments from Burrows, Chapter Seven, this volume, in relation to sex offenders and 'giving back'). Consequently, this subject warrants more sustained and critical attention than it has so far been given. This section therefore attempts to bring together key ideas and thoughts about generative potentials and areas of interest for both practice and further research.

The concept of generativity was first proposed by Erik Erikson (1950) as part of his eight-stage theory of psycho-social development. This suggests that individuals move through, and have to resolve, a series of conflicts or crises associated with particular ages and life-stages. Current thinking favours the idea of individuals accomplishing a more diverse range of developmental tasks and not progressing through stages in this discrete and linear way. Nevertheless, three of Erikson's 'ages of man' are of interest to the discussions in this volume.

First, in Erikson's fifth stage of adolescence, the focus is on *identity v role confusion*. Here, the individual works to establish stability in personal qualities and character traits, in terms of both understanding of self and self-presentation/acceptance by others. Although Erikson proposes a kind of psychological and ideological moratorium, allowing for experimentation rather than long-term commitment to specific ideas and values, ultimately the object for the individual during this period is to achieve a degree of consistency and congruence: as he puts it, 'the accrued confidence that the inner sameness and continuity prepared in the past are matched by the sameness and meaning for others' (1950, 261). In contrast, those unable to develop a secure emerging identity experience 'role confusion' characterised by poorly defined sense of self, personal priorities and goals.

Second, the central concern for the following stage is *intimacy v isolation*. Essentially this refers to the developing capacity to sustain intimate relationships and the ability to give to others in the spirit of subsidiarity, solidarity and reciprocity suggested by Weaver (2016). Interestingly Slater (2003) adds extra dimensions from later research, which include the suggestion of lower level crises to be resolved: *being needed v alienation* which denotes capacity for inter-dependence, and, following Josselson (1996), *responsibility v ambivalence*. It is evident that, in Eriksonian terms, many young people involved with offending and substance use are struggling with these developmental challenges, typically meeting a 'biographical impasse' (Thomson, 2011).

The third and most relevant stage is Erikson's seventh, which he frames as *generativity v stagnation*. Although he attaches this to mature adulthood (from age 40), traces of later stages may be present during earlier decades of life, and this may be particularly the case in relation to parenting. However, in general

> 'The adult stage of generativity has broad application to family, relationships, work and society. "Generativity, then is primarily the concern in establishing and guiding the next generation…the concept is meant to include…productivity and creativity" (Erikson, 1950, 267)' (Slater, 2003, 57).

For McAdams (1993), an important motivation for generative activity is the desire to leave some sort of legacy. However, this must be pursued in a way that is achievable and accessible, as well as meaningful to the individual. This may in part explain the attraction of working or volunteering in a social capacity, especially within the addictions field (see Farrall et al, 2014; Best, Chapter Eight, this volume). Relatedly, Maruna notes that

> Going straight, therefore, does not seem to be about defiant rebels turning into diligent working stiffs. Instead, defiant rebels are able to find social roles or occupations that can provide them with the same sense of empowerment and potency they were seeking (unsuccessfully) through criminal behaviour (2001, 121).

Aside from the therapeutic benefits that might accrue to the helper (Maruna, 2001), roles as 'professional ex' have a function in certifying and legitimating change. However, this may happen some distance down the line and more muted ways of adopting the 'wounded healer' role may emerge in the first instance. For example, LeBel's (2007) research with ex-prisoners found that many of them reported behaviours or intentions consistent with a wounded healer orientation (which seemed to be associated with strong identification with other prisoners and sense of remorse for past crimes). These included sharing experiences with others, acting as role models, mentoring and developing future care-related career plans. A minority of this same sample group (predominantly older members) were also activists or taking advocacy roles, suggesting a proactive stance towards system change within a form of 'identity politics' (LeBel, 2009).

Of course, not all generative activity relates back to an offending or substance-using past, at least in a formal or organised way. In Weaver's (2016) study, Adam, who had been one of the leading gang members, was instrumental in helping some of her other participants relocate from the West Coast of Scotland to London. Through his intervention (often by employing them on contracts he had obtained), they gained work experience which enabled them to learn the trade of steel fixing and establish their own contacts in the trade. This practical help was bolstered by emotional support and sharing of common experiences in the context of strong relational bonds.

Weaver (2016; 2013a) also points to the potential role of religion in change, and Calverley (Chapter Six, this volume) explores the influence of different faiths. There is an established literature linking spirituality to recovery and growing interest in its relationship to desistance (Maruna et al, 2006). However, what is significant here is that conversion to Christianity provided two of Weaver's participants with both benefits from the generative efforts of others, and opportunities to engage in their own generative activities through supporting others and ministry. As a side-note, there seems to be a real connection noted here and even more so in Halsey and Deegan (2015), with experiences of receiving care and attention to needs, and also exercising self-care (see also Goodwin, Chapter Four, this volume). Further research may be needed to confirm these initial indications that generative activity must be underpinned by a sufficiency of feelings of self-worth.

Despite the above examples, the desistance literature suggests that generative activity is most commonly found in parenting roles. This may reflect the age profile in many studies who are typically younger than the participants in Maruna's (2001) Liverpool Desistance Study (for example, Healy and O'Donnell, 2008). As Sloan (Chapter Three, this volume) notes, fatherhood may represent a further resource for the performance of masculinity and a new social role post-offending. Given their imprisonment, her participants were anticipating the emotional satisfactions of parenthood rather than engaging actively in fathering, but the projective nature of their hopes and aspirations may still be conceived as generative (see Robinson, Chapter Five, this volume). It is interesting that at least some of the women in Goodwin's study (Chapter Four, this volume) did not seem to find the same level of satisfaction in caring, perhaps because this is more expected of women and does not carry the same social rewards. Nevertheless, as she notes, such roles do provide a ready-made script or blueprint, if you like, for a new and recognised social self. What is not explored here, and may be relevant, is the stress associated with the context in which these women were carrying out their caring roles, and how poverty, environmental factors and surveillance by social workers, for example, might diminish their sense of competence and pleasure in parenting.

Generativity is not an inherent property of particular activities, but is found in the social relations and sense of meaning invested in them. Being over-burdened with caring responsibilities – or caring, for example, in difficult circumstances – can be depleting, rather than self-enhancing. Irving (Chapter Nine, this volume) also presents an instance where an AA sponsor had to cope with the suicide of her sponsee, noting that roles that are otherwise generative may have a darker side and in themselves present risks to the individual.

Generative activities may be most powerful where they provide a route towards 'normalcy' and wider social, even civic, engagement. In this respect, the intervention of 'normal-smiths' at key points in desistance and recovery may be highly significant. Both Maruna (2001) and Farrall et al (2014) draw on the notion first put forward by Lofland (1969) that individuals who confirm the essential normality of an individual can play a significant part in encouraging and enabling change:

> Social actors who can facilitate the ascription of normal status play an important role in the transition from deviant to normal…The normal-smith requires a far less onerous "proof" of the deviant's essential normality than society and consequently they convey to the deviant actor that they can change (Farrall et al, 2014).

'Normal-smithing' is not necessarily connected with generative activity. However, in some instances it may be the means by which a person in recovery or a would-be-desister hears of an opportunity and is supported to seize it, benefiting from the confidence imparted by the 'normal-smith'. These individuals may have formal roles or be informal contacts, and their impact will no doubt vary according to the nature of the relationship (interestingly, Halsey and Deegan (2015) even put themselves squarely 'in the generative frame' as researchers). Yet 'normal-smiths' may be in a good position to publicly recognise change. Maruna tellingly draws a parallel with Braithwaite's (1989) argument in favour of 're-integrative shaming', stressing the salience of generative activities as a means of redeeming a previously 'de-generative' lifestyle. In contrast to a 'deviant-smith' – for example, a probation officer, social worker or community member focused on the negative aspects of the individual's past – a 'normal-smith' can productively help in a 'de-labelling' process (Maruna et al, 2009). Again, this is another area that justifies further research efforts and there are possibly helpful linkages with the role of 'community connector' in asset-based community development approaches.

## Researching the intimacies of personal change

Reflecting on the evolution of desistance research necessarily means acknowledging the role of large-scale research endeavours tracing crime, substance use and other forms of delinquency over time. Major work tracking study samples from an early age include the *Cambridge study in delinquent development* (see Farrington et al, 2006) and the *Dunedin multi-disciplinary health and human development study* from which Terrie Moffitt (1993) derived her taxonomy of adolescent-limited and life-course persistent offenders. Meanwhile, school cohorts have been followed through key life stages in the *Edinburgh study of youth transitions and crime* (McAra and McVie, 2010) and other examples such as the *Peterborough youth study* (Wikstrom and Butterworth, 2007). Despite their considerable contribution to understanding of crime over the life course, these and other similar examples (see Soothill et al, 2009, for an overview) are largely quantitative in methodology and tend to be more focused on onset and persistence of offending rather than the end of the criminal career (but see, for example, McAra and McVie, 2012).

Other research has focused rather more on the life trajectories in early and later adulthood of known offenders. Here the seminal contributions of Sheldon and Eleanor Glueck's *Unravelling juvenile delinquency* (1950) built upon by Sampson and Laub (1993) and Neal Shover's *Aging criminals* (1985) and *Great pretenders* (1996) deserve special mention. Further step-changes in the understanding of personal change and desistance followed in the light of: Laub and Sampson's (2003) revisiting of their previous work and proposed theory of age-graded social control; Maruna's (2001) conceptualising of the ways that individuals 'make good' an offending or drug-using life story; Giordano et al's (2002) 'cognitive shifts'; and Maruna and Farrall's (2004) distinction between primary and secondary forms of desistance. Meanwhile, Farrall et al (2014) have found suggestions of long-term influences – or 'imprints' – left by probation officers that desisters may be able to recall years after supervision has ended. It remains to be seen whether Halsey and Deegan's (2015) and Weaver's (2016) research will have equivalent impacts to these major studies. Both do, however, have stand-out methodological features, in the one case because of the longitudinal design, and in the other, the focus on group relationships.

The relatively modest studies in this volume have no pretensions about being ground-breaking in that same way. Yet they add to a body of smaller studies that is growing, patchwork fashion, and is beginning to accumulate critical mass. That said, there are still many gaps in knowledge or areas where small-scale studies only serve to show how much more there might be to explore. In the next section, I highlight a select few promising avenues for future enquiries. Meanwhile the rest of this section reflects upon the methods used in the studies featured in this volume and across the wider desistance and recovery literatures that we have traversed. I also focus on interesting methodological considerations for future research and attempts to reach diverse populations and take new angles on important questions of identity and change. These tend to involve collection of narratives as a key component of the methodology, so I begin with reflections on seeking participants and creating conditions that encourage the sharing of self-stories.

## Researcher/participant relationships

A central issue within qualitative research centres on sameness and difference between the researcher and participants, and how these might facilitate or inhibit their contributions. Certainly research with young participants generally involves having to bridge an age gap as well as potential differences in gender, class and other social characteristics (Heath et al, 2009) (which may include being a known 'young offender' or drug-user). While it is possible to use participatory methods and peer researchers (Murray, 2006), this may be time and resource intensive. A minority of researchers may have personal histories involving experiences in the care system, in offending or in substance use that means that they are effectively 'insiders', but for many this will not be the case. In some instances the sheer length of time that researchers spend in contact with participants allows for the growth of relationships of trust (see Sloan, Chapter Three, and Goodwin, Chapter Four, this volume). In other situations, however, researchers are able to gain a degree of 'quasi-insider' status by virtue of their past professional lives or personal contacts.

Of note here is Hamilton's study (Chapter Two, this volume) which benefited from her experience as a probation officer in terms of both credibility with her offender participants, and the skill set that she brought to her interviews. The unique quality of her interviews allowed her to explore the emotional aspects of her participants' experiences in surprising depth. This was not without challenges, including the temptation to slip into counsellor or helper mode (Hamilton and Albertson, 2013) and the potential to 'do rapport' in a manipulative way (Duncombe and Jessop, 2002). Elsewhere, Marsh (2011) used his role as a drugs worker to recruit a small sample of long-term desisters in Dublin. He was interested in the influence of twelve step programmes on identity change, specifically the narrative template that they provide, and his pursuit of this was clearly enhanced by his knowledge of the field and his established relationships with his participants. Both these examples show the need for a good degree of researcher reflexivity. Nevertheless, drawing on professional roles in this way does open up possibilities for candid accounts of self that might not be available to other researchers (as well as offering insight at the analysis stage).

## Who to involve in the research?

It may be less evident in relation to recovery in its association with mutual aid, but one of the main criticisms of desistance research is its recurring tendency to see change in terms of processes that take place on an individual level. Beth Weaver's (2016) focus on the dynamics of a delinquent group and their relationships therefore stands in stark contrast to other studies. Research looking at peer relationships in offending and drug using groups in adolescence are not unusual (see, for example, McAra and McVie, 2012; France et al, 2012). But Weaver sets out to explore the relational aspects of desistance and how members of a group might influence and support others, drawing on their own experiences of change as they do so. Ideas of relational investments and shared concerns provide new insights into motivations and abilities to sustain change and to develop new identities-in-relation. Indeed, as she remarks, 'while desistance may be one of the *ends* (or objectives) of correctional services, for the would-be-desister, desistance seems to emerge rather as the *means* to actualising their ultimate or relational concerns, with which continued offending is more or less incompatible' (Weaver, 2012, 406, emphasis in original).

Reflecting on Weaver's research highlights two main points. The first is that she used a personal connection with one of her participants to engage other former members of 'The Del'. This gave her a degree of 'insider' status as well as assisting with questions of trust and confidence which is reflected in the honesty of the narratives she presents. The second is that, while her interest is in group relationships, the narratives she collects are individual retrospective accounts of these relationships, rather than observed dynamics and interactions. So, although this is a marked step forward, particularly in her analysis, there are perhaps further opportunities for exploring change processes and their connections to group relations, whether a friendship/kinship group as in this instance, or a group that has come together for other purposes.

A further interesting innovation can be seen in Halsey and Deegan's (2015) longitudinal study in South Australia. This is remarkable because of the level of contact with their participants over almost a decade, and also because the research design required participants to nominate up to three people whom they regarded as significant who were also periodically interviewed. It is not too unusual for research designs to incorporate professional perspectives (Farrall, 2002; King, 2014), but rather more rare to see systematic attempts to involve parents, partners and others. Given that, except for the most isolated individuals, lives are lived in the context of family relationships, intimate partnerships, work groups and so on, it seems astonishing that so little attention has been paid to the major relational influences and networks that might support (or thwart) desistance and recovery. And, of course, as an individual undergoes change, that may have practical, emotional and other impacts on family members, friends and, most likely, partners. (Indeed, multi-systemic therapies are based on this understanding!) So widening the scope of research design to include the perspectives of those most intimately connected with research participants may be another fruitful development.

## Thoughts on longitudinal studies

Long-term qualitative studies have clearly made huge contributions to our understandings of personal change. And this applies not only to desistance and recovery but also related areas such as youth transitions (for example, Henderson et al, 2007; MacDonald and Marsh, 2005). Farrall et al (2014) provide a thoughtful review of the major desistance studies and reflect upon the merits of qualitative longitudinal research, particularly those with prospective designs. They rightly emphasise the significance of large-scale studies with rigorous methodologies and successful follow-up of a substantial proportion of participants. However, the investment of time and resources means that such studies are relatively rare and, in any case, their importance should not be allowed to diminish the contribution of smaller studies. I have three key points to add on this subject.

First, longitudinal research does not inevitably involve a long period of fieldwork, but rather is characterised by successive stages or sweeps of data collection (Saldana, 2003). So, when charting a process of change, longitudinal methodologies allow opportunities for analysis both across the sample group at any particular point of data collection and in terms of individual histories or themes over time (Thomson and Holland, 2003). However, the extent of cross-sectional or diachronic analysis (Thomson, 2007) will depend upon the study design. Giordano et al's research (2002; 2007), for example, extended over more than 20 years, but with large gaps between participant interviews in 1982, 1995 and 2003. Although the rate of follow-up was impressive across a large sample group, this inevitably had some effect on their detailed exploration of change. In contrast, Goodwin (Chapter Four, this volume) refers to her work as a micro-longitudinal study, denoting a compressed timescale albeit one in which she collected a considerable amount of data. Naturally, a shorter length of time for the study will affect the realistic aims of the research. For example, participants making contact with drug services might be tracked through the most intense period of transition, effectively their contemplation, preparation and action stages of change (Prochaska et al, 1992), rather than the whole process of recovery.

Second, prospective research designs do need careful forward planning in the interests of consistency. New sources of funding that enable additional sweeps of data collection may not be anticipated at the outset, but robust design would allow such opportunities to be grasped when they do come along. An excellent example of continuity over time is the *Inventing adulthoods* study (Henderson et al, 2007) which maintained the same study team over a decade throughout successive phases of the project, providing both rich (re)analyses of their data and reflection on the qualitative research process and relationships (Thomson and Holland, 2003; 2005; Thomson, 2007).

Finally, longitudinal studies may involve small cohorts, particularly those lasting over long periods of time with groups where high rates of attrition might be expected. That does not in itself pose a problem, if the quality of the data and the analysis is good. Halsey and Deegan's (2015) study, for example, reported on only 12 of their participants but with depth and insight. Indeed, they showed great tenacity in keeping track of a group of young men whose lives, at least in the early stages of the study, were chaotic and lacking in stability.

### Capturing narratives

It can be argued that criminology is relatively 'straight-laced' in terms of its approach to qualitative data collection, and this may be particularly so in terms of drawing out narratives. The essence of pure narrative inquiry is to allow participants to determine the pace and the direction of their interviews, and much of its subject matter (perhaps with some initial prompts) (see Hamilton, Chapter Two, this volume; Lieblich et al, 1998; Reissman, 2008). However, narratives form part of data collection in a much wider variety of research methodologies. Researchers with a previous background as practitioners in social care or similar, may be familiar with using pictorial methods such as genograms, relational maps and activity charts. Some desistance studies have drawn on elements of these (for example, Farrall et al, 2014), but in general more imagination could be used, particularly to capture the narratives of individuals where there are barriers in communication or simply confidence. Elsewhere (Robinson, 2015), I have written about the potential for exploring the visual and mobile methods developed in youth studies, social geography, anthropology and other fields. These are already proven to be helpful with young people, but may also have value for individuals, for example, with learning difficulties or mental health issues, or perhaps in contexts where research participants might have particular concerns about trust and feeling that they genuinely have a 'voice'.

## Opportunities in ethnography

It is already established that ethnographic approaches are capable of giving access to hard-to-reach populations and what would otherwise be sensitive situations. Two outstanding examples are Sophie Day's (2007) *On the game* and Teela Sanders' (2005) *Sex work: A risky business*, both exploring lives lived in the context of prostitution. Through Sanders' observations and 'ethnographic conversations' (Davies et al, 2011) – often snatched with sex workers in brothels and licensed saunas between 'punters' – she examines their negotiations of risk, including reputational risk, and what this work means for sexual identities.

Elsewhere, ethnographies have examined the occupational identities of prison officers (Crawley, 2004) and workers in a newly formed youth offending team (Souhami, 2007). The latter is particularly pertinent as Souhami considered the essential 'flux, ambiguity and complexity' (2007, 189) of identity in the context of change. In this case, she was referring to an organisation in transition as practitioners were brought together to form a multi agency team. However, ethnographies may have a wider application in looking at identity change within processes of desistance, recovery and, for example, exiting prostitution. That was not the primary purpose of Sloan's prison ethnography (Chapter Three, this volume), but her insights do reveal how data collection through participant observation and interviews over a period of time could enhance our understanding of change. It is also worth noting that ethnographies provide opportunity to look at the social context and the relationships in the immediate environment that might help or constrain identity change, thus providing fresh views on its essential dynamics.

## The value of individual stories and histories

Best (Chapter Eight, this volume) presents short case studies that exemplify the process of change and development of professional identities in two of his participants. As more extensive methodologies and space in publications have allowed, case studies in other work have been used to good effect to give close up accounts of lives and lived experiences. Where the 'narrative turn' and the 'biographical turn' (Roberts, 2002) intersect, this is perhaps at its most powerful. This chapter has talked already about the studies by Weaver (2016) and Halsey and Deegan (2015). Both involve extensive detail about the lives of their participants but, in Weaver's case, this is derived from reflective narrative interviews whereas the other study has brought together details collected over a number of years. This necessarily implies a process of interpretation, selection and analysis on behalf of the researchers, in part because of the sheer volume of data collected, but also to draw out salient points and themes. In this regard, Rachel Thomson, reflecting on the research process within the longitudinal *Inventing adulthoods* study (Henderson et al, 2007) comments on the opportunity to move beyond an illustrative case study to a more exploratory case history. She makes a key distinction in remarking that 'where the aim of the former is to summarise events and actions, the aim of the latter is to interrogate how and why events and actions took place as they did' (2007, 573). Elsewhere she has explained this as an attempt 'to provide a compelling account of the connected individual, of how and why events unfolded as they did, the transformation of the individual over time, and the dance between personal agency and interdependence' (2011, 24).

Of course, integral to this is the sense that out of the participant's story, the researcher is creating his or her own narrative of events, and thus is engaging in his or her own process of meaning-making. This is not set in stone any more than participant's self-narratives are fixed, but rather can be subject to reflexive reappraisal and alternative viewpoints. The important quality from a researcher perspective is whether any individual analysis is valid based on the 'evidence' and is thus credible and authentic in its own terms.

Finally, any discussion of individual stories must inevitably include autobiographical accounts that, according to Weaver and Weaver, offer the possibility of 'properly rounded offender (or ex-offender) perspectives' (2013, 260) This contributes to the body of knowledge and understanding of desistance, but also, for Allan Weaver, now working as a criminal justice social worker, writing an autobiography required him to reflect upon his personal 'journey' and its impact upon his professional practice. This perhaps begs the question about whether making stories public, and offering your understandings of your own process of change, may constitute a further form of generative activity. Here the question of audience may be pertinent to the presentation of public and private selves, particularly in the assessment and evaluation of life experiences (Roberts, 2002).

## Where next for research?

Throughout the chapters in this volume, and in the earlier sections of this chapter, there are indicators of useful areas for future study. These include: the impact of masculinities and ethnicities on desistance and recovery; the experiences of women in recovering identities 'spoiled' by offending, drug use, victimisation and sexual exploitation; the needs of those who 'specialise' in certain types of offending, rather than the generic offender; the nature and the role of generative activity in supporting change; and the significance of relational contexts. Rather than rehearsing these, this section outlines three separate areas for development in research. First, addressing the relative lack of attention to identity itself in desistance research (and even more so in the recovery literature). Second, the possibilities in reaching out to the youth transitions research to further explorations in identity development and change, both conceptually and methodologically. Third, the benefits of cross-fertilisation between the fields of desistance and recovery which have remained so distinct.

### Exploring identity

Hamilton in Chapter One (this volume) outlined two approaches to identity taken within the desistance and recovery movements, with the emphasis on internal processes in the one theoretical strand, and externalities in the other. She also highlighted social interactionist perspectives that, by focusing on self-perception and reflexivity, perhaps help us better to appreciate the essential conundrum of agency versus structure. Both play a part in the development and on-going negotiation of identity, as we are irreducibly social and embodied entities, not abstractions. Yet for all the brouhaha about identity in the social sciences, identity per se is relatively under-conceptualised in the desistance literature, and arguably even more so in recovery.

The cause of this lack of explicit theoretical attention to identity may be twofold. First, the primary concern in criminal justice agencies and addiction services is behavioural change, and resources and institutional processes are focused, in that sense, on outcomes – fewer offences, less alcohol-related disease, reduced harm to individuals in the context of street sex work, drug cultures and domestic violence. Addiction studies have followed a different trajectory, but in the academic world attention to crime over the life course certainly concentrated in its early days in onset and persistence of anti-social behaviour and offending. A shift of gaze towards cessation of offending came somewhat later, and the idea that identity change accompanies behavioural change, still later. Although interests have diversified in a busy field of desistance research, much of the theorising is around such processes as 'de-labelling' (Maruna et al, 2004; 2009), readiness to grasp 'hooks for change' (Giordano et al, 2002) and ambivalence/ambiguity in change (Healy, 2010; King, 2014). Meanwhile in recovery, which has a less cerebral orientation in any case, the developing impetus is around 'recovery capital' (Best and Laudet, 2010), professional help and communities of activism. In some senses this is entirely right and proper, as there are both practical and moral imperatives to use knowledge to respond to social problems (in this case, crime and addiction). But it has resulted in some considerable leaps of faith when it comes to identity, what constitutes identity, and the mechanisms that link identity to behavioural change.

The other reason, I would suggest, for the relatively simple ideas about identity at the heart of more complex theorising about processes of change, is the reluctance to be pinned down by the sorts of identity models proposed in social psychology. Cote and Levine's simplified identity formation theory (SIFT) (2016), for example, suggests too neat a separation between their proposed elements of ego identity (or the executive self), personal identity and social identity. Clearly for researchers interested in subjectivities and the lived experience, adopting such a model would be a positivist step too far. Conversely, other ways of looking at identity might prove too abstract and philosophical for researchers in fields that are applied by their very nature.

Nevertheless, the point that identity itself deserves a more critical focus is a valid one. After all, the transformations that take place from 'deviant' to prosocial identities, can surely only be appreciated fully from the basis of a nuanced understanding of identity (selfhood, personhood and all its other suggested parts). As thinking about identity change becomes more sophisticated, so should the underpinning concepts of identity. Moreover, there may be useful alignments with the knowledge and insights into identity development from youth and transition studies – a hitherto neglected link.

## Transitions to desistance, recovery and adulthood

It is striking that desistance studies have drawn so little on the healthy tradition in youth transition research, which is particularly ironic given the enduring evidence of the 'age-crime curve'. Perhaps it is assumed that there is little value there, that young people may certainly cease their offending and drug use but that they do not undergo that all-important process of 'secondary desistance' (Maruna and Farrall, 2004). Not that young people's identities are static: clearly most are engaged in 'identity work' well into their early adulthood. It does, therefore, seem a missed opportunity to look more closely at processes of identity change and social relationships, exploring interests that are broader than crime and substance misuse. The renowned 'Teesside Studies' have brought sociological and criminological interests together and, indeed, Robert MacDonald concludes that 'it was not possible to understand the onset and consolidation of the most serious forms of criminal careers revealed in these studies without attending to wider aspects of youth transitions. The same applied to processes of desistance from crime' (2015, 214). He further notes that

> A proper understanding of how criminal careers commence and desist for young people necessitates a broad investigation of youth transitions that incorporates not just aspects of offending but also encompass elements of school to work, housing, family, leisure and drug-using careers. There are benefits in trying to incorporate this sort of youth sociology into criminology. (2015, 217)

There may also be benefits for desistance researchers in looking at the methodologies employed in youth transitions research. The 'Teesside Studies' are an outstanding example of longitudinal research, as is the *Inventing adulthoods* study (Henderson et al, 2007) referred to elsewhere in this chapter. Youth research may also provide insights into methodologies that invite group participation or at least observation of groups and their dynamics in the process of change. More generally, there is merit in looking outside narrow disciplinary – and in terms of our arguments here, sub-disciplinary – boundaries for inspiration for new methods, lines of enquiry and important linkages.

## Desistance or recovery. Or is it recovery and desistance?

Here we come – at last – to the central question for this volume. Are the processes of change – the transformations – similar in ceasing crime and problematic substance use? What happens when crime and substance use co-exist? It is strange that so little work has tackled this question head on, although perhaps not surprising given the origins of recovery in the field of medicine and mental health, and the genesis of desistance-thinking in crime studies. Of course, there is inevitably some cross-over. Researchers have used concepts from desistance to explore recovery from substance use (for example, Marsh (2011) and self-narratives). Similarly, criminologists have explored the substance misuse of young desisters (Barry, 2006) and the longer-term desistance trajectory of drug-using offenders (Farrall et al, 2014), to give just two examples. Colman and Vader Laenen's (2012) study of desistance and recovery in a sample of drug-using offenders remains one of the few studies in this area, yet their conclusion – that 'recovery came first' – may not be generalisable to other populations, given the heterogeneity of drug use (and drug users). More recently Bachman et al (2015) found evidence of intentional self-change of identity in desisters among a sample of long-term drug involved offenders, although for them the question of whether desistance precedes recovery, follows it or occurs at the same time, remains unsettled. They call for further research on identity transformation and desistance, based on their conclusion that

> For both desistance and recovery, the process of breaking
> from self-harmful behaviour involves a change in how one
> views oneself, as well as maintaining productive activities
> and supportive social networks that lead to and sustain the
> new lifestyle (2015, 21)

We are conscious that in this volume, while including chapters on both desistance and recovery, to some extent we have replicated the divide in desistance and recovery thinking. Our difficulty in comprehensively bringing the two together does exemplify the enormity of engaging in that project in a meaningful way. It is possible to say glibly that the identity transformations have similarities. However, that may seriously underplay the significance of the social and institutional contexts in which they take place and what they mean for individuals in terms of initiating and sustaining change, the norms and values that are internalised, and their access to supportive relationships. The salient difference is between the orientation of criminal justice processes towards reduction in crime and public protection, and of recovery agencies towards 'health and well-being and participation in the rights, roles and responsibilities of society' (UK Drug Policy Commission, 2008). The latter, apart from being framed more positively, is inherently more person-centred (Allan, 2014).

Services delivering drug and alcohol treatment may be based on traditional medical models, and treatment allied to criminal justice services is imbued with its own system of power relationships. However, the field of addictions does encompass an ethos of mutual aid and service user involvement that is perhaps somewhat uneven, but certainly present in a way that is largely unknown in penal processes. The opportunities for empowerment, generative activity and outward, visible expression of a changed self are thus more readily available. In contrast, penal services tend to discourage probationers and former prisoners from mixing with each other unless they are supervised within groups or Approved Premises. This may limit damage from unhelpful associations, but it also prevents helpful sharing of experiences of change and overcoming obstacles, not to mention empathic encouragement from peers. The early stages of change – marked often by ambivalence, low confidence and fluctuating motivation (Burnett, 2004; Healy, 2010; King, 2014) – may then be more challenging and more individualised. And the later processes of developing a new social self, and receiving social recognition for that new self, seems inherently more difficult due to assumptions about the enduring nature of 'offenderhood'.

That said, leaving substance misuse behind is no easy matter. The recovery movement itself is not a panacea, although it perhaps provides a more helpful environment for change for those individuals who engage with it than penal services. The voluntary nature of engagement may be significant here (although, according to Bean (2008) those in recovery are still likely to feel some degree of pressure, even coercion). However, the impetus around activism, peer-led initiatives and recovery champions in the more radical parts of the recovery movement (Allan, 2014) means that associated concepts and understandings of identity are less developed than for desistance, which has remained, relatively speaking, an academic preserve (notwithstanding new work by Buckingham and Best, forthcoming). So, while desistance researchers and criminal justice practitioners have much to learn about generativity, empowerment and collaboration from the recovery side, there is potential for learning to go in the opposite direction too.

So where is the common ground? The chapters in this volume do attest to different experiences of change for individuals according to their physical, social and relational context, as well as the pressures acting upon them and the supports available. Desistance has been described as a 'complex, contingent, individualised, reflexive and relational process' (Weaver, 2016, 121) and that would seem true of all efforts to recover a 'spoiled identity' and establish a new social self. What drives change and what it means is unique to each individual. Yet the accumulated narratives of change suggest some necessary ingredients: motivation; capacity to develop a vision of a future different to the past; recourse to help and support, practical and emotional, to achieve desired change; recognition of change that is subsumed into self-perception (and therefore self-presentation and willingness/capacity to engage in an expanded range of social roles); and, it might be added, a great deal of tenacity. As Burnett (2010) notes, the individual aspiring to change needs both 'the will and the ways' to achieve and to sustain it.

## Concluding remarks

In that same editorial article, Burnett refers to a way of viewing hope that sees it as incorporating both '[A]gency-thinking (motivation and commitment to reaching one's goals, as expressed in "I can do this" and "I'm not going to be stopped") and *pathways thinking* (the perceived availability of successful pathways relating to goals, as conveyed in "I'll find ways to get this done")' (2010, 664).

This neatly captures the essential requirements for change: agency, opportunity and resource. Our focus in this volume has been specifically on identity change – or transformations – as individuals seek more successful lives. These transformations are will-ful, in the sense of being intentional, but the will can only be made to count if there is a space that allows for the possibility of change and a sufficiency of support for it to happen. The interplay between an individual's readiness to change and personal agency on the one hand, and the social relations or structures that might assist (or impede) on the other, is complex. The chapters in this volume have made some attempts to unravel a few of these complexities, but inevitably new complications and issues emerge in the process. One such is the question of whether individuals exiting sex work, surviving sexual or domestic abuse, or dealing with other causes of 'ill repute', undergo comparable identity transformations to those in desistance and recovery. Thirty years ago, Jim Orford in

*Excessive appetites* (1985), presented a compelling argument that there are commonalities across a range of compulsive behaviours – effectively that addiction is not a property of the drug itself, or of the sexual act, but that there are similar psychological underpinnings to excessive eating, drinking, drug use, sexual behaviours and exercise. Perhaps it is time for a similar wide-sweeping view across a spectrum of 'deviance' and the work involved in recovering previously tainted identities.

## References

Allan, G, 2014, *Working with substance users: A guide to effective interventions*, Basingstoke: Palgrave Macmillan

Bachman, R, Kerrison, E, Paternoster, R, O'Connell, D, Smith, L, 2015, Desistance for a long-term drug-involved sample of offenders: The importance of identity transformation, *Criminal Justice and Behaviour*, doi: 10.1177/0093854815604012

Barry, M, 2006, *Youth offending in transition: The search for social recognition*, Abingdon: Routledge

Bean, P, 2008, *Drugs and crime* (3rd edn), Cullompton: Willan

Best, D, Laudet, A, 2010, *The potential of recovery capital*, London: RSA

Best, D, Beckwith, M, Haslam, C, Haslam, D, Jetten, J, Mawson, E, Lubman, DI, 2015, Overcoming alcohol and drug addiction as a process of social identity transition: The social identity model of recovery (SIMOR), *Addiction Research and Theory*, early online, doi: org/10.3109/16066359.2015.1075980

Braithwaite, J, 1989, *Crime, shame and reintegration*, Cambridge: Cambridge University Press

Buckingham, S, Best, D, forthcoming, *Addiction, behavioural change and social identity*, Abingdon: Routledge

Burnett, R, 2004, 'To re-offend or not to re-offend? The ambivalence of convicted property offenders, in S Maruna and R Immarigeon (eds) *After crime and punishment: Pathways to offender reintegration*, pp 152–80, Cullompton: Willan

Burnett, R, 2010, The will and the ways to becoming an ex-offender, *International Journal of Offender Therapy and Comparative Criminology* 54, 5, 663–6

Calverley, A, 2013, *Cultures of desistance*, Abingdon: Routledge

Colman, C, Vander Laenen, F, 2012, 'Recovery came first': Desistance versus recovery in the criminal careers of drug-using offenders, *The Scientific World Journal*, doi: 10.1100/2012/657671

Cote, JE, Levine, CG, 2016, *Identity formation, youth and development*, Hove: Psychology Press

Crawley, E, 2004, *Doing prison work: The public and private lives of prison officers*, Cullompton: Willan

Davies, P, Francis, P, Jupp, V, 2011, *Doing criminological research*, London: Sage

Day, S, 2007, *On the game: Women and sex work*, London: Pluto Press

Duncombe, J, Jessop, J, 2002, 'Doing rapport' and the ethics of 'faking friendship', in M Mauthner, M Birch, J Jessop, M Miller (eds) *Ethics in qualitative research*, pp 108–23, London: Sage

Erikson, E, 1950, *Childhood and society*, New York: Norton

Farrall, S, 2002, *Rethinking what works with offenders*, Cullompton: Willan

Farrall, S, Hunter, B, Sharpe, G, Calverley, A, 2014, *Criminal careers in transition: The social context of desistance from crime*, Oxford: Oxford University Press

Farrington, D, Coid, J, Harnett, L, Jolliffe, D, Soteriou, N, 2006, *Criminal careers up to age 50 and life success up to age 48*, London: Home Office, http://www.crim.cam.ac.uk/people/academic_research/david_farrington/hors299.pdf

France, A, Bottrell, D, Armstrong, D, 2012, *A political ecology of youth and crime*, New York: Palgrave Macmillan

Giordano, PC, Cernkovich, SA, Rudolphe, JL, 2002, Gender, crime and desistance: Towards a theory of cognitive transformation, *American Journal of Sociology* 107, 4, 990–1064

Giordano, P, Schroeder, RD, Cernkovitch, SA, 2007, Emotions and crime over the life-course: A neo-Meadian perspective on criminal continuity and change, *American Journal of Sociology* 112, 6, 1603–61

Glueck, S, Glueck, E, 1950, *Unravelling juvenile delinquency*, New York: Commonwealth Fund

Halsey, M, Deegan, S, 2015, *Young offenders: Crime, prison and struggles for desistance*, Basingstoke: Palgrave Macmillan

Hamilton, P, Albertson, K, 2013, Reflections on values and ethics in narrative inquiry with (ex)-offenders, in M Cowburn, M Duggan, A Robinson, P Senior (eds) *Values in criminology and community justice*, pp 329–42, Bristol: Policy Press

Healy, D, 2010, *The dynamics of desistance: Charting pathways through change*, Abingdon: Routledge

Healy, D, O'Donnell, I, 2008, Calling time on crime: Motivation, generativity and agency in Irish probationers, *Probation Journal* 55, 1, 25–38

Heath, S, Brooks, R, Cleaver, E, Ireland, E, 2009, *Researching young people's lives*, London: Sage

Henderson, S, Holland, McGrellis, S, Sharpe, S, Thomson, R, 2007, *Inventing adulthoods: A biographical approach to youth transitions*, London: Sage

Jenkins, R, 2006, *Social identity*, London: Routledge

Josselson, RL, 1996, *Revising herself: The story of a woman's identity from college to mid-life*, New York: Oxford University Press

King, S, 2014, *Desistance transitions and the impact of probation*, Abingdon: Routledge

Laub, J, Sampson, R, 2003, *Shared beginnings, divergent lives*, London: Harvard University Press

LeBel, TP, 2007, An examination of the impact of formerly incarcerated prisoners helping others, *Journal of Offender Rehabilitation* 46, 1–2, 1–24

LeBel, TP, 2009, Formerly incarcerated person's use of advocacy/activism as a coping mechanism in the reintegration process, in BM Veysey, J Christian, D J Martinez (eds) *How offenders transform their lives*, pp 165–87, Cullompton: Willan

LeBel, TP, Burnett, R, Maruna, S, Bushway, S , 2008, 'The 'chicken and egg' of subjective and social factors in desistance from crime, *European Journal of Criminology* 5, 2, 131–59

Lieblich, A, Tuval-Mashiach, R, Zilber, T, 1998, *Narative research: Reading, analysis and interpretation*, London: Sage

Lofland, J, 1969, *Deviance and identity*, Englewood Cliffs, NJ: Prentice Hall

McAdams, DP, 1988, *Power, intimacy, and the life story: Personological inquiries into identity*, New York: The Guildford Press

McAdams, DP, 1985, *Power, intimacy and the life story: Personological enquiries into identity*, New York: Guildford Press

McAdams, DP, 1993, *The stories we live by*, New York: William Morrow

McAra, L, McVie, S, 2010, Youth justice and crime: Key messages from the Edinburgh study of youth transitions and crime, *Criminology and Criminal Justice*, 10, 2, 179–209

McAra, L, McVie, S, 2012, Negotiated order: The groundwork for a theory of offending pathways, *Criminology and Criminal Justice* 12, 4, 347–75

MacDonald, R, 2015, Youth transitions, criminal careers and social exclusion, in B Goldson, J Muncie (eds) *Youth and crime* (2nd edn), London: Sage

MacDonald, R, Marsh, J, 2005, *Disconnected youth? Growing up in Britain's poor neighbourhoods*, Basingstoke: Palgrave Macmillan

Marsh, B, 2011, Narrating desistance: Identity change and the 12 step script, *Irish Probation Journal* 8, 49–68

Maruna, S, 1999, Desistance and development: The psychosocial process of going straight, The British Criminology Conference: Selected Proceedings, vol 2, pp 1-25.

Maruna, S, 2001, *Making good: How ex-convicts reform and rebuild their lives*, Washington, DC: American Psychological Association

Maruna, S, Farrall, S , 2004, Desistance from crime: A theoretical reformulation, *Kolner Zeitschrift fur Soziologie and Sozialpsychologie*, 43, 171–94

Maruna, S, Roy, K, 2007, Amputation or reconstruction? Notes on the concept of 'knifing off' and desistance from crime, *Journal of Contemporary Criminal Justice* 23, 1, 104–24

Maruna, S, LeBel, T, Mitchell, N, Naples, M, 2004, Pygmalion in the reintegration process', *Psychology, Crime and Law* 10, 3, 271–81

Maruna, S, Wilson, L, Curran, K, 2006, Why God is often found behind bars: Prison conversions and the crisis of self-narrative, *Research in Human Development* 3, 2–3, 161–84

Maruna, S, LeBel, TP, Naples, M, Mitchell, N , 2009, Looking glass identity transformation: Pygmalion and Golem in the rehabilitation process, in BM Veysey, J Christian, DJ Martinez (eds) *How offenders transform their lives*, pp 30–55, Cullompton: Willan

Mead, GH, 1934, *Mind, self and society from the standpoint of a social behaviourist*, Chicago, IL: University of Chicago Press

Moffitt, T, 1993, Adolescent-limited and life-course-persistent anti-social behaviour: A developmental taxonomy, *Psychological Review* 100, 4, 674–70

Murray, C, 2006, Peer-led focus groups and young people, *Children and Society* 20, 273–86

Orford, J, 1985, *Excessive appetites: A psychological view of addictions*, Chichester: Wiley

Paternoster, R, Bushway, S, 2009, Desistance and the 'feared self': Towards an identity theory of criminal desistance, *The Journal of Criminal Law and Criminology* 99, 1, 1103–56

Prochaska, JO, Diclente, CC, Norcross, J, 1992, In search of how people change: Applications to addictive behaviours, *American Psychologist* 47, 9, 1002–114

Reissman, CK, 2008, *Narrative methods for the human sciences*, London: Sage

Roberts, B, 2002, *Biographical research*, Maidenhead: Open University Press

Robinson, A, 2015, Life stories in development: Thoughts on narrative methods with young people, *British Journal of Community Justice* 13, 2, 59–77

Saldana, J, 2003, *Longitudinal qualitative research: Analysing change through time*, Walnut Creek, CA: AltaMira Press

Sampson, R, Laub, J, 1993, *Crime in the making: Pathways and turning pints through life*, Cambridge, MA: Harvard University Press

Sanders, T, 2005, *Sex work: A risky business*, Cullompton: Willan

Shover, N, 1985, *Aging criminals*, London: Sage

Shover, N, 1996, *Great pretenders: Pursuits and careers of persistent thieves*, Boulder, CO: Westview Press

Slater, CL, 2003, Generativity versus stagnation: An elaboration of Erikson's adult stage of human development, *Journal of Adult Development* 10, 1, 53–65

Smith, DJ, 2007, Crime and the life course, in M Maguire, R Morgan, R Reiner (eds) *Oxford Handbook of Criminology* (4th edn), Oxford: Oxford University Press

Soothill, K, Fitzpatrick, C, Francis, B, 2009, *Understanding criminal careers*, Cullompton: Willan

Souhami, A, 2007, *Transforming youth justice: Occupational identity and cultural change*, Cullompton: Willan

Thomson, R, 2007, The qualitative longitudinal case history: Practical, methodological and ethical reflections, *Social Policy and Society* 6, 4, 571–82

Thomson, R, 2011, *Unfolding lives: Youth, gender and change*, Bristol: Policy Press

Thomson, R, Holland, J, 2003, Hindsight, foresight and insight: The challenges of longitudinal qualitative research, *International Journal of Social Research Methodology* 6, 3, 233–44

Thomson, R, Holland, J, 2005, Thanks for the memory: Memory books as a methodological resource in biographical research, *Qualitative Research* 5, 2, 201–19

UK Drug Policy Commission, 2008, *A vision of recovery*, www.ukdpc.org.uk

Vaughan, B, 2007, The internal narrative of desistance, *British Journal of Criminology* 47, 3, 23–39

Weaver, A, Weaver, B, 2013, Auto-biography, empirical research and critical theory in desistance: A view from the inside out, *Probation Journal* 60, 3, 259–72

Weaver, B, 2012, The relational context of desistance: Some implications and opportunities for social policy, *Social Policy and Administration* 46, 4, 395–412

Weaver, B, 2013a, Desistance, reflexivity and relationality: A case study, *European Journal of Probation* 5, 3, 71–88

Weaver, B, 2013b, Co-producing desistance: Who works to support desistance?, in I Durnescu, F McNeill (eds) *Understanding penal practice*, pp 193–205, Abingdon: Routledge

Weaver, B, 2016, *Offending and desistance: The importance of social relations*, Abingdon: Routledge

Wikstrom, POH, Butterworth, DA, 2007, *Adolescent crime: Individual differences and lifestyles*, Cullompton: Willan

# Index

**Note:** Page numbers in *italics* indicate figures.